Repositioning
the Hong Kong Government

A series on socio-economic and cultural changes in Hong Kong

HONG KONG CULTURE AND SOCIETY

Series Editors

Tai-lok Lui	Department of Sociology, The University of Hong Kong
Gerard A. Postiglione	Faculty of Education, The University of Hong Kong

Panel of Advisors

Ambrose King	The Chinese University of Hong Kong
Alvin So	The Hong Kong University of Science and Technology
Siu-lun Wong	The University of Hong Kong

Other titles in the series

The Dynamics of Social Movements in Hong Kong
Edited by Stephen Wing-kai Chiu and Tai-lok Lui

Consuming Hong Kong
Edited by Gordon Matthews and Tai-lok Lui

At Home with Density
Nuala Rooney

Toward Critical Patriotism: Student Resistance to Political Education in Hong Kong and China
Gregory P. Fairbrother

Changing Church and State Relations in Hong Kong, 1950–2000
Beatrice Leung and Shun-hing Chan

Collaborative Colonial Power: The Making of the Hong Kong Chinese
Law Wing Sang

Desiring Hong Kong, Consuming South China: Transborder Cultural Politics 1970–2010
Eric Kit-wai Ma

Repositioning the Hong Kong Government

Social Foundations and Political Challenges

Edited by
Stephen Wing-kai Chiu and Siu-lun Wong

香港大學出版社
HONG KONG UNIVERSITY PRESS

Hong Kong University Press
14/F Hing Wai Centre
7 Tin Wan Praya Road
Aberdeen
Hong Kong
www.hkupress.org

ISBN 978-988-8083-49-7 (*Hardback*)
ISBN 978-988-8083-50-3 (*Paperback*)

British Library Cataloguing-in-Publication Data
A catalogue record for this book is available from the British Library.

10 9 8 7 6 5 4 3 2 1

Printed and bound by Goodrich Int'l Printing Co., Ltd. in Hong Kong, China

Contents

Series foreword

Most past research on Hong Kong has been generally aimed to inform a diverse audience about the place and its people. Beginning in the 1950s, the aim of scholars and journalists who came to Hong Kong was to study China, which had not yet opened its doors to fieldwork by outsiders. Accordingly, the relevance of Hong Kong was limited to its status as a society adjacent to mainland China. After the opening of China, research on Hong Kong shifted focus towards colonial legitimacy and the return of sovereignty. Thus, the disciplined study of Hong Kong was hindered for almost half a century, and richness of a society undergoing dramatic economic, social and political change within the contemporary world was not sufficiently emphasized.

The unfolding of culture and society in Hong Kong is no longer confined by the 1997 question. New changes are shaped by local history as much as by the China factor. Rather than being an isolated entity, Hong Kong is an outcome of interaction among local history, national context, and global linkages. An understanding of the future development of Hong Kong requires sensitivity to this contextual complexity.

The volumes in this series are committed to making Hong Kong studies address key issues and debates in the social sciences. Each volume situates Hong Kong culture and society within contemporary theoretical discourse. Behind the descriptions of social and cultural life is a conceptual dialogue between local agenda, regional issues, and global concerns.

This series focuses on changing socio-economic structures, shifting political parameters, institutional restructuring, emerging public cultures and expanding global linkages. It covers a range of issues, including social movements, socialization into a national identity, the effect of new immigrants from the Mainland, social networks of family members in other countries, the impact of the colonial legacy on the identity of forthcoming generations, trade union organization within the shifting political landscape, linkages within Southeast Asian societies, Hong Kong's new role between Taiwan and the Chinese mainland, the transformation of popular culture, the globalization of social life, and the global engagement of Hong Kong's universities in the face of national integration.

Gerard A. Postiglione
Tai-lok Lui

Series General Editors

Acknowledgements

The editors would like to thank the Central Policy Unit of the Hong Kong Special Administrative Region Government for its support of this project. Professor Lee Ming-kwan, a full-time member of the unit, had been instrumental in conceiving the project and has been behind it throughout its execution. The Central Policy Unit has played a significant role in fostering dialogues between academic researchers and policymakers in Hong Kong; this book can certainly be viewed as a product of its many efforts.

We are indebted to the authors for contributing their chapters to this volume, for updating the text at our request, and for persevering with us (since their valuable works had many suitors). The Public Policy Research Centre at the Chinese University of Hong Kong provided much assistance to the editors for the duration of the project. Thanks are also due to the able editorial staff of Hong Kong University Press, especially Christopher Munn, for their patience and guidance.

Contributors

Peter Tsan-yin CHEUNG is associate professor, director of the Master of Public Administration Programme, and former head of the Department of Politics and Public Administration, the University of Hong Kong. He is the coordinator of the Research Area on the Greater Pearl River Delta and Hong Kong, the Strategic Research Theme on Contemporary China Studies, and the convener of the China Area of Inquiry of the Common Core Curriculum at the university. His research interests focus on the relations between Beijing and the Hong Kong Special Administrative Region (HKSAR), the management of cross-boundary cooperation in south China and the politics of policy making in Hong Kong. He is also a former consultant, part-time member, and research and planning director of the Central Policy Unit of the HKSAR government.

Stephen Wing-kai CHIU received his doctorate from Princeton University and is currently professor in the Sociology Department, the Chinese University of Hong Kong and associate director, the Institute of Asia-Pacific Studies, the Chinese University of Hong Kong. His research interests include development studies, industrial relations, social movements and the comparative study of the East Asian Newly Industrialized Economies. Among his recent publications is *Hong Kong: Becoming a Chinese Global City* (co-authored with Tai-lok Lui, 2009).

Peter B. EVANS is professor of sociology at the University of California, Berkeley. His current research interest focuses on the comparative political economy of national development in the Global South. His recent books include *Embedded Autonomy: States and Industrial Transformation* (1995), an edited collection entitled *State-Society Synergy: Government and Social Capital in Development* (1997), and another edited collection entitled *Livable Cities: Urban Struggles for Livelihood and Sustainability* (2001).

Agnes Shuk-mei KU is associate professor of social science at the Hong Kong University of Science and Technology. She is also affiliated with the Centre for Cultural Sociology at Yale University. She specializes in cultural sociology, civil society, citizenship, urban space and Hong Kong studies. Her publications include *Remaking Citizenship in Hong Kong: Community, Nation and the Global City* (co-edited with Ngai Pun, 2004), and *Hong Kong Mobile: Making a Global Population* (co-edited with Helen F. Siu, 2008).

James Kin-ching LEE is professor of social policy and chair of the Department of Applied Social Sciences at the Hong Kong Polytechnic University. He specializes in comparative social and housing policy in East Asia. His research focuses mainly on comparative social development and social policy in East Asia, and in particular, on institutional arrangements that facilitate the attainment of social and economic objectives. He publishes in international journals such as *Housing Studies, Pacific Review, Policy & Politics, Environment & Planning, and Economic Geography*. He has also published several books in housing policy and social welfare, which include *Housing, Home Ownership and Social Change in Hong Kong* (1999), *Housing and Social Change: East West Perspectives* (with Ray Forrest, 2003), and *The Crisis of Welfare in East Asia* (with K. W. Chan, 2007).

Eliza Wing-yee LEE is associate professor in the Department of Politics and Public Administration, the University of Hong Kong. She obtained her BSocSc from the Chinese University of Hong Kong and her PhD from Syracuse University. Prior to joining the University of Hong Kong, she taught at the Chinese University of Hong Kong. Her current research interests are the politics of social policy development, civil society organizations, participatory governance, public management and gender, with particular focus on Hong Kong and its comparison with selected Asian states. Her articles have appeared in *Governance, Policy and Politics, Journal of Social Policy, Voluntas, Public Administration Review, Asian Survey*, and *International Review of Administrative Sciences*. She is a member of the editorial board of *Voluntas* and an associate editor of the *Asian-Pacific Journal of Public Administration*.

Tai-lok LUI is chair and professor of sociology at the University of Hong Kong. His research interests are in the areas of class analysis and economic restructuring. His recent publications include *Hong Kong, China: Learning to Belong to a Nation* (2008) and *Hong Kong: Becoming and Chinese Global City* (2009).

MA Ngok is associate professor of government and public administration at the Chinese University of Hong Kong. He received his BSSc and MPhil from the Chinese University and PhD from the University of California, Los Angeles. His research interests include Hong Kong government and politics, democratization, parties and elections, political economy, and transformation in Eastern Europe. His recent publications include *Political Development in Hong Kong: State, Political Society and Civil Society in Hong Kong* (2007).

Alvin Y. SO received a bachelor of social science degree from the Chinese University of Hong Kong and an MA and PhD degree in sociology from the University of California, Los Angeles. He has taught at the University of Hawaii before joining the Hong Kong University of Science and Technology in 1998. His research interests include development, social movements and class conflict. His writings include: *The South China Silk District* (1986), *Social Change and Development* (1990), *East Asia and World Economy* (co-authored with Stephen Chiu, 1995). *Hong Kong's Embattled Democracy* (1999). His co-edited volume (with William Tay) entitled *The Handbook of Contemporary China* is forthcoming from World Scientific.

Siu-lun WONG obtained his bachelor of social sciences degree from the University of Hong Kong in 1971, his MPhil degree from the Chinese University of Hong Kong, and his BLitt and DPhil degrees from the University of Oxford. His academic career began with teaching in the Department of Sociology at the University of Hong Kong where he was later appointed professor and head of department. He has recently retired from the directorship of Centre of Asian Studies at the University of Hong Kong. His research interests include the study of entrepreneurship, business networks, migration, social indicators, and the development of sociology in China. He is the author of, among others, *Emigrant Entrepreneurs: Shanghai Industrialists in Hong Kong* (1988), *Chinese Family Enterprises in Hong Kong: Case Studies* (with Victor Zheng, 2004), and *A History of the Hong Kong Rice Trade* (with Victor Zheng, 2005).

Introduction
Repositioning the post-colonial Hong Kong government
The interplay of state, market and society

Stephen Wing-kai Chiu

Contrary to popular mythology that upheavals of epic proportions would mark the end of the millennium, the twenty-first century actually dawned far less spectacularly than the doomsayers had predicted. Yet, it proved no less eventful as we all know. In particular, the world has witnessed a number of dramatic changes over the past few decades that have reverberated throughout the globe—the end of the Cold War and the dissolution of the Warsaw Pact bloc undoubtedly the most dramatic. The acceleration of the process of global integration turns out to be equally consequential, especially in the realms of economic flows since roughly the same time as the fall of the Berlin Wall. Stepping into the new century, we also witnessed the unprecedented September 11 terrorist attack upon the USA homeland in 2001 and rising tension between the Islamic and Anglo-American worlds.

Chinese traditions also believed that extraordinary natural phenomena precede major political upheavals, signalling heavenly unrest or dissatisfaction towards the ruler on earth. Nevertheless, contrary to this view, the secular event of Hong Kong's return to Chinese sovereignty in 1997 took place utterly uneventfully, with none of the popularly imagined and feared social and political disturbances surrounding the handover. Yet, the new Special Administrative Region (SAR) government soon faced a number of unprecedented challenges. In 1997, the spread of the Asian Financial Crisis to Hong Kong burst the asset bubbles of the 1990s, thus puncturing the long period of prosperity that coincided with the last years of colonial rule. From 1997 to 1998, an outbreak of avian influenza ("bird flu") resulted in eighteen confirmed human cases and six deaths. Hong Kong authorities managed to contain the disease only by slaughtering over one million chickens. As Hong Kong was nursing the wounds caused by the double blows of the recession and the 1997 epidemic, an even more mysterious infectious disease struck Hong Kong in 2003. Between February and May, the Severe Acute Respiratory Syndrome (SARS) outbreak in Hong Kong took 299 lives and infected 386 health care workers. Prompted by popular dissatisfaction with the government's performance in tackling challenges like the SARS outbreak, over a million people marched in the streets of Hong Kong. In March 2005, the first Chief Executive of the SAR government under Chinese rule, Tung Chee-hwa, resigned (on medical grounds), replaced by the then Chief Secretary for Administration, Donald Tsang.

Of course, supernatural forces might have less to do with this unprecedented political upheaval than the mundane dynamics of the society and polity. Yet, the case suggests that, despite its past reputation as the stable and prosperous crown jewel of the British Commonwealth, post-colonial Hong Kong may not be an easy place to govern. The Tsang team has continued to face similar challenges to its governance and still explores ways to reposition itself vis-à-vis the economy and the society in the post-colonial era. While seeking to mobilize public support for its policies through strengthened political communication, it has continued to pursue an incremental approach to democratization instead of rapidly deepening the channels of political participation. The creeping spread of state interventionism that started during the late-colonial period and that persisted into the Tung era observably continues during the Tsang era—so much so that an attempt to legislate for the minimum wage in 2010 led the neo-liberal *Economist* to declare the end of the free-market experiment in Hong Kong (*The Economist* 2010).

This volume includes nine original essays that help shed light on the challenges facing the Hong Kong SAR government in the new century. With the exception of Peter Evans, all our contributors, each a locally-born scholar, have experienced the ups and downs of Hong Kong in recent decades and stay deeply concerned about the future of the local community. As we shall see, despite all the claims about the demise of the state in an era of globalization, we believe that the government remains a major force in this new century and that any effective policy measures offered to solve Hong Kong's problems must somehow involve it. Embedded social and political conditions, difficult to alter in the short run, made governance more than merely a matter of technique or skills. It is therefore essential for the Hong Kong community to reflect on and discuss the political foundations of its governance and the appropriate roles of the Hong Kong government in the new century.

Beyond the state-market antinomy

In this volume, we have chosen to step aside from the belaboured constitutional *cum* political battles of the search for a new political order in Hong Kong (see Lau 2007 for a review of such issues), and to start instead from a more macroscopic perspective of the challenges facing the Hong Kong government in its relationship to the society. Our chapters have undertaken to address these challenges, in various ways, from two directions, namely, the changes in the domestic society and in the global economy. As in most newly developed societies, changes in the domestic political economy have given rise, on the one hand, to debates over the appropriate role of the state in the society while, on the other hand, changes in the global economy have also generated new problems for states to tackle.

On the first question, regarding the appropriate role of the state, during much of the post-war years, the key issue has consisted of whether the state or the market should drive developmental outcomes. In the early post-war years, neo-liberal prescriptions prevailed in the development literature resulting in favouring a market-led model of development with East Asia taken as the prime example of the success of this strategy. The *World Development Report 1987* offers an explicit statement consistent with the mainstream neoclassical view in economics that supports the free-trade and free-market model of development. In its lending policy, as in that of other multilateral financial bodies such as the International Monetary Fund, it also strives to coax developing states to adopt a more "market-friendly" programme of development.

The writings on the East Asian NICs (EANICs) by economists associated with the World Bank best represent the accounts of East Asian development emphasizing the importance of market forces.[1] In this model, the state assumes the relatively limited role of serving as a catalyst and as corrector of market failures. Private entrepreneurs who respond eagerly to market stimuli occupy the centre stage, capitalizing on a cheap, plentiful supply of labour. This interpretation begins with a free-trade regime, under which national policy allocates resources in accordance with the country's existing comparative advantages. Thus, Little (1981) stresses the positive effects of "almost free trade conditions for exports" in EANICs' success. By "getting the price right" through trade liberalization and exchange rate reform, EANIC states provide the optimal environment for the growth of private enterprise (Little 1981, 42).

In the case of Hong Kong, for instance, it posits that the maintenance of a free-trade regime accounts for the city's successful industrialization. Freed from the fetters of government intervention and capitalizing on their comparative advantages, the EANICs then embarked on export-oriented, labour-intensive industrialization. Government stability also vitally provides stable, long-term time-horizons for private business calculations. It sees a regulatory framework and infrastructural capacity as beneficial, but any interference into private decision-making as not (see for example, Balassa 1988). In other words, it portrays private entrepreneurs as the protagonists of the East Asian industrialization narrative with the state's role best conceived of as catalytic rather than "pervasive" (Ranis 1985).

By the 1980s, however, a revisionist interpretation of the East Asian experience, epitomized by the concept of the developmental state, provided an alternative account diametrically opposed to the neoclassical perspective (Johnson 1987; White and Wade 1988). This new intellectual paradigm draws historical sustenance from the argument that successful "late development" takes a very different form from that of earlier industrializers (Gerschenkron 1967, 443–59); the former's developmental process becoming less "spontaneous", with the state assuming the role of the major agent of social transformation. Partly in reaction to the neoclassical onslaught, two major studies on East Asian industrialization have devoted themselves to this theme (Wade and White 1984 and Deyo 1987). Likewise, Deyo concludes his volume on the "new East Asian industrialism" by proposing a "strategic capacity" model (1987, 227–48). Instead of emphasizing free markets, trade liberalization, private enterprise and the restricted role of the state, the statist perspective contends that states have a strategic role to play in taming domestic and international market forces and harnessing them to national ends (Gerschenkron 1962; Rueschemeyer and Evans 1985).

Since the late 1990s, and especially after the 1997 Asian Financial Crisis, observers have increasingly placed the statist model under critical scrutiny. Drawing on the cases of Korea and, to a lesser extent, Thailand and Indonesia, they have raised the possibility of the "crony state" and spoken of the dangers of the state meddling in the market. They claim that state interventions would lead to collusion between it and private business, giving rise to rent-seeking behaviour by special interest groups. The backlash against the arguments for a strong and autonomous state, therefore, quickly led to a theoretical reaction that emphasizes the nature of the interactions and the institutional linkages between the state elite and societal actors (Kohli 2004; Migdal, Kohli and Shue 1994).

In the discussion of East Asian development, scholars hold a similar view stressing the *interdependence* of state and business. Weiss calls it the "governed interdependence theory", premised on the proposition that "the ability of East Asian firms and industry more generally to adapt quickly to economic change is based on a system that socialises risk and thereby coordinates change across a broad array of organizations—both public and private" (Weiss 1995, 594). Governed interdependence refers to a system of central co-ordination in which the government and industry co-operate and communicate to bring about innovation and realize competitive potentials. This model has both analytical and policy implications, since it simultaneously generalizes about state-business co-ordination in East Asia and how this relationship has contributed to the economic success of the region.

This approach departs from the state-led model in its insistence that states cannot simply *impose* development policies upon the private sector. Doing so would compromise their effectiveness since the most optimal ones consist of those formulated in consultation with the private sector and implemented with the willing co-operation of firms. "Co-ordination" comprises the key to this system. Why is industrial co-ordination possible? Apart from the autonomy emphasized so much in the state-led models, Weiss pins down the institutional capacities for co-ordination to developing the efficaciousness of state-industry linkages. She argues that Korea, Taiwan and Japan have established an elaborate matrix of institutional linkages between state agencies and the private sector. Such "policy networks" "provide a vital mechanism for acquiring information and for co-ordinating agreement with the private sector" (Weiss 1995: 600). In Japan, for example, the Ministry of International Trade and Industry (now renamed Ministry of Economy, Trade and Industry) benefited from the work of over 250 deliberation councils that enable the state to consult the private sector and to collect valuable information. Only by doing so can a strong ministry avoid formulating policies insulated from the private sector and act in concert with industry (see also Samuels 1987; Okimoto 1989).

Social embeddedness and the challenges of good governance

Going beyond the opposition between the state and the market in the debates that occurred during the 1980s, the leading discussions in the 1990s on the role of state in development highlighted the contributions of good governance. "Governance" constitutes a nebulous term that has come to assume very different meanings. Development studies commonly assert its importance. As the United Nations Development Program (UNDP) states, "[h]uman development cannot be sustained without good governance" (UNDP 1997, iv). In the development context, the definition of governance the World Bank proposed and adopted by many development agencies and institutions, prevails: "the manner in which power is exercised in the management of a country's economic and social resources for development" (World Bank 1992, 3; UNDP 1997).

The World Bank and other development agencies typically identify four inter-related attributes of good governance: capacity building, participation, predictability and transparency. *Capacity building* implies "the capacity to provide citizens with an acceptable level of public services, in an effective and efficient manner" (Asian Development Bank 1995, 26). They consider greater accountability essential to enhance governing capacity. The involvement of the governed lies at the heart of *participation*; a participatory approach will enable beneficiaries and other affected parties to have "the opportunity to improve the design and implementation of public programs and projects" (Asian Development Bank 1995, 5). The principle of *predictability*, on the other hand, often more concretely expresses itself in the establishment of the legal framework for development, but can also extend to the entire regulatory and policy matrix relating to public and private activities. To ensure predictability, government and organizations must apply rules and laws as uniformly and impartially as possible (Asian Development Bank 1995, 6). Finally, agencies often link *transparency* to the provision of information. "Transparency improves both the availability and the accuracy of market information and thereby lowers transaction costs" (World Bank 1994, 29). These four elements of good governance obviously support and reinforce themselves mutually.

The concept of governance has aroused much controversy.[2] On the one hand, the Bank uses a definition clearly neo-liberal in origin as it assumes a narrow band of policy areas that the state should engage in. In this respect, the Bank has received criticism for focusing entirely on the narrow administrative level of governance and neglecting the power or regime dimension. Nevertheless, in spite of its neo-liberal origins, even those less inclined to favour a reduced range of state interventions in development have found the concept useful since it highlights the importance of state actions in development administration. In this view, good governance can provide a vehicle for administrative reforms that enable the state to intervene more effectively in a statist manner, rather than restraining state actions. Therefore, the concept does not inherently restrict itself to expanding the role of free markets. Whatever its ideological underpinnings, the idea of governance, like that of state-society interdependence, does throw sharp relief on the interconnectedness of state actions and societal interests, and downplays the notion of the state as an autonomous entity standing above the society.

With respect to participation, Fung and Wright (2001) respond to the conservative assertion of an alleged trade-off between participation and efficiency in democratic institutions by coining the notion of "empowered deliberative democracy" (EDD). They document a series of reforms in local level governance that seek to "deepen the ways in which ordinary people can effectively participate in and influence policies that directly affect their lives" (Fung and Wright 2001, 7). They generalize from these case studies to derive three political principles, three design characteristics and one primary background condition for EDD. While they agree that it is premature to draw conclusions regarding the final results of these experiments, they suggest that EDD has the potential to effectively solve problems, to generate fair and equitable outcomes and to facilitate broad and deep participation.

Fung and Wright's discussion overlaps with Peter Evans' notion of empowerment and participation in his chapter for this volume and has also inspired a number of other contributions here. Our chapters demonstrate that public policy and good governance must embed themselves in the society in complex ways, even if one even leaves out the issue of democratization. Ma Ngok's chapter traces the increase in state interventions to the state's co-optation of a new crop of political appointees into the elite ranks of its governmental machinery. Chiu and Lui's chapter documents the declining cohesiveness of the capitalist class in Hong Kong over the 1980s and 1990s and considers its effect on policy-making. Eliza Lee highlights how the top-down business-oriented approach to urban planning could reduce the capacity for smooth policy implementation. Ku discusses the ways in which the Hong Kong government has shaped, and, in turn, successive images of citizenship have shaped it. From a comparative perspective, So and Chiu also show the manner in which the nature of Korean democracy has allowed for an effective response to the Asian Financial Crisis in restructuring large corporations and in eliminating their dependence on state handouts.

Globalization and the end of the state?

Apart from examining the changing nature of and expectations for governance, our chapters also address the impact of globalization on government and, in particular, whether it has contributed to the alleged demise of state power. As Held and McGrew put it, globalization "denotes the expanding scale, growing magnitude, speeding up and deepening impact of transcontinental flows and patterns of social interaction". It refers to a shift or transformation in the scale of human organization that links distant communities and expands the reach of power relations across the world's regions and continents" (2003,

4). While globalization is taking place in many realms of social life, economic globalization typically takes the centre stage in many of the analyses. We normally view expansion of international trade; rapid flows of inward and outward foreign investment; the multi-nationalization of corporate activities; the growing integration of international financial markets; the movements of labour and talent and the formation of global policy regimes governing cross-border transactions as processes normally associated with globalization. Yet, we must resist the temptation to equate globalization with the growing integration of the global economy per se, as the accelerated growth of social interactions and the integration of human organizations across political and spatial units in the world does not confine itself to economic transactions. Globalization has also resulted in the diffusion of values and cultural phenomena, while the formation of global governance institutions does not remain restricted solely to regulating economic flows.

Globalization has given rise to numerous debates, even in response to the very basic question of whether it genuinely exists and constitutes a new phenomenon. Unsurprisingly, given the modern state's roots in national sovereignty and the establishment of national boundaries, debates have also occurred surrounding the role of the state in the developmental process in the alleged new age of globalization. At one extreme lies the "end of the state" thesis proposed by what Held et al. (1999) call the "hyperglobalists", which posits that the contemporary processes of globalization have rendered the nation-state obsolete. In Kenichi Ohmae's view, nation-state "has become an unnatural—even dysfunctional—organizational unit for thinking about economic activity. It combines things at the wrong level of aggregation" (1995, 16). His arguments for the end of the nation-state, once novel, have now become commonplace. He observes the nature of the four "I's" (investment, industry, information technology, and individual consumers) has so changed as a result of globalization that they require "region states" that border on several national territories conduct economic activities. "They may lie entirely within or across the borders of a nation state. That does not matter. It is the irrelevant result of historical accident. What defines them is not the location of their political borders but the fact that they are the right size and scale to be the true, natural business units in today's global economy. Theirs are the borders—and the connections—that matter in a borderless world" (1995, 5).

Certainly, such extreme views associated with hyperglobalism have not met with widespread acceptance. What Weiss (2003) identifies as the "globalization-as-constraint" thesis employs a more sophisticated approach, one often viewed as "standard", for understanding the transformation of governance under globalization. According to Weiss, this thesis asserts: "(a) that the world is becoming more interconnected through increasing economic openness and the growth of transborder networks that accompany that process, and (b) that this interconnectedness is increasing the power of global (economic and political) networks of interaction *at the expense of* national (economic and political) networks" (2003, 5; emphasis in original). Further, Strange (1996) offers a sophisticated but forceful version of this thesis. The argument found there largely coincides with the "globalization-as-constraint" view in that "the impersonal forces of world markets, integrated over the post-war period more by private enterprise in finance, industry and trade than by the cooperative decisions of governments, are now more powerful than the states to whom ultimate political authority over society and economy is supposed to belong" (1996, 4). It identifies the accelerating pace of technological change and financial integration as the primary causes of the shift in the state-market balance of power though such a shift occurs before our eyes in spite of three paradoxes that apparently mask it.

The first paradox—while its power is declining, the state has become more active and intervenes constantly in the daily lives of citizens. The second paradox—although existing states are suffering from a progressive loss of real authority, political entities aspiring to sovereign statehood are increasing. The final paradox—while the governments of advanced western societies appear to be retreating from intervention into the society, many Asian states have apparently gained power through their active role in the developmental process. Strange considers these paradoxes as either illusory, e.g., the view that more interventions mean more power, or dismisses them as temporary phenomena, as in the case of the ascendancy of Asian states under the Cold War system. She asserts that, in the longer run, the forces of change in the international political economy continue to unmistakably transform the balance of state-market power leading to a diffusion of authority to non-state institutions and associations, and to local and regional bodies (Strange 1996, 5–7).

Weiss herself contests these views and, instead, highlights the other, "enabling" face of globalization. Her thesis rests on two main arguments. First, "[s]trong exposure to world markets (qua globalization) has a tendency to heighten insecurity among broad segments of the population, which in turn generates demand for social protection" (2003, 16). Such generalized insecurity would prompt states to compensate for the social costs of globalization through social policies in order to maintain the social contract. The second suggests that increased global competitive pressure on businesses has heightened firms' need for governmental support. Rather than "coming of age" and weaning themselves from public assistance, they clamour for more governmental action that would allow them to gain advantages over their competitors in the global marketplace, whether they consist of tax incentives, technological diffusion or support for training and human capital investment. The combined effects of these two forces, rather than significantly constraining and reducing the states' scope for actions, would, instead, prompt a variety of responses from the state both to compensate the losers and to groom winners in global competition. For example, Hobson (2003) demonstrates that the tax burden on corporations in the Organisation for Economic Co-operation and Development has generally increased rather than declined in the period of accelerated globalization, suggesting that the latter process has not diminished overwhelmingly the extractive capacity of the state.

Peter Evans' essay in this volume accords largely with this line of thought, but also adds to the theoretical basis for a discussion of the role of the state in Hong Kong's development. Starting with three new developments in economic theories of growth, namely, the endogenous growth approach, institutional approaches and the capability approach, he underlines their convergence through their common emphasis on "institutions that set collective goals, provide collective goods, and maintain general rules and norms" (this volume). With this observation, he returns to the theory of the developmental state he pioneered in his various path-breaking works and highlights the role of bureaucratic capacity and the presence of dense ties between the state and the entrepreneurial elites in shaping developmental outcomes.

He then asks: does this form of the developmental state, that is, with high bureaucratic capacity and dense connections to entrepreneurial elites, remain relevant in the twenty-first century? The question becomes important since the character of economic growth has experienced a radical transformation during the twenty-first century. What he calls the "bit-driven" growth that centres on intangible production and the delivery of direct inter-personal services to consumers underlies the phenomenon of the decline of manufacturing and the rise of services. He argues that the requirements of the bit-driven economy will make private sector elites less reliable allies than in the previous era. For example, developmental states in the industrial century tended to create and protect monopoly rights, albeit temporarily, that would encourage the private sector to invest and expand production. In the era of bit-driven growth, such political protection of monopoly rights might seriously strangle innovation and slow down the overall rate of growth.

Evans echoes the capability approach with its emphasis on the expansion of the capabilities of people to lead the kind of lives they value. These capabilities represent, at the same time, both the goals of development and the primary means of attaining them. Fostering private and public investment in the knowledge and skills of individual citizens as key inputs of growth therefore becomes the critical task for the new century's developmental state. In discharging this task, the state also needs to embed itself in a network of public deliberations that would help it choose among the range of capabilities available for expansion and the means of achieving them. In other words, broad-based political participation and some forms of democratic "deliberative" political institutions remain important for the new breed of developmental states. While this new vision of development does not necessarily condemn the "old" developmental states to the dustbin of history, it does mean that political elites have to make considerable adjustments if they wish to deal effectively with the task at hand.

In a similar vein, So and Chiu analyze the post-war transformation of another archetypical developmental state, namely, South Korea in this volume. The state's active intervention into the economy, a competent and meritocratic bureaucracy, its control of the financial sector and its dominance over the *chaebols* (large diversified family-owned conglomerates) and all other classes characterize the Korean developmental state. As in the case of many others, the Korean version was created on the foundation of a strong state, weak market and weak society in the Cold War era. However, this kind of state-market and state-society relationship began to change in the 1980s. Nurtured by the developmental state for three decades, the *chaebols* had grown immensely in both size and power. Globalization policies, as for example, liberalization and de-regulation of financial markets, empowered them even further, giving them the capacity to evade or challenge the policies of the developmental state. Democratization, too, weakened the foundations of a developmental state based on authoritarianism and the repression of civil society.

The authors then document how a critical event arising from the new globalized economy, the Asian Financial Crisis, further transformed the relationship among the state, market and society. With the *chaebols* weakened by the Crisis, the ascendance to power of the popularly elected Kim Dae Jung government enabled it to pursue neo-liberal reforms to reinvigorate the market, reforms to re-strengthen the state and reforms to involve the civil society under the name of "participatory democracy". The state also put forward a massive welfare programme in response to high unemployment, social polarization and rising tensions in Korean society.

In broad brushstrokes, the authors thus validate Evans' vision for the developmental state. Rather than assuming the zero-sum conception of a "strong state, weak society" foundation for the developmental state, they point to the Korean case as an example of the new "mutual empowerment" relationship between the state, market and society since Kim's government seeks to invigorate the market, to empower the state and to activate the civil society concurrently. So and Chiu also emphasize how the South Korean case points to the importance of appreciating the political conditions for the developmental state, encapsulated by Evans (1995) under the concept of "embedded autonomy". The South Korea experiment in "mutual empowerment" appears to come at a time when the Asian Financial Crisis heightened state autonomy and the rise of the civil society accentuated state embeddedness. Democratic participation has strengthened the capacity of the state to regulate the market, while state policies have geared themselves toward enhancing the capabilities of the citizenry to respond to the new bit-driven economy in developmental states.

James Lee's chapter on public housing also testifies to the continuing relevance of public policy in discussing the shaping of Hong Kong people's life chances and the economy. Peter Cheung then assesses the Hong Kong government's responses to globalization directly through an examination of its role in managing cross-border transactions between Hong Kong and mainland China. So and Chiu's chapter certainly deals with the issue of the ways in which globalization created challenges for the Korean state to deal with, while Lui and Chiu also argue that Hong Kong's economic restructuring that accompanied the new wave of globalization since the 1990s has led to realignments in the governing coalition that, in turn, fundamentally reshaped the parameters of governance in Hong Kong.

The Hong Kong story

One should craft the Hong Kong story of the changing role of the government in the developmental process certainly with reference to the intellectual currents and issues within the larger theoretical and comparative literature on the role of the state in the global economy. In this respect, we can see that the local contributions to this volume pay particular attention to the role of the state-society relationship and democratic participation in shaping the capacity of the state to respond to globalization and the new economy. While globalization stands out as a common background to much discussion of state-society relations, Hong Kong contrasts sharply with the advanced countries because of its status as a polity undergoing democratization. It also exists not as a full-fledged sovereign state but as a special administrative region with a high degree of autonomy under the People's Republic of China. As a result, though on the one hand, the political impact of globalization appears to impinge on Hong Kong as in many other advanced countries, on the other, it faces political challenges not commonly found in the industrialized world.

Ma Ngok's chapter starts the Hong Kong story by outlining the contours of the transformation of governance since the colonial era. He first seeks to debunk the myth of Hong Kong's colonial *laissez-faire* policy as the result of ideological adherence to the free market. Instead, he contends, it resulted from, along the lines advanced by a handful of other scholars, a carefully forged strategy of legitimizing colonial rule. After 1997, the state form of Hong Kong changed as a consequence of decolonization, democratization and economic restructuring. Continued efforts to incorporate new political elites into the state machinery have an eclectic, increasingly fragmented, corporatist structure. A type of what he labelled as "organizational feudalism" therefore leads to ad hoc and particularistic sectoral intervention in the post-colonial era.

In a similar vein, the chapter by Lui and Chiu looks at the changing relationship between the government and big businesses in Hong Kong. They begin by describing the colonial political order as one built on their close partnership. A cohesive business community composed of a dense network of major corporations, among other factors, made this alliance possible. The consensus of the business community (or at least the dominant segments of it) on major policy issues, positive non-interventionism prominent among them, formed the pillar of the colonial governance, making it easier for the colonial government to forge social support for its policies.

While this characterization of the colonial political order looks familiar, it breaks new ground in its analysis of the evolution of the government-business alliance. Based on a new data set of the network of big businesses developed through their interlocking directorships from the 1980s to the late 1990s, they argue that, since the 1990s, the degree of cohesion in the business community has declined, due, first, to the rise of Chinese business groups and, second, to the process of deregulation which led to the intrusion of business groups onto each other's turfs resulting in intensified competition. With the breakdown of the business network, the SAR government could no longer position itself as an impartial arbiter of any conflicts of interests between the big businesses, but has found itself dragged into taking sides in the rivalries among the business groups.

Returning to the question of the viability of the developmental state in the new century, both Ma and Lui and Chiu review the recent debate in Hong Kong regarding the alleged demise of the "positive non-interventionist" approach to economic management, perhaps illustrating the double bind the government has discovered itself caught in. They observe that, while the Hong Kong government has been trying vigorously to articulate a viable development strategy and carve out a new direction for Hong Kong's development, a cross-fire of conflicting demands and interests has trapped it. They argue that such conflicting demands do not emanate merely from the process of democratization or the popular demands for participation or welfare, as commonly believed, but also symptomize the underlying changes in the power structure. The weakening of state governance capacity should not be attributed therefore simply to democratization but also to increasing fragmentation of the governing coalition or, in Ma's words, the eclectic corporatism in Hong Kong. To construct a viable governing coalition that supports the quest for strong governance, they contend, the government must seek a way to overcome the fragmentation of business interests and forge broad-based support and legitimizing its major development policies. The first four chapters in this volume illustrate the prominent theme of the possibility of creating a positive feedback loop between democratization and the state's capacity to forge a viable developmental strategy in the new century.

Agnes Ku's chapter looks at the issue of governance from the perspective of the changing conceptions of citizenship in Hong Kong. Beginning with a review of the idea of modern citizenship and, especially, the Marshallian view, she next examines how the rise of neo-liberalism impinges on it. Ku views the Marshallian conception of citizenship as one built upon the state-based mode of equality that seeks to redress the inequality of power between capital and labour in a capitalist society. She then documents the evolution of colonial governance and the subsequent underlying conceptions of citizenship since the colonial era. Though a *laissez-faire* ideology dominated the colonial state's mode of governance, the concept of citizenship there remained underdeveloped except in the market sphere and implicitly concerned itself much more with law and order than with rights and entitlements. In particular, the idea of social rights almost did not exist, and welfare provisions developed with a "residualist" character, although the role of the colonial state in collective consumption did expand gradually in the post-war era.

The same forces since the 1960s that pushed the colonial state to expand provisions of welfare also drove a gradual revision of the broader mode of governance into one that emphasized social consensus. The colonial government sought to mobilize public consent to and support for its policies as well as the very system of its rule. Political institutions still circumscribed opportunities for open democratic participation and did not promote the concept of political citizenship. Instead, the colonial state employed its active involvement in the everyday lives of its people to boost its legitimacy and forge a social consensus without actually allowing their participation in policy-making arenas.

The process of decolonization since the 1980s, however, opened the floodgates of democratization and, by implication, a new understanding of political citizenship. A pro-democracy movement also emerged in response to the new political opportunities. A new discourse that emphasized the rights of individual citizens and a broadening of political participation came to contest citizenship, and the hegemonic discourse of administrative efficiency leading to economic prosperity and political stability. In the post-handover period, changing circumstances have led to a more interventionist style of "active and strong" governance in the SAR government. Ku pinpoints its reliance on active and assertive interventions without the articulation of a new conception of political citizenship as the key feature of this new mode of governance. Both Tung Chee-hwa and Donald Tsang's governments appear to have adopted many of the colonial strategies of consensus building without genuine dialogue with and incorporation of the diverse voices into the society. In conclusion, to resolve the political stalemate in Hong Kong, she calls for the development of a democratic citizenship that allows for more effective public political participation.

Eliza Lee also takes up the issue of governance but shifts her attention to the local level. She begins her chapter with an historical overview of the development of local governance in Hong Kong, summarizing its central features as the prevalence of state intervention in and the penetration of local communities, state absorption of civic association and confinement of community initiatives to administratively-defined arenas. In the post-colonial era, the government has continued to rely on the political machinery the colonial state constructed as the basis for its support and legitimacy. Moreover, the rise of pro-Beijing local organizations has marked their entrance into local political sphere as the so-called "pro-establishment" forces. Mobilization by the political parties, however, means that new grassroots associations have proliferated. Centring on the District Councils, a "Hong Kong-style pork-barrel" local politics became visible. She contends that the post-colonial government has relied on clientelism to maintain the loyalty of the pro-establishment political forces.

She then turns her attention to the so-called "H15" urban renewal project that would redevelop certain old areas in Wanchai demolishing old buildings to make way for modern high-rises. The Urban Renewal Authority, a public organization overseeing the project, set out to buy out the buildings in the area for redevelopment. As an old community, resistance began to brew as the area's residents and small business owners who had lived and worked there for a long time expressed great reluctance to move. Residents and business owners with the help of a local NGO eventually formed an organization, the H15 Concern Group. Some stakeholders mobilized around the Concern Group, and demanded, among others, more compensation for their properties and a relocation plan that would allow them to maintain their existing community networks. Eliza Lee observes that a largely defensive, instrumental movement quickly turned into a "journey of self-discovery" for the participants. The activists began to demand a participatory people-oriented approach to urban renewal and sought to preserve the cultural heritage of the local community. With the help of planning professionals, the Concern Group proposed its own alternative redevelopment plan that embraced the sustainable development and cultural conservation. While the resistance turned out to be futile when the government refused to budge, Lee argues that it has important ramifications for local governance and signifies the beginning of a new mode of local participation and mobilization.

Another set of questions our authors address concerns those arising from an examination of the proper role of the state in Hong Kong's development. Consistent with a comparative discussion, they largely agree that the Hong Kong government has a significant role to play above and beyond the neo-liberal minimalist conception. Even under accelerated globalization, it remains critical for the SAR government to actively involve itself in the economy and society. One example involves housing policy. The post-colonial government inherited a sizable presence in the provision of housing from the colonial era resulting in debates over whether it should continue with that role or beat a retreat. In his chapter, James Lee first reviews the conceptual justifications for state intervention in the housing market. He observes that even a neoclassical perspective justifies state intervention on efficiency and/or equity grounds. For efficiency, the existence of market failures in the form of monopoly or oligopoly justifies state intervention. For equity, ensuring equitable access to housing and home finance, especially for low income households, justifies state action. Going beyond neoclassical precepts, Lee suggests that housing policy can serve an integral role in the social security system while fulfilling multiple social goals.

His chapter then examines several key issues in housing policy. It starts by charting the government's crucial role in regulating the supply of land through its formal ownership of all land in Hong Kong as well as demonstrating the importance of revenues generated from the sale and use of land in public finance. For Lee, the system of land allocation by auction with its goal of maximizing land value contains serious flaw since it results in housing-cost inflation and over-investment by the real estate sector. Through the regulation of land supply and the construction of public housing, the government has sought to maintain a delicate balance between revenue generation and stabilization of the housing market. In the aftermath of the Asian Financial Crisis, the government's misguided effort to respond to it by increasing land and public housing supply to address the housing shortage prior to the bust soon turned into a major political and economic blunder. He also observes the pronounced instability of housing prices in Hong Kong that remain subject to major swings. In the most recent decades, housing has also become extremely unaffordable for many families. People in Hong Kong highly value home ownership leading to government policies adopted to promote this ideal. In the post-Crisis era, the government is also leaning towards the private sector as the primary vehicle for meeting the demand for home ownership. Yet, the author points out that home ownership has risks given the volatility of housing prices. The boom and bust in the housing market can then have serious repercussions for the entire economy, given the exposure of home owners to mortgage loans. Lee implies that state cannot avoid intervention into the housing sector in Hong Kong in order to address the efficiency and equity issues and that the government must forge a new set of housing policies less-focused on home ownership.

Moving beyond the confines of the territory, Peter Cheung explores the role of government in managing cross-boundary co-operation between Hong Kong and mainland China since 1997. He observes that cross-border relations between Hong Kong and South China have moved from a tentative, initial phase after the handover to one of intensified co-operation since 2003. The phenomenal growth of these transactions have also prompted the government to revamp and expand its institutional framework for their management and for the co-ordination and liaising between the central government and Hong Kong as well as between Hong Kong and the various levels of local governments on the Mainland.

As a result, the government has been taking a more active role in policy co-ordination leading toward economic integration, signified by the signing of the Closer Economic Partnership Arrangement (CEPA) in 2003. It has also pushed forward the promotion of mainland tourism into Hong Kong, the building of Hong Kong into a financial centre for China, deeper co-operation in infrastructural development and the inclusion of considerations about Hong Kong's role in regional and national plans. Furthermore, deepening social and economic integration has also given rise to a host of new issues that require a concerted response from governments in Hong Kong and South China, such as arranging boundary crossings, protecting the environment and containing the spread of health and food safety hazards of the type associated with SARS and bird-flu. He concludes that the phenomenal growth of cross-border interaction between Hong Kong and mainland China have contributed to recasting the role of government in the society and the economy. It has moved governance further away from *laissez-faire* or even the so-called "positive non-interventionism" and towards an activist local state. In response to the pressures involved in managing the growing flows of people, capital and traffic, the SAR government has gradually developed a greater capacity as well as the intention to regulate them.

We certainly do not claim we have exhausted the intellectual terrain relevant to an analysis of the changing governance in Hong Kong. Much work remains in order to foster a more comprehensive understanding of this complex issue. In particular, while our chapters have largely "bracketed" the effect of democratization upon shaping governance, it looms large in the background and will continue as an unavoidable issue in the near future. Though the constitutional stalemate will stay with us for some time, the democratization process has recently progressed while all concerned parties have committed themselves to move ahead, even though much disagreement still exists over its pace and direction. How would such incremental (and still limited) movement toward democratization affect public policies? A more complete answer will have to await another volume, but we stay confident that even with accelerated democratization, future governments of Hong Kong will have to come to terms with a largely similar set of challenges and parameters of governance to those this volume outlines. We hope it will pave the way for many more studies of the critical issues of state-society relations in Hong Kong in the new century.

1

What will the twenty-first-century developmental state look like?

Implications of contemporary development theory for the state's role

Peter B. Evans

What role will the developmental state play in the twenty-first century? What state structures and political institutions will best equip nations trying to enter the ranks of "developed" countries? I offer two interconnected propositions. The first stresses continuity: the "developmental state" will continue to play a crucial a role in economic growth and social transformation in the twenty-first century, just as it did in the latter half of the twentieth century. The second offers a more radical answer: successful twenty-first-century developmental states will have to depart fundamentally from existing models in order to achieve success. Growth strategies focused primarily on traditional capital accumulation will no longer suffice. State-society ties can no longer focus narrowly on relations with capitalist elites.

Understandings of the role of the developmental state have changed, first of all, because development theory has evolved. In addition, the historical context of development has changed. New challenges, seen through the lens of new theories, point toward a twenty-first-century developmental state quite different from its twentieth-century predecessor.

I will begin by reviewing the new streams of thinking that currently dominate development theory, starting with the "new growth theory" as put forward by theorists like Lucas (1988) and Romer (1986, 1990, 1993a, 1993b and 1994), and developed by a range of economists like Aghion (1999) and Helpman (2004). "Institutional approaches" to development, as elaborated by a wide-ranging set of development economists, including Rodrik (1999), Stiglitz (2002), Acemoglu and Robinson (2005 and 2006) among others, offer an equally important perspective. Perhaps most important of all are the convergences between these theories of growth and the "capability approach" to development as pioneered theoretically by Amartya Sen (1999), and at a more practical level by Mahbub Ul Haq.[1]

I will then review the models of the twentieth-century developmental state built around the studies of the archetypal cases of Korea and Taiwan by Amsden (1989, 1999 and 2001), Wade (1990) and many others (including myself). The success of these developmental states still remains incontestable, whether using the Human Development Index (HDI), growth of GDP per capita or more specific measures of industrial competitiveness as indicators. Following the perspective that I laid out a dozen years ago in *Embedded Autonomy* (Evans 1995), I will highlight two facets of the twentieth-century developmental state: bureaucratic capacity and "embeddedness".

Following this discussion of the twentieth-century developmental state, I will try to summarize some of the shifts in the historical character of development particularly relevant to the role of the state. I will argue for a partly mythical character of the narrative of "development" that emerged out of the "Golden Age of Capitalism" in the rich countries of the North that we can no longer sustain. This vision, in which the expansion of machine-production and a "blue-collar middle class", anchored relatively comfortable lives for a broad cross-section of the population never fit the realities of the Global South. In the twenty-first century, it is patently unsustainable in either the North or the South.

A narrative must ground itself in the fact that growth has become increasingly "bit-driven". Value added comes more from new ways of arranging bits of information in formulas, software code and images and less from the physical manipulation of materials to make tangible goods.[2] Even in the Global South, manufacturing employs a shrinking proportion of the population. Most people's livelihood depends on delivering intangible services. For a small minority, this entails highly rewarded "business services". For most, it means poorly-rewarded personal services.

The confluence of endogenous growth theory with institutional approaches to development and the capability approach jibe nicely with the shifting historical context. Together they suggest that twenty-first-century development will depend on generating intangible assets (ideas, skills and networks) rather than on stimulating investment in machinery and physical assets oriented to the production of tangible goods. This makes investment in human capabilities (which include the factor traditionally known as "human capital") more economically critical. At the same time, new development theories assume that economic growth depends on political institutions and the capacity to establish collective goals. The capability approach sets out the political argument most firmly, contending that only public interchange and open deliberation can effectively define development goals and elaborate the means for attaining them.

All of this has powerful implications for the institutional character of the developmental state, which I will develop in the final substantive section. Expanding investment in human capabilities depends, above all, on public investment, the efficient allocation of which requires much broader capacity to collect information. Implementation requires "co-production" of services by communities, families and individual.[3] The state-society ties required correspond nicely with the political propositions of new development theories, but stand in contrast to those utilized by traditional developmental states.

In short, viewing shifts in the historical character of economic growth through the lens of modern development theory suggests that state capacity will have an even greater role to play in societal success in the coming century than it did in the last one. But, it also suggests much broader, much more "bottom up" set of state-society ties to secure developmental success in the current century must replace the specific kind of "embeddedness" or "state-society synergy" crucial to twentieth century success—dense networks of ties connecting the state to industrial elites.

The recent evolution of development theory

We have left behind the days when development theory fixated on capital accumulation as the necessary and sufficient bedrock of growth. In what Hoff and Stiglitz (2001) call "modern economic theory", "[d]evelopment is no longer seen primarily as a process of capital accumulation but rather as a process of organizational change" (Hoff and Stiglitz 2001, 389).

Two interconnected strands of the "modern economics" of growth exist. They are: (1) the "new growth theory" which emphasizes the increasing returns to ideas as the real key to growth, and (2) the "institutional approach", which focuses on the key role of enduring shared normative expectations or "rules of the game" in enabling forward-looking economic action. If we combine the two, the central question for growth becomes, "What kind of institutional arrangements will best enable societies to generate new skills, knowledge and ideas and the networks needed to diffuse and take advantage of them?" I will start with the "new growth theory" (now two decades old) and then consider "institutional approaches".

In the late 1980s, theories of "endogenous growth" or the "new growth theory",[4] helped reorient theoretical discussions of growth. Its basic premises make intuitive sense. The dismal logic of diminishing returns, which limits development strategies based on physical capital (and even more thoroughly those based on land and natural resources), does not apply to knowledge and ideas. Since the cost of reproducing an idea effectively approaches zero, multiplying the use of valuable ideas generates returns that increase indefinitely with the scale of the market.

The new growth theory's emphasis on the centrality of idea production (rather than the accumulation of physical capital) fits well with the comparative empirical evidence on growth amassed over the course of the second half of the twentieth century.[5] Nonetheless, a still-large residual remains in most growth equations usually labelled as changes in "total factor productivity".[6] Trying to account for it provided one impetus for the institutional approaches that now dominate the mainstream of development economics.[7]

The "capability approach" supplies the third element in the renovation of development theory. Among all the recent contributions to development theory, it takes most seriously the universally accepted proposition that growth of GDP per capita serves not as an end in itself, but, instead, as a proxy for improvements in human well-being valuable only insofar as it empirically connects to improved well-being. Sen argues that we should evaluate development in terms of "the expansion of the 'capabilities' of people to lead the kind of lives they value—and have reason to value".[8] Because it rejects reduction of developmental success to a single metric, the capability approach identifies "public deliberation" as the only analytically defensible way of ordering capabilities and puts political institutions and civil society at the centre of developmental goal-setting.

An interesting convergence between the capabilities conceptualization of development and the new growth theory also occurs. Sen (1999) emphasizes that the expansion of capabilities represents simultaneously the primary *goal* of development and a principle *means* through which to achieve development. The emphasis of new growth theorists upon the knowledge and skills embodied in the capabilities of individuals (and the networks that connect them) as key inputs to growth, buttresses the idea of "capability enhancement" as a principal input to growth.[9]

At the same time, a different sort of convergence takes place between institutional approaches and the capability approach. Advocates of the institutional turn increasingly focus on the causes and consequences of the kind of collective goal-setting that Sen puts at the centre of the capability approach. Rodrik (1999), for example, argues for democracy as a "meta-institution" promoting the "high-quality institutions" which in turn promote growth.

What do taking these strands of the "modern economics" of development and applying them to the question, "What is the most effective role for the state in the process of development imply?" These theories accord central importance to institutions that set collective goals, provide collective goods and maintain general rules and norms, vindicating those who have argued that the effectiveness of state institutions remains central to developmental success. But, we need to go beyond this generic assertion. In order to derive more specific implications, we need to first review the institutional character of the twentieth-century developmental state.

The twentieth-century developmental state

To understand the implications of the new development theories for the twenty-first-century developmental state, we must set them within the context of existing models of the twentieth-century developmental state. While a variety of twentieth-century states have played important roles in promoting development, theorizing with regard to the twentieth-century developmental state has drawn most heavily on post-World War II East Asia (e.g. Amsden 1989; Wade 1990).[10] The East Asian Tigers (including the "city state tigers" of Hong Kong and Singapore) managed to change their position in the world economic hierarchy, moving from "underdeveloped" to "developed" in the course of two generations. This kind of shift is not only unprecedented among twentieth-century developing countries, but exceptional in an even broader context that includes the historical experience of Europe and the Americas.

To focus on the East Asian developmental states entails concentrating on the importance of the capacity of public bureaucracies. Nearly every analyst agrees that when they compare East Asian public bureaucracies with those of developing countries in other regions, they more closely approximate the ideal-typical "Weberian bureaucracy". Meritocratic recruitment to public service with those careers offering long-term rewards commensurate with the ones obtainable in the private sector constituted the institutional cornerstones of the East Asian economic miracle.[11]

A few years ago, Jim Rauch and I undertook a simple empirical exercise to confirm the importance of bureaucratic capacity (Evans and Rauch 1999). We collected estimates of the extent to which the core organizations of economic administration in a sample of developing countries, conformed to the basic features of true bureaucracies as originally identified by Max Weber: whether recruitment to public positions involved impersonal meritocratic criteria and whether those recruited into these organizations could expect long term career rewards that approximated those available in the private sector, providing they performed well.

In our sample of developing countries, investments in improving bureaucratic capacity had very large consequences. Roughly speaking, an increase of one-half of a standard deviation in the "Weberian" score resulted in a 26 percent increase in GDP from 1970 to 1990 (controlling for human capital and initial GDP per capita). Likewise, an increase of one standard deviation in the Weberian score equalled roughly a shift in average years of education in 1965 from three years to six years (controlling for initial GDP per capita).

Despite the centrality of bureaucratic capacity, no student of the twentieth-century developmental state assumed ivory-tower bureaucrats constructing policy in isolation from society. Given a capable, internally coherent state bureaucracy, the next challenge became connecting bureaucrats and corporations. East Asia made the connection on at least two quite different levels. On the most general level, East Asian governments managed to generate a sense that they had genuinely committed themselves to a collective project of national development. Despite political divisions and governmental missteps, this sense of a national project gained surprisingly widespread credence and constituted one of the most important "collective goods" provided by the state. A dense set of concrete, interpersonal ties that enabled specific agencies and enterprises to construct joint projects at the sectoral level provided the essential complement to this broad ideological connection. The standard portrayal of the twentieth-century developmental state relies as much on "embeddedness" as on bureaucratic capacity.

Embeddedness never produced a tension-free symbiosis. Based on the prior performance of local business, state officials assumed that the private sector's "natural" strategy involved "rent-seeking", looking for officially sanctioned niches that would allow them to buy cheap and sell dear without having to brave entry into newer, more risky sectors. Therefore, the developmental state had to avoid political capture by its partners, in order to keep private elites oriented toward national projects of accumulation rather than their own consumption. Maintaining dense ties to entrepreneurial elites while avoiding capture and remaining able to discipline them[12] constitutes a defining feature of East Asian development states, distinguishing them from the less successful ones in Asia and Africa (see Kohli 2004).

East Asian's crucial ability to maintain autonomy from local industrial elites did not represent simply the fruit of bureaucratic competency and coherence. The revolutionary violence and chaotic geopolitics of the mid-twentieth century had the developmentally propitious consequence of wiping out landed elites as politically effective class actors in national politics in post-World War II East Asia. They also resulted in weak local industrial elites, both economically and politically, and transnational capital largely absent from domestic processes of accumulation. Consequently, state could construct a form of embeddedness in which national projects of transformation carried strong weight relative to the particular interests of private actors.

Despite the ambivalent character of the twentieth-century developmental states' relations with industrial elites, connections to other social groups did not offset ties to these elites. To the contrary, the state excluded civil society as a whole from the process of "state-society synergy". It saw private industrial elites as key collaborators in enabling industrial transformation as well as key sources of information regarding the feasibility of specific industrial goals. Other social groups lay outside, if not threatening, to this exclusive state-society partnership.

The basic vision of the twentieth-century developmental state remains compelling. A coherent, capable state apparatus pairs with dense ties to private entrepreneurial elites to produce forward-looking investments that enhance productivity, grow incomes and lead to increased well-being. This narrative certainly coincides with the "institutional turn" development theory, which emphasizes that functioning markets require a complex of underlying institutional arrangements in which the state likely plays central role.

The conventional model of the twentieth-century developmental state does not, however, appear to fit with either an emphasis on investment in capability-expanding services, as implied by the capability approach, or opening access to intangible assets, as implied by the "new growth theory". The new emphasis on collective goal-setting, particularly alien to conventional descriptions of state-society relations under the twentieth-century developmental state, remains central to both Sen and to institutionalists, as for example, Rodrik. Squaring the conventional institutional model of the twentieth century with the demands of growth and welfare enhancement as seen through the lens of new development theory becomes even more difficult when we add recent shifts in the historical context of development to the equation.

A historical shift in the character of development

Development in the current century will differ from the twentieth-century version along a wide variety of dimensions. Looking at the changing sector dynamics offers a way of highlighting the differences. Focusing on the declining centrality of manufacturing and the increasingly strategic role of services provides an empirical bridge between changes in development theory and the transformation of the role of the developmental state.

In the conventional twentieth-century narrative of how development occurred in the rich countries of the North, machine-production plays a starring role. In a very simplified (and slightly caricatured) form, the story runs something as follows: a massive shift of employment from agriculture to manufacturing takes workers out of a sector characterized by declining marginal returns and into one in which learning by doing, spill-over effects and greater possibilities for technological progress enable long-term, secular increases in labour productivity.

At the same time, machine-production lends itself to political organization, both because workers concentrate socially and they occupy a position from which they can hold hostage the machines on which profits depend. This, coupled with the option that industrial capitalists enjoy of increasing their profits by investing in increased productivity, creates an opening for progressive change. Political organization in the form of unions and associated political parties enables a substantial part of the work-force to capture a share of the productivity gains generated by machine-production and see relatively broad increases in incomes.

In sum, it posits machine-production as creating the possibility of a broad-based expansion of incomes by means of two simple, plausible propositions: 1) if you can move a substantial people out of agriculture into manufacturing, and continually give them better machines to work with, their productivity will increase; 2) Marx correctly suggested that machine-assisted production facilitated political organization, leading to at least partially successful demands for a more equitable share of this increased productivity.

Looking at the evolution of twentieth-century manufacturing economies in the North, it becomes plausible to argue for a connection between industrialization and general increases in well-being. By the end of World War II, a combination of rising productivity and political struggle had produced, in the rich, industrialized countries, a "Golden Age of Capitalism" which allowed a relatively large blue-collar working class to share in many of the amenities of middle-class life. If the twenty-first century appeared likely to sustain this paradigm in the North and extend it to the Global South, projecting the role of the twenty-first-century developmental state would become much simpler. Unfortunately, neither theoretical analysis nor empirical evidence supports such a positive scenario.

By the late twentieth century, manufacturing was going the way of agriculture in the rich countries of the North—a source of employment for an ever-shrinking minority of the working population. In the Global South, even impressive increases in manufacturing output (see Amsden 2001) proved incapable of generating a blue-collar class of a size and prosperity sufficient to anchor general increases in well-being.

The actual numbers belie the images, popular in the North, that the Global South is vastly expanding its manufacturing employment (at the presumed expense of Northern workers). As Ghosh (2003) points out, in most countries of the Global South, globalization has destroyed more local manufacturing jobs than it has created. Carson (2003) notes that, between 1995 and 2002, manufacturing payrolls dropped globally by twenty-two million. A quick look at trends in two of the world's star export manufacturers should suffice to drive this point home.

Korea, a small country in which we could expect manufactured exports to exercise more weight than in larger developing countries, will serve to illustrate the point. In the original "workshop of the world", Britain, manufacturing provided employment for a third or more of the work-force for almost a century (from 1840 to 1940). In Korea, manufacturing briefly managed to employ about one quarter of the work-force in the early 1990s but immediately fell back below that level. By the end of the 1990s, almost two out of three Koreans were working in the service sector and manufacturing employment declined toward the level of agriculture employment.

China offers an even more telling case. Looking at the actual evolution of employment structures in China suggests that being the most dynamic manufacturing power of the twenty-first century contains quite different socio-political implications than those of the nineteenth and early twentieth centuries. Employment in Chinese manufacturing peaked at about one worker in seven in the mid-1990s and had already begun to decline by the end of the decade (Evans and

Staveteig 2009). An independent analysis by economists at Alliance Capital Management found that between 1995 and 2002, China lost, on net, fifteen million manufacturing jobs (Carson 2003).

The field observations of researchers, as for example, William Hurst (2004) and Ching Kwan Lee (2007) give us a sense of the dynamics that underlie these statistical changes. The much more technologically advanced and comparatively more labour-saving joint-ventures and foreign-owned firms of the Southeast have replaced the relatively more labour-absorbing, state-owned manufacturing firms of the Northeast as the dominant form of industrialization resulting in increasing output but falling employment in manufacturing.

Other successful manufactured exporters in the Global South confirm this general picture. In Brazil, for example, manufacturing's share of employment peaked in the 1980s, accounting for one in five jobs and began to decline at the end of the 1990s as service jobs came to account for the majority of employment. South Africa tells the same story. Manufacturing peaks at about one job in six at the end of the 1990s and services become the source of livelihood for the majority of the work-force (see Evans and Staveteig, 2009).

A Global South in which manufacturing employs a shrinking minority of the population while most depend on the service sector undercuts the twentieth-century story of increased general well-being built around machine-production. To figure out what new narrative makes sense, we must go beyond shifts in the structure of employment to the changes in the distribution of economic opportunities and returns that underlie those shifts.

"Bit-driven growth", growth driven more by ideas and information (both as means of production and objects of consumption) than by the physical transformation of nature, represents the fundamental component of the changing profile of economic activity.[13] Its rising role corresponds to the theoretical propositions of the "new growth" theory and econometric observations of differential returns in the latter half of the twentieth century which show growth and productivity as driven primarily by changes in the stock of ideas and in people's capacity to take advantage of them (i.e., levels of education and training).

The possibility of indefinitely increasing returns creates unparalleled possibilities for profit, especially in a global market:

possibilities which accrue primarily to Northern corporations which have secured proprietary rights to the most profitable ideas. The changing bases of profits within sectors that produce tangible goods also reflect the tendency for higher returns to accrue to ideas and information. In manufacturing, design, on the one hand, and market, on the other, becomes key sources of high returns. "Financialization" (Krippner 2005), the tendency for financial returns to take increasing priority over returns from the so-called "real" economy, further reinforces the returns to command over information and communications technology, even among ostensibly "industrial" corporations.

The increasing importance of "intangible assets" (ideas, brand images, etc) has, in turn, powerful political implications for the role of the state. Securing the appropriation of returns from ideas poses notoriously difficult problems, requiring intensive, politically-enforced protection of monopoly property rights. Consequently, for the most powerful economic actors in a bit-based economy, the key role of the state remains maximal enforcement of their monopoly rights to returns from their intangible assets.

When the ideas in question consists of "producer goods", such as computer software or the chemical formulas involved in the production of medications, enforcing monopoly rights likely has anti-developmental effects, quite different from those of the exclusive ownership of physical capital. Ownership of physical assets only reduces their productivity if the owner uses them inefficiently. Ideas are different. Use of steam engines constitutes a zero-sum proposition—if others use my steam engine, I can't use it at the same time. As long as I use mine productively, my rights don't pose a drag on development. Ideas comprise non-rival goods—an indefinite number of people can use them simultaneously. When monopolists exclude others from using their ideas, they rob society of potential production, diminish the possibility that other users will find innovative, new uses for the ideas and slow the overall rate of growth.[14]

Negative distributional implications occur as well. The political protection of monopoly rights to productive ideas restricts people's access to the key tools, diminishes their ability to make use of their own "human capital" and reduces the number of actors who can participate in the overall process of innovation. Without politically imposed restrictions on the use of ideas, entrepreneurially inclined citizens could have access to the intangible equivalent of a variety of steam engines (Weber and Bussell 2005), a vision perhaps best exemplified by the case of open-source software (see Weber 2004).

The Global South displays a particularly sharp contradiction between providing monopoly protection of traditional property rights and expanding people's access to productive opportunities. "Human capital" constitutes its most abundant potential economic resource, one currently underutilized much more severely than in the rich countries of the North. Markets likely invest even less in human capabilities in the South than in the North. Conversely, current political protection of monopoly control over ideas benefits Northern corporations at the expense of Southern access. Monopoly returns to intangible assets create a drain on the South's resources as they flow to corporate headquarters in the North. As Ha-Joon Chang (2002) points out, governments in the North historically responded to this dilemma by essentially ignoring the property rights of corporations based outside their borders. Today's increasingly globalized property rights regime makes it more difficult for governments in the Global South to take advantage of this obvious strategy.

Taking into account bit-driven growth and the increasing focus of profits on intangible assets and financial assets helps illuminate the consequences of the service sector's dominance as the source of modern employment, e.g. the bifurcation of the service sector from the point of view of workers' incomes. For a small minority of service sector workers, employment constitutes an opportunity to share in the returns from intangible and financial assets. Privileged workers in the business and financial services sectors and the "symbolic analysts"[15] who manipulate key information in other sectors enjoy a comfortable share of the returns from "bit-driven" growth. For the vast majority of those who work in the service sector, they encounter a very different situation. Most service sector workers engage in delivering some kind of inter-personal services—ranging from retail trade to education to health, the bulk of them under-rewarded.

For most workers, the current shift from employment in manufacturing to service sector jobs lacks the promise of the earlier one from agriculture to industry. A narrative built around the transition from an industrial to a service economy seems likely to be marked, not by the creation of a new, relatively affluent working class, but by the expansion of inequality and the stagnation of wages for the majority of workers.

Looking at the dis-privileged majority of workers in the bifurcated service sector also points to a contradiction between its structure, in practice, and, in theory, its optimal form from a capability perspective. If the expansion of human capabilities constitutes both the key means and central goal of development, then, rewarding capability-expanding services and increasing their supply should continue as a developmental priority. Yet, in practice, capability-expanding services, as for example, health and education remains undersupplied as well as under-rewarded.

This hardly represents a paradox from the perspective of market logic. Since the expansion of human capabilities yields substantially higher social returns than private ones, they consistently and perennially under-invest in human capabilities. Instead, markets channel investment to other areas with lower total returns although private returns appear higher, particularly true in the case of the most fundamental capability-expanding services. Early childhood education, where the capabilities generated will impact production only in the distant future provides the best example.

When capability arguments connect back to "new growth theory" arguments, the disjunction between market logic and developmental logic becomes even more apparent. Human heads generate ideas and, through their interaction, expanding human capabilities becomes part and parcel of accelerating growth in the stock of ideas. Yet, for a private investor, investing in a human being poses a much greater risk than in machines.

Very likely, machines do what they are supposed to do. People make choices (constrained choices, but choices nonetheless). No one who "invests" in a person's capabilities can count on their "investment" choosing to eventually exercise their resulting talents in the way that will deliver specific returns to the particular investor. In short, private investors will under-invest in "human capital" because they cannot fully control the human being in whom it is embodied. Therefore, markets will chronically fail to supply optimal levels of the "human capital" crucial to bit-driven growth.

All of this brings us back to the third stream of developmental theory—institutional approaches to development. Looking at the changing historical character of development in the twenty-first century from the perspective of both the new growth theory and the capability approach, suggests that twentieth-century institutions will require substantial overhaul if they plan to confront the challenges of twenty-first-century development. Among the institutions challenged by the shift in the historic character of development, the state stands at centre-stage.

The challenge of transforming the developmental state

If the developmental state proved essential to twentieth-century economic success, it will acquire much more importance for twenty-first-century success. New theoretical perspectives have alerted us to the underlying reasons for the state's increasing centrality. Historic changes in the character of the economy have increased the salience of the state's role, making it more difficult at the same time. Citizens of the South, even more than their counterparts in the North, need aggressive action by entrepreneurial public institutions if they are to realize their potential productivity and enjoy the levels of well-being that the twenty-first-century economy can provide. Since the core twenty-first-century challenges comprise issues of political economy, the state's ability to shift strategies will rest upon reconstructing political connections to society.

The basic arguments for the increasing significance of the state's role have already been set out. Accelerating economic growth in the twenty-first century requires expanding access to the existing stock of ideas, increasing effective utilization and generating new ideas suited to a country's specific circumstances. All of this depends on the growth of human capabilities. Left to themselves, markets will not deliver an optimal supply of capability-expanding services. Only aggressive and efficient entrepreneurial engagement by public institutions can meet that need. At the same time, states must find ways to resist the traditional logic of political economy which pushes them to over-protect monopolies' control of the existing stock of ideas, restricting access and utilization and, thereby, reducing both growth and well-being.

More aggressive state action must obviously starts with ramping up the effective delivery of capability-expanding services. Since all modern states play a central role in the provision of health and education, public institutions cannot escape this task in any case. The question lies in whether they undertake it in the aggressive developmental fashion warranted by its central economic importance. Since the under-remuneration of capability-expanding services also introduces a distortion that reduces the well-being of a growing portion of the work-force, aggressive action in this arena becomes a growth strategy with immediate positive welfare effects.

None of this implies tossing aside the institutional achievements of the twentieth-century developmental state. Instead, reflecting on them in the light of twenty-first-century challenges, suggests that the traditional emphasis on industrial production neglected some key features of the state's contribution. Without denying the importance of their ability to promote industrial prowess, in retrospect, twentieth-century developmental states clearly also pioneered in capability expansion. The East Asian Tigers achieved renown for their levels of investment in human capital. They began their periods of accelerated economic growth with education levels that made them outliers for countries at their income levels and continued to invest in the expansion of education throughout the period of their rapid growth. In this optic, late twentieth-century China, which also invested heavily in human capability expansion, looks more like a developmental state. Its exceptionally broad-based investments in health and education laid the foundations for its subsequent ability to exploit industrial opportunities.

Twentieth-century developmental states offer also interesting examples with regard to accelerating the production of ideas and expanding access to the existing stock of ideas. "Industrial policy" in both Taiwan and Korea never restricted itself to subsidizing investments in plant and equipment. It always focused on increasing the access of local firms to productive ideas and creating networks and incentives to push entrepreneurs toward a greater emphasis upon the production of new knowledge. In addition to finding ways to transplant and exploit the stock of knowledge—ostensibly the property of Northern corporations—the East Asian Tigers, like China, resisted the over-protection of ideas monopolized by Northern corporations, leading to cries of "piracy" from the North, but expanded access by their citizens to productive ideas.[16]

Finally, these states possessed another capacity critical to capability expansion. They managed to extract revenues from their own private elites at a level sufficient to maintain the integrity of their own apparatuses and to finance necessary investments in capability-expansion. As EVK Fitzgerald (2006) has pointed out, one of the principle differences between Asian developmental states and their less successful counterparts in Latin America, lies in their inability of the latter to tax their own elites, despite the fact that, in Latin America, they appropriate larger shares of the collective national product for themselves (see also DiJohn 2006). Having the organizational capacity and political will necessary to collect adequate revenue served as the pre-requisite to investing in both capability-expansion and industrial transformation.

None of this makes twentieth-century developmental states twenty-first-century models in disguise. Nor should it lead us to expect that twentieth-century success will continue smoothly into the twenty-first century without traumatic institutional transformation. Capable and coherent twentieth-century public bureaucratic apparatuses supply an invaluable but insufficient foundation for the additional capacities that states need to construct to meet twenty-first-century challenges.

More problematically, twentieth-century success has shifted the balance between public and private power in ways that could undermine future institutional transformation. Developmental success has strengthened private capital and increased the domestic political role of transnational capital. Deeply-established reliance on local private economic elites, the growing centrality of transnational capital to local accumulation and the proliferation of alliances between local and transnational capital have transformed the political landscape into something quite different than it was forty years ago.

The shifting balance of public and private power runs directly counter to the requirements of twenty-first-century strategies, which demands a stronger, more capable, public sector than the twentieth-century version. In the twentieth-century manufacturing-focused development project, states found the symbiosis between private profitability and a shared national project easier to execute. Shared projects around industrialization depended on counterbalancing private risk aversion and pushing private perspectives toward a longer time horizon, but the eventual productive capacity accorded well with a profitability-focused market logic. Capability-expansion fits less easily into a shared project with private capital. When it becomes the goal, risk abatement and horizon extension have difficulty making up for the persistent gap between social and private returns. Precisely, because of the large "collective goods" element in capability-expansion, productive alliances with private capital prove less easily constructed. State-society ties remain, nonetheless, critically important.

The twentieth-century model of the developmental state found embeddedness important as a source of information and, also, because implementation of shared projects depended on private actors. In the twenty-first-century version, the same dynamics hold but the interlocutors and the character of the networks both differ. Efficient allocation of capability-expanding investment requires a much broader set of information than that for the allocation of investments in plant and equipment.

In the case of industrial investment, the key information involved figuring out which projects were feasible and how much it depended upon overcoming "collective action problems" among firms. Capability-expansion requires the same kind of information, but it must be gathered from more numerous and less organized constituencies. In addition, a simple technocratic measure, such as rate of return on investment or projected market share cannot assess the value of a project, such as rate of return on investment or projected market share. The worth of a project depends, in large measure, on how well its results correspond to the collective preferences of the communities being served.

The skills and organization required to aggregate and assess this kind of information demand qualitatively more capable state apparatuses. Nonetheless, accurate information on collective priorities at the community level remains the *sine qua non* of a successful twenty-first-century developmental state. Without multiple channels receiving accurate information, the developmental state will end up investing inefficiently and wasting precious public resources.

Engaging social actors in implementation stays as crucial to capability-expanding strategies as getting information on goals from them. As Ostrom (1996) has emphasized, their "recipients" always can produce capability-enhancing services. For example, students (and their families) co-produce education while patients, their families and their communities co-produce health. The state needs their active engagement in the delivery of those services in order to insure that the investments produce the desired effects. Delivery to passive recipients produces sub-optimal results at best, and sometimes counter-productive. Once again, the skills and organizational capacities required to stimulate this kind of engagement prove more complex and harder to construct because of their more political rather than technocratic nature.

In order to be able to create effective state-society linkages, the state must facilitate the organization of its counterparts in "civil society." The twentieth-century development state's interaction with industry gave industrial elites a reason to become a more collectively coherent class. The twenty-first-century developmental state must do the same for a much broader cross-section of society. It won't be easy. "Civil society" is a complicated beast, full of conflicting, particular interests and rife with individuals and organizations claiming to represent the general interest. Still, shared interests in capability-expansion run broad and deep. In addition, since capture poses less of a danger in building ties with non-elites, public institutions can concentrate on the positive side of this political project.

Returning to the political dimension of state capacity brings us back to institutional and capability approaches to development. Institutional approaches have increasingly emphasized the political dimensions of the institutions that support growth. Rodrik provides an archetypal example with his argument (1999, 19) that it may be "helpful to think of participatory political institutions as meta-institutions that elicit and aggregate local knowledge and thereby help build better institutions". For Rodrik, developing institutions that allow effective social choice stay central to enabling societies to develop the capacity to "build better institutions" of other kinds.

Political institutions serve an even more foundational purpose in the capability approach. Sen argues democratic deliberation offers the only way to adequately define what the desired economic ends might be. In addition, since the capability of making choices encompasses one of the most important of all human capabilities, "processes of participation have to be understood as constitutive parts of the *ends* of development in themselves (1999, 291)".

The centrality of dense connections to civil society and the construction of democratically deliberative institutions would at first seem to make the twenty-first-century developmental state the political antithesis of the twentieth-century version. A closer look suggests that the classic twentieth-century developmental states have already begun to change the character of their embeddedness. For example, Joseph Wong's (2004) analysis of the expansion of health care over the course of the 1980s and 1990 shows Taiwan and Korea managing to shed enough of their authoritarian traditions to allow public deliberation to move policy priorities in the direction of capability-centred development. Failure to reconstruct political institutions in order to expand the scope of state-society ties may still undercut the developmental capacities of twentieth-century developmental states, but we should not dismiss prematurely their institutional capacity to "reinvent themselves".

At every level, comparisons of the requirements for twenty-first-century success with those of the twentieth century's are sobering. In order to effectively develop, the twenty-first-century state must take more responsibility, achieve greater autonomy in relation to private elites and construct more complex and demanding forms of embeddedness. Given that only a small set of states managed to merit the label of "developmental," what prospects does the emergence of the twenty-first century have?

Conclusion: Prospects for a twenty-first-century developmental state

Claiming to predict the precise institutional forms that successful twenty-first-century developmental states will adopt would be foolish. Hegel's dictum that "the owl of Minerva spreads its wings only with the falling of the dusk" holds as much truth in this case as in any other. Scholars did not fully appreciate nor effectively incorporate into theories of development the role of the twentieth developmental state in the economic transformation of the East Asian Tigers, in the period from the end of World War II through the 1980s, until the beginning of the 1990s. Effective understanding of and theorizing about the role of the twenty-first-century developmental state will likely to arrive only after its effects are already being experienced.

Nonetheless, the assumption that we can contribute to useful theory or effective policy simply by sticking with old models, analyzed in terms of past theoretical formulations seems even more foolish. The owl of Minerva should not excuse resting content with knowingly outmoded analyses. Starting with an appreciation of how theory and the historical character of development itself are changing, no escape exists from trying to formulate plausible propositions on how the state must change in order to enjoy success in the century to come. Some firm conclusions remain possible.

Neither new theories of development nor recent transformations in the character of economies diminish the centrality of the state as a developmental institution. The vision of bureaucratic capacity as one of the keys to effective state involvement established in analysis of twentieth-century developmental states stands fully intact, as does the key role of state-society ties. Beyond these reassuring general continuities, new theories and a new historical context impose severe demands upon institutional change.

The "new growth theory" forces development policy to focus on ideas and knowledge. The "bit-driven" character of twenty-first-century growth implies an expansion of the state's role relative to that required by the "machine production" of nineteenth-and early twentieth-century growth. Countries that lack public effort and investment in an era of bit driven growth will suffer the fate of economic marginalization. Ensuring maximum possible access to ideas that serve as tools for the further expansion of knowledge requires active state involvement, sometimes in opposition to the private owners of those assets. In short, to facilitate twenty-first-century bit-driven growth, the state must be agile, active, resourceful and able to act independently of private interests whose returns depend on restricting the flow of knowledge.

The capability approach dovetails with the new growth theory and further expands the demands on the state. The bureaucratic capacity required for the delivery of capability-expanding collective goods must join with the very broad range of state-society ties necessary for the effective delivery of capability-expanding services.

Institutional approaches to development remind us that re-formulating policy goals alone cannot achieve these changes. The only way to produce a state with the capacity to meet twenty-first-century requirements lies with transforming public institutions. Bureaucratic and organizational capacity remains crucial but, in order to deliver, new political capacities must couple with them. Institutional approaches and the capability approach converge around the centrality of democratically deliberative institutions to developmental success. For the capability approach, deliberative institutions and the broad-based connections between state and civil society that they entail offer the only way to ensure either the flows of information necessary to guide the allocation of public resources or the "co-production" necessary for the effective delivery of capability-expanding services.

Realistically, no twenty-first-century state is likely to fully achieve the required transformation, not even those that best managed to meet twentieth-century requirements, but this should not represent a pessimistic conclusion. As in the case of the twentieth-century developmental state, even very partial approximations to ideal-typical institutional models can deliver impressive results. Celebrating whatever institutional changes make the state more capable of meeting twenty-first-century demands makes more sense than bemoaning the difficulty of achieving all the requisites of the ideal-type. Unless contemporary development theory misses the mark completely, countries that do manage to move in the direction of the required institutional transformations will receive the reward of more productive and dynamic economies. They will also better enable their citizens to "lead the kind of lives they value—and have reason to value".

2

State-market realignment in post-crises East Asia

From GNP developmentalism to welfare developmentalism?

Alvin Y. So and Stephen Wing-kai Chiu[*]

As a critique of the neoclassical economic perspective, the statist literature (Johnson 1982; Amsden 1989; Wade 1990; Evans 1995) argues that the developmental state—not the market—that explains the success of East Asian development. The following features distinguish developmental states:

- *Active Intervention in the Economy.* For example, a pilot agency, the Economic Planning Board (EPB), in South Korea or the Ministry of International Trade and Industry (MITI) in Japan established to develop a range of policy tools which ensure the nurturing and management in the overall "national interest" of indigenous business. The developmental state serves as the engine that powers economic growth. It allocates resources for strategic development; sets prices and regulates capital movement; and shares risks and underwrites research and development.

- *A Competent and Meritocratic Bureaucracy.* Analysts describe the developmental state as approaching the ideal of a Weberian bureaucracy, with bureaucratic elites recruited from among the technically most highly-qualified in the system. Highly selective, meritocratic recruitment and long-term career rewards create commitment and a sense of corporate attachment among them. A highly competent bureaucracy dedicates itself to devising and implementing planned economic development.

- *Embedded Autonomy.* The state must establish institutionalized channels for the continued negotiation and re-negotiation of goals and policies, sufficiently close to allow it to implement policy, but not so close that it risks "capture" by vested economic interests. The state has powerful policy tools at its disposal which make the co-operation of indigenous business more likely: access to cheap credit, protection from external competition and assisted access to export markets all act as levers that states can use to ensure business compliance with governmental goals.

- *Control of the Finance Sector* (the nerve centre of the developmental state). In South Korea, the state nationalized the banking system, controlling 96 percent of the country's financial assets by 1970. Through it, the Korean developmental state found a method of developing a set of "carrot and stick" policies to implement its strategic polices and developmental plans. It used subsidies or cheap credits to promote strategic industries or firms, and penalized those unable to meet targeted goals. In the 1950s and 1960s, South Korean exporters received a 50 percent tax cut on earnings, while any large exporting firm could easily obtain subsidized credit. Since the South Korean firms had high debt/equity debt ratios, even the threat of the withdrawal of subsidized credit would result in serious consequences (Minns 2001).

In highlighting the techniques and economic success of East Asian developmental states, the statist literature may have unintentionally overlooked their configuration of power, their authoritarianism and their historical geo-political origins (Lie 1991; Berger 2004). Instead of taking East Asian developmental states for granted, the following section will critically examine the nature of a developmental state, the reasons some states want to establish economic growth as their highest priority, and factors that make East Asian developmental states strong and autonomous. Before we move on to a discussion of the transformation of developmental states in the 1980s and 1990s, however, we first provide a brief sketch of their distinctive features in the post-World War II era.

The rise of the developmental state in the post-World War II era

We argue here that the Cold War and American struggles with communism for hegemony played a singularly important role in the genesis of developmental states in South Korea and Taiwan.

We must bring Cold War dynamics back in order to understand the origins, the distinguishing features and the trajectory of East Asian developmental states.

What is a developmental state?

By definition, a developmental state consists of one in which its bureaucratic elites place its highest priority on economic growth. In a developmental state, they single-mindedly pursue the growth of GNP at all costs (what we call "GNP developmentalism"), disregarding other important goals, including equality, welfare, democracy and human rights.

However, we must avoid exaggerating the vision and foresightedness of elites in developmental states. Although many states aspire to become developmental, only a few will succeed in the end. In this respect, we cannot know whether a state has become developmental until many years later, i.e., until after it has achieved rapid economic growth and status as a Newly Industrializing Economy (NIE). For example, in the 1960s and 1970s, doubts always existed about the authenticity of South Korean industrialization, whether South Korea was simply the same as any other third world country and whether the South Korean economy would break down at the first sign of a global recession. Only in the 1980s, after South Korea had become a NIE, did researchers finally agree to label South Korea as a developmental state.

Why does state want to become developmental?

Every state, of course, wants to promote economic growth. But why do some states want to strive for it so desperately that they willingly sacrifice other important goals in order to attain this one? Here, Woo-Cumings (1999) insightfully points out that East Asian developmental states represent an historical by-product of the Cold War and revolutionary nationalism. World War II and the Cold War brought the issues of nationalism and national survival to the fore when the US defeated Japan, and Korea and China turned into divided nations. Nations then conceived developmental states as a revolutionary national project to make themselves strong and powerful as soon as possible, in order that they could withstand immanent attacks from their communist counterparts within the other half of their countries (South Korea by North Korea and Taiwan by mainland China).

The continual siege mentality of the Cold War helps us understand the reasons East Asian developmental states place their highest priority upon economic growth — rather than equality, welfare, democracy or human rights. Subsequently, GNP developmentalism and nationalism became the twin bases of legitimacy for the East Asian developmental states. However, because of its emphasis on the bureaucrats' technical expertise, the statist literature often forgets that East Asian developmental states came historically out of the Cold War, anti-communism and fervent nationalism.

Why did the developmental state become the dominant player?

A strong state but a weak/dependent capitalist class (and a weak society) distinguish East Asian developmental states. Since no other agent in the society could take the lead, the strong state became dominant player by default. But what explains the existence of a strong state in East Asia in the first place?

Here, the Cold War laid the foundation of the strong East Asian developmental state. Needless to say, the extended fighting they lived through during World War II substantially weakened East Asian states. Their ability to quickly rebuild themselves in the aftermath of the war resulted mostly from American anti-communist policies. In order to transform Japan, South Korea and Taiwan into bulwarks against communism, the US not only provided them with military aid, tolerated their authoritarian policies and supported their militaristic regimes, but also injected significant amounts of economic assistance while offering them lucrative American business agreements. The arrival of American industrial orders needed for the Korea War in the early 1950s, for example, helped lift the Japanese economy out of a recession and put it on a course of rapid growth. In South Korea and Taiwan, foreign economic assistance in the 1950s figured heavily in alleviating huge government budget deficits, financing investment and paying for imports.

The massive influx of US aid and business empowered the East Asian states to develop their market economies. As they faced intense global competition in the era of late industrialization, they could not afford to take the time to nurture their small capitalist classes. Thus, developmental states needed to take a more "catalytic" role to hatch capitalists, to govern the market and to promote the economy.

Why did state intervention succeed?

The Cold War also provided breathing room for developmental states to try out their economic policies. In the South, since transnational corporations had already gained a foothold in their domestic markets, it proved difficult for domestic corporations to build up sufficient strength to compete with the transnationals. Cheap, high-quality foreign imports easily destroyed domestic products.

However, in East Asia, as a result of the Cold War, the US willingly instituted an unusual arrangement that operated contrary to the interests of American corporations. The US allowed its East Asian Cold War allies to close their markets to American imports in order to strengthen their domestic industries. At the point where their industrial products grew competitive enough for sale in the world economy, the US generously opened the American market in order to support East Asian states' export-led drive to industrialize. The US market provided critical impetus to the growth of East Asia states as their largest single market throughout the 1960s and 1970s. The geo-political strategy of the US during the Cold War, therefore, explains the reasons why, despite their infamous closed domestic markets of South Korea and Taiwan, their exports could still enjoy unrestricted access to the American market for so long.

Because of this American open-door policy, East Asian developmental states expended great effort on export-led industrialization in order to capture this competitive market. On the one hand, the developmental states provided incentives such as bank loans, subsidies, technical assistance and tax incentives to encourage exports. On the other hand, the developmental states disciplined their domestic corporations for their failure to meet the stringent export requirements. Thus, Amsden (1989) asserts that Korea differs from other late industrializing countries in the discipline it exercised over its private firms.

What is the dark side of developmental states?

In the end, the Cold War resulted in endorsing the authoritarianism of East Asian developmental states. It permitted East Asia's generals and military regimes to stay in power and impose martial law in the name of anti-communism and national security. As a result, East Asian developmental states repressed civil society, banned labour strikes and outlawed labour unions on the grounds that they had ties to communists. It also censored newspapers and arrested dissidents and movement activists.

They used labour subordination as an important method of making workers docile, their wages low and their hours long, since otherwise East Asian developmental states' exports would not sell so cheaply and competitively in the global market. In highlighting the techniques of developmental states, the statist literature seldom discusses its dark side.

Since the developmental states in East Asia derived historically from the Cold War, they faced great challenges when it ended. In the following section, we will focus on South Korea to illustrate the profound transformations in developmental states and state-market relationship during the past two decades.

The transformation of the developmental states at the end of the twentieth century

The end of the Cold War and globalization

By the late 1980s, the favourable geo-political environment which had seen the US privilege systemic strategic issues over national economic interests came to an end. Subsequently, the US became increasingly concerned about economic competition from successful East Asian developmental states, and more willingly used its economic and political leverage to pursue trade agreements designed to remedy expanding trade deficits between the US and the East Asia. Now, freed from strategic concerns, the US could more actively promote market-oriented reforms which threatened the very basis of East Asian developmental states (Beeson 2003; Berger 2001; Woo-Cumings 1998).

The end of the Cold War coincided with a new, increasingly global environment. Beginning in the 1980s, neo-liberal economists advocated a globalization project that opted for unfettered free markets, trade and capital account liberalization, a reduced role for the state, dismantling barriers to international trade in goods and services and integration into the global economy as the best model for development. Policy circles came to know this as the "Washington Consensus". International financial institutions, the World Bank and the International Monetary Fund (IMF) pressed developing countries to conform to this model as a condition for their loans (Öniş and Aysan 2000; Levinson 2000).

However, until the 1970s, the Korean financial system stayed relatively insulated and autonomous from the global economy. The Korean developmental state controlled the domestic banking system in order to ensure the co-operation of indigenous financial institutions to provide funds to industry. Business complied with this arrangement since it allowed them access to capital at "artificially" low interest rates, a potentially important advantage over established rivals elsewhere.

Korean financial market reform started gradually in the early 1980s, but accelerated upon the waning of the Cold War in the late 1980s and 1990s. Globalization pressures from international organizations, foreign financial institutions and particularly from the US government pushed it to open up its financial market (Erdogdu 2002; Zhang 2002).

In response to global pressures and prompted by the pressure to apply for Organization of Economic Co-operation and Development (OECD) membership, the Kim Young Sam government accelerated financial liberalization and deregulation through its *Segyehwa* (globalization) drive that included, among other things, interest rate deregulation, abolition of policy loans, granting more autonomy to banks, reduction of entry barriers to financial activities and, most importantly, capital account liberalization. In 1994, the pilot agency of Economic Planning Board (EPB) was merged to form the Ministry of Finance and Economy (the MOFE), signalling an abandonment of the planning and co-ordination function, long a powerful instrument of the developmental state's intervention in the economy (Chung 2001).

In the 1970s and 1980s, the *chaebols* (the big business conglomerates of South Korea) closely followed state planning directives. When the state's long-term strategic developmental project conflicted with the *chaebols'* short-term profit-taking, the state always had its way. However, the very success of the South Korean developmental state undermined its power base. By the 1980s, the *chaebols* had grown immensely as a result of the state's support. Their sheer size, diversity, increasing control of finance and importance to the economy as a whole had made it difficult for the state to arrest their further expansion and to discipline or restructure them.

The rise of the chaebol

By the 1980s, the greater global reach of their activities and the intertwining of their links to foreign capitalist corporations empowered the *chaebols*. By the end of 1994, South Korean *chaebols* had begun 2,650 projects overseas, involving investment of US$4.2 billion (Minns 2001). The foreign location of a significant proportion of their businesses made the *chaebols* less willing to accept state directives.

In this fashion, privatization of banks and non-bank financial institutions (NBFIs) and financial deregulation in the 1980s further enriched the *chaebols*. Despite a 10 percent legal ceiling on bank ownership, the ten largest *chaebols* soon held up to 52 percent of all bank shares as a result of their control of NBFIs and by the registering of bank shares in the names of the family members of *chaebol* owners.

Furthermore, after the dismantling of the EPB, *chaebols* focused much less on the national project of industrialization. Short-term profit-taking, rather than long-term capital investment, increasingly dominated their activities. Freed from state discipline, *chaebols* diverted a large proportion of their investment into speculative areas, especially, the Seoul real estate market and money-lending to exploit the difference in interest rates between bank loans and the unofficial market.

In short, since the *chaebols* had now gained direct access to the global capital market and acquired controlling interests in minor banks and NBFIs, they became financially independent. In addition, they could expand their direct investment abroad as a result of the relaxation of financial regulation, and further venture into new business areas the economic concentration rules following the lessening of market-entry standard previously restricted.

As the *chaebols* diversified their business without disposing of poorly-performing subsidiaries, their financial situation grew worse because of high levels of short-term foreign debt. In the 1990s, *chaebols* borrowing soared totally out of control. Between 1992 and 1996, overseas funds loaned to South Korea rose by 158 percent (Minns 2001), a large portion of them short-term (up from 34 percent in 1992 to 63 percent in late 1996). Some *chaebols* even developed a debt/equity ratio of as high as 20 to 1. Their excessive borrowing caused South Korea's external debt to nearly treble between 1993 and 1997 (Erdogdu 2002).

The 1997 financial crisis

In retrospect, *chaebols'* massive foreign borrowing of short-term loans led to South Korea's financial difficulties (Wade and Veneroso 1998). As the Asian crisis spread throughout the Asian region in 1997, South Korea became a victim of self-fulfilling speculative attacks and contagion (Moon and Mo 2000).

In the aftermath of the financial crisis, more than one-quarter of the *chaebols* collapsed. In 1998, the top five alone sacked over eighty thousand workers. South Korea's unemployment rate rose from 3.1 percent in December 1997 to 8.5 percent in 1999. Subsequently, South Korea required the largest IMF bail-out in history: US$57 billion in December 1997 with another $10 billion to follow (Minns 2001).

From this perspective, too little, rather than too much, government regulation caused the financial crisis. The neo-liberal model (the abolition of industrial policy and excessive and premature financial liberalization without adequate regulations) failed, not the East Asian developmental state model (Öniş and Aysan 2000; Erdogdu 2002; Wade and Veneroso 1998).

In spite of the previous account, mainstream literature tends to identify developmental states as the cause of the Asian Financial Crisis. It argues that close state-business relations not only equate with corruption and inefficiency ("crony capitalism"), but they appeared incompatible with the sort of dynamic competitive pressures associated with "globalization" (Bello 1998; Mauro 1997; Fischer 1998).

The comeback of the developmental states after the financial crisis

In December 1997, South Korea elected Kim Dae Jung, the veteran opposition leader, as its new president during the height of the financial crisis. While a movement leader, Kim criticized Korean developmentalism as focusing too narrowly on GNP, and also the all-too-obvious growth of the *chaebols*.

However, in the aftermath of the financial crisis and under pressure from the IMF, Kim Dae Jung seems to have pursued free-market liberalism by promoting competition and liberalizing foreign investment barriers, downsizing the state bureaucracy and introducing a more flexible labour market. Kim's new book entitled *DJnomics* spelled out his neo-liberal economic policies (Kim 2005).

Observing them, some researchers (Lee 2005 and Kim 2005) have described the Kim's government as market-oriented—one that has lost its interventionist capacity to manage the economy. Thus, they have portrayed the Korean state after the Asian Financial Crisis as one transformed into a "post-developmental state" (Kim 2005; see also Minns 2001).

Nonetheless, this chapter argues that the Kim Dae Jung government managed to exploit a critical moment in the economic crisis by pushing for reforms to re-regulate the market, to control the *chaebols* and to expand the welfare sector. In this respect, the developmental state in South Korea not only has experienced a comeback, but has also moved beyond the "GNP developmentalism" of the 1960s and 1970s.

Kim's government successfully carried out its reforms as a result of democratization and empowerment of Korean society.

Participatory democracy and the empowerment of the civil society

The Kim government (1998–2003) and, later, Roh Moo-Hyun's government (2003–08) promised a *"people's government"* and *"participatory democracy"* to encourage the citizenry's active participation in the policy-making process and the democratization of industrial relations in order to build a more equitable economy for all Koreans.

In 1998, the Kim government passed the Assistance for Non-Profit and Non-Governmental Organization Act to aid the operations of NGOs. Through the Ministry of Government and Home Affairs (MOGAHA), it disbursed 7.5 billion *won* (US$6.3 million) to civil society organizations in 1999 and 2000. Later, the Ministry of Labour gave 4.4 billion *won* (US$3.7 million) to labour-related NGOs (Lee 2005). Principally, the Kim government's desire to use NGOs both as an advance guard for change and as a lever for political reform against the *chaebols* fuelled its support for the NGOs. Since Kim's government needed political allies for its reform policies, it chose civil society organizations for that purpose. With the Kim government's support, Korean NGOs now took up the role of whistle-blowers, monitoring both businesses and the market.

In addition to the NGOs' scrutiny, the Asian Financial Crisis further significantly undermined the *chaebols* economic and political power. Koreans identified *chaebols'* reckless foreign borrowing as the primary cause of the economic crisis. In addition, the *chaebols* found themselves having to depend on the Kim government to resolve their high debt load and over-investments.

Nationalism, too, rose in the aftermath of the crisis, as Koreans blamed the IMF's austerity policies for exacerbating the financial crisis.

A rising tide of nationalism and participatory democracy, therefore, gave sufficient power to Kim's government in order to carry out the following reforms that moved beyond the IMF's neo-liberal policies (Chung 2001).

Financial reforms

Cleaning up non-performing loans and recapitalizing the financial institutions presented an immediate task for Kim's government. First, the Kim government created the Financial Supervisory Commission (FSC), a powerful regulatory agency to preside over financial and corporate reform. The FSC held unchecked power with legal authority to grant market entry into the financial industry; inspect and sanction financial institutions and oversee the securities and futures markets.

The government also shut down five major banks and a large number of non-banking financial institutions. In total, the Kim government spent sixty-four trillion *won* to clean up non-performing loans and recapitalize viable financial institutions. In addition, it implemented regulatory reforms in the banking sector to increase transparency and open it up to foreign capital.

Using the FSC and re-regulation, the Kim government managed to regain control of the Korean financial sector and to break the corrupt links between government-controlled banks and *chaebols*. Next, the Kim government strove to democratize the market, i.e., to reform the unequal, *chaebol*-oriented economic structure.

Corporate reforms

First, the Kim government demanded a "Big Deal", meaning the swap of key subsidiaries among the leading *chaebols* in order that each would emerge stronger in their area of core competence. Before the financial crisis, the *chaebols* had over-diversified and invested in large numbers of industries totally unrelated to their central business. The Big Deal represented an effort to induce *chaebols* to specialize in their primary business, to reduce overlapping investments and to allow the closure of surplus production capacity over time.

Second, the government asked *chaebols* to reduce their debt/equity ratios to by as much as 200 percent by the end of 1999 in the case of the largest *chaebols*.

Third, the administration proposed a variety of corporate governance reforms for the *chaebols* that promoted a "free and fair market order", including equity investment ceilings, bans on mutual investment and payment guarantees between affiliated firms, enhanced public participation in governance, the option of class-action suits by minority shareholders, vesting regulatory power in the Fair Trade Commission, an all-inclusive inheritance and gift tax. It moved to establish a "power balance" between business and labour.

As opposed to the previous largely top-down *chaebol* reform, this time, the Kim government operated from both the top-down and the bottom-up as it has actively involved civic movement organizations. For example, groups including the People's Solidarity of Participatory Democracy (PSPD) and the Citizens Coalition for Economic Justice (CCEJ) have played an important role in alerting the Korean people to the *chaebols'* family-based governing structure and informing them of their minority shareholders' rights. The PSPD monitored *chaebols* ownership (in particular, Samsung) to determine if they illegally bequeathed their wealth to the next generation. The CCEJ also initiated a watchdog campaign to identify any *chaebols'* attempt at avoiding fair competition and/or heightened market monopolization.

Empowering civil society and participatory democracy

The involvement of civil society organizations in monitoring the *chaebols* signalled a new form of state-market-society relations. Kim's state sought to foster civil organizations as a "third sector" that balanced the state-market relationship.

Kim's participatory democracy emphasized coexistence among a strong society, a strong (i.e., efficient) market and a strong state. The participatory approach did not necessarily do away with market liberalization, insofar as it used the latter to dissolve *chaebol* monopolies created during the Cold War era. In this sense, the Kim government wanted to couple liberalization with re-regulation to realize participatory democracy, i.e., it wanted to take advantage of liberalization and the democratization drive after the Asian Financial Crisis to break up the corrupt ties the developmental state had formed with *chaebols* through the "GNP developmentalism" strategy.

In short, the Korean developmental state has tried to achieve a comeback by re-regulating the financial sector, regaining control over the *chaebols* and bringing in civil society organizations to support its reform measures.

Nevertheless, the developmental state that re-emerged under Kim Dae Jung took a different form than the previous one. Popularly elected during the Asian Financial Crisis, Kim had to respond to the wishes of his supporters who suffered unemployment, job insecurity and a lowering of living standards as a result of the globalization policies of the previous Kim Young Sam government. Subsequently, the Kim Dae Jung government put forward the following labour and welfare policies.

Welfare reforms

The financial crisis in 1997 brought about massive unemployment, greatly lowering workers' income and quality of life. The unemployment rate skyrocketed from 2.2 percent in 1994 to 8.5 percent in early 1999. In response, Kim's government took a more consensus-based approach to the labour problem than the previous government's by establishing a Tripartite Commission consisting of business, labour and government. Further, the Kim government widened the social safety net and reformed the social security system in order to protect vulnerable groups during the adjustment of the economic structure.

Before the Asian Financial Crisis, only a small number of workers working for the *chaebols* enjoyed unemployment benefits. After his election at the end of 1997, Kim's government quickly expanded unemployment benefits coverage to include, first, workers in small business, then, finally, all regularly-employed workers.

In addition, the Kim government initiated a large scale public works programme to absorb the unemployed. In 1999, it spent 3.2 percent of national GDP on unemployment measures and 16 percent in public works to lessen the pain of the IMF's austerity policy (Chung 2001). According to an OECD report (OECD 2000), the Korean government's efforts to relieve the unemployed seemed quite impressive even from the perspective of the OCED countries.

Apart from the policies mentioned above, the Kim government also expanded coverage of other social insurance programmes to marginal sectors: The national pension programme grew to cover the entire public (including the urban poor and the self-employed) from 1999 onwards. The industrial injury compensation insurance programme also expanded its coverage from businesses with five employees to all businesses. It set up the National Health Insurance Corporation (NHIC) to provide medical insurance to all those working in rural and urban areas (including those in the urban informal sector). It adopted a public assistance programme to provide poor people with minimum income as a right, whether or not they have the ability to work.

The Kim government labelled its own welfare reform as "productive welfarism", aiming to increase the effective utilization of human resources (i.e., human capital investment), the productivity of workers (through job training) and an expansion of employment opportunities (through re-employment and structural reform to facilitate job-hunting). The concept of a "productive welfare state" originated in the Scandinavian countries that closely linked economic and social welfare policy via active intervention in the labour-market and universal income protection for its citizens. In short, "productive welfare" strove to provide adequate income support while also encouraging benefit recipients to participate in the labour market.

Conclusion

This chapter examines the transformation of state-market relationships in South Korea. In the post-World War II era, the Cold War geopolitical environment gave rise to a new developmental state which single-mindedly pursued growth of GNP at all costs (what we call GNP developmentalism). The state's active intervention into the economy, a competent and meritocratic bureaucracy, its control of the financial sector, and its dominance over the *chaebols* and all other classes characterized the Korean developmental state. In sum, the developmental state built itself on the basis of a strong state, a weak market and a weak society in the Cold War era.

However, these types of state-market and state-society relationships began to change in the 1980s. Nurtured by the developmental state for three decades, the *chaebols* had grown immensely in size and power. Globalization policies including liberalization and deregulation of the financial market had empowered them further, giving them the capacity to evade or challenge the policies of the developmental state. Democratization, too, had weakened the foundation of the developmental state (based, itself, on authoritarianism and the repression of the civil society). Observing this kind of state-market, state-society relationship, researchers began to describe the period as the fall, the decline, the retreat or the dismantling of developmental states.

The Asian Financial Crisis further transformed the relationships among the state, the market and society. First, the *chaebols* became significantly weakened after the crisis because of their high level of debt, and they incurred criticism for causing the Asian financial crises.

Second, the developmental state achieved a dramatic comeback. The popularly elected Kim Dae Jung government managed to pursue both neo-liberal reform (deregulation, privatization and downsizing the state) to reinvigorate the market and re-strengthen the state (to re-regulate the market) and reforms to activate the civil society (under the name of "participatory democracy"). The state-*chaebol* nexus formed under the Kim's government reflected new state-market relationships predicated on a democratic model emphasizing participation, equity and productive welfare. The participatory democratic logic of corporate reform assumed that civic organizations, as for example, the People's Solidarity of Participatory Democracy (PSPD), functioned as watchdogs and whistle-blowers to correct any unequal market structures. The state also put forward a massive productive welfare programme in response to high unemployment, social polarization and rising tension in the Korean society.

Theoretical reprise

We want to note that the case of Kim's government may shed new light on our understanding of state-market, state-society relationships. Assuming a zero-sum game, the developmental state literature tends to present a "strong state, weak market" or a "strong state, weak society" analysis.

Kim's experience in South Korea, however, seems to point to a new "mutual empowerment", rather than a "zero-sum" relationship. Kim's government sought to invigorate the market, to strengthen the state, and to empower civil society simultaneously. It wanted to liberalize the market economy so it could compete better in the global economy; it also wanted to strengthen the state in order that it could regulate the market; finally, it wanted to empower civil society for it to serve as a "watch dog" or a "whistle-blower" to supervise the *chaebols* and the state bureaucracy. Kim seemed to assume the "mutual empowerment" of state market, and society: As civil society grows more robust, it enhances the capacity of the state to govern, and "if expansion of competitive markets is the aim, the state must be institutionally reinforced, not shrunk or dismantled" (Evans 1993, 518; Migdal, Kohli and Shue 1994).

The South Korean case points to the importance of appreciating the political conditions of the developmental state. Evans (1995) encapsulates them under the concept of "embedded autonomy". The South Korea experiment in "mutual empowerment" appears to come at a time when the Asian Financial Crisis heightened state autonomy and the rise of civil society accentuated state embeddedness. When we say that the developmental state is alive and well, we do not intend to generalize from it to East Asia as a whole. For example, while we believe the politically unchallenged Singaporean government is still assuming a steering role for the economy and remains fairly effective in discharging this role, the other two East Asian NIEs are not performing as well in this respect. The Hong Kong SAR government is still struggling to find a viable role acceptable to elites and the society, while political cross-fires have paralyzed the Taiwanese government which largely failed to play a meaningful role in economic development. The East Asian developmental states share certain similarities but they also diverge in other respects. Where their paths will take them certainly depends on how the political economy in each society plays out.

The future of state-market relationship in South Korea

Turning back to Korea, it remains too early to determine whether the government will fully implement and institutionalize Kim's policies of *chaebol* reform, participatory democracy and productive welfare with lasting effect. Obviously, South Korea is now at a crossroads and can move in a variety of directions.

For example, South Korea could take the path of "democracy" in politics, the economy and society. Once empowered, participatory democracy will continue on, until it conquers all institutions. Given the legacy of the authoritarian developmental state, the concentration of wealth in the hands of *chaebols*, and the novelty of civil society in South Korea, however, this democratic path seems most unlikely, as the long history of Confucianism (and authoritarianism) acts as a dead weight that will pull down any tendency toward democracy.

South Korea could also move to the path of a "*chaebol*-dominated economy". The policies of Kim's government operate only as temporary crisis-management, soon forgotten when the Asian Financial Crisis recedes. Moreover, the *chaebols* have stayed too strong and too powerful to allow regulation by the Korean state. The global economy in the twenty-first economy has also undermined the capacity of the Korean state to exert power beyond its national boundaries.

Finally, South Korea could move back to a path of "the developmental state," with its active intervention into both the economy and the society. The victory in the 2007 presidential election by Lee Myung-Pak, obsessed with mammoth infrastructure projects and launching a campaign of national economic revival, who implicitly suggested himself as a would-be Park Chung-Hee for the twenty-first century, makes this path a possibility.

3
Eclectic corporatism and state interventions in post-colonial Hong Kong

Ma Ngok

Years of political co-optation have built a corporatist network in Hong Kong which has fundamentally changed the role of the state after 1997. It led to a form of "eclectic corporatism" created by a multilateral bargaining framework, making the post-1997 Hong Kong state more susceptible to particularistic interventionist demands from major interest groups after 1997. With weakened state capacity and no popular mandate, this eclectic corporatist state could not impose coherent top-down reform packages, but would instead resort to *ad hoc* intervention measures which prove effective in helping Hong Kong adjust to the challenges of the global economy. As only a partially-democratic regime with an over-represented business sector, this new interventionism and corporatism brought about a new legitimacy crisis for the post-colonial government.

Neo-liberal economists usually saw Hong Kong's economic success as the best proof of the superiority of a *laissez-faire* or non-interventionist economic strategy. This chapter points out that we should not regard Hong Kong in colonial times simply as "non-interventionist". The relatively low level of intervention in the early colonial times constituted part of a governing and legitimating strategy. It did not originate from a free-market ideology; instead, the political power formation and the development needs of colonial times shaped it. The political transition and the change in power-structure since the 1980s altered state formation, with evolving developmental needs, democratization and privatization leading to expansion of the state and more diversified organizational forms. The need to foster a governing elite after 1997 drove Beijing to build a massive corporatist network for the purpose of co-optation, which, in the end, reinforced the business dominance of the regime. This business-dominated corporatist government, however, created new legitimacy problems for a partially-democratic system.

The three images of the Hong Kong state

For decades, the colonial government has claimed that its economic management philosophy consisted of free-market capitalism. The government attributed its post-war economic success to its adherence to a *laissez-faire* philosophy or "positive non-interventionism", and invariably refused demands for redistribution or regulation from interest groups on ideological grounds. More detailed study of Hong Kong's economic history, however, would show that the colonial state played much more than a minimalist or night-watchman role during the economic take-off.

Neo-liberal economists commonly saw Hong Kong as a prototypical *laissez-faire* state. This dominant image derives more or less from Milton Friedman's famous formulation:

> We may well ask whether there exists any contemporary examples of societies that rely primarily on voluntary exchange through the market to organize their economic activity and in which government is limited . . . Perhaps the best example is Hong Kong . . . Hong Kong has no tariffs or other restraints on international trade . . . It has no government direction of economic activity, no minimum wage laws, no fixing of prices . . . Government . . . enforces law and order, provides a means for formulating the rules of conduct, adjudicates disputes, facilitates transportation and communication, and supervises the issuance of currency. (Friedman and Friedman 1981, 54–5)

Studies of the East Asian Tigers often saw Hong Kong as an anomaly that managed to promote export-led growth under a *laissez-faire* system, unlike other Tigers that relied on state intervention to make a "big push" (Haggard 1990; Deyo 1987). Aikman (1986) claimed that Taiwan and Hong Kong "demonstrates just how faithful, conscious or not, the rulers of these two countries have been to American conceptions of free enterprise". Decades of government propaganda reinforced this view, as successive financial secretaries of Hong Kong repeatedly emphasized their commitment to a free-market ideology. John Cowperthwaite, Financial Secretary in the 1960s, spelled out this neo-liberal logic quite clearly,

> For I still believe that, in the long run, the aggregate of the decisions of individual businessmen, exercising individual judgment in a free economy, even if often mistaken, is likely to do less harm than the centralized decisions of a government; and certainly the harm is going to be counteracted faster . . . *[t]he community's scarce economic resources can be efficiently allocated only by the price mechanism.* (italics mine) (Hong Kong Government 1966, 216, 218)

Philip Haddon-Cave, Financial Secretary of Hong Kong in the 1970s, coined the term "positive non-interventionism", which quickly became the standard catch-phrase for Hong Kong's economic strategy. Haddon-Cave (1980, xii) claimed that, "in the great majority of circumstances it is futile and damaging to the growth rate of the economy for attempts to be made to plan the allocation of resources available to the private sector". To Haddon-Cave, "positive non-interventionism" did not strictly equate to *laissez-faire*, as the government would intervene "positively" in cases of market failure or crises (1980, xii).

In contrast, scholars studying the Hong Kong take-off experience have shown that the colonial state played a significant role in helping economic growth. Although not in the "developmental state" manner, this second image viewed the colonial Hong Kong state as, in fact, quite interventionist or developmental. Castells, Goh and Kwok (1990) described various hidden state subsidies in the realms of collective consumption, which helped keep labour costs low during the export-led growth period. Public housing provided a rent subsidy of as high as approximately 70 percent of monthly wages to manufacturing workers. Intervention in the private housing market took the form of rent control, which stipulated that rents in private premises could rise by no more than 21 percent every two years. The Hong Kong state also provided a major proportion of education and medical services in post-war years, with citizens paying minimal fees for basic services (Youngson 1982).

For many years the colonial government believed that a reliable supply of food would provide the key to colonial stability, and spared no pains to control food supply and subsidized food prices to ensure their stability. It has imposed a rice control scheme since 1955, allowing only licensed merchants to import rice, and strictly regulated stock-holders in order to ensure ample rice stocks at all times (Schiffer 1991; Youngson 1982). From the 1950s to the 1970s, Hong Kong imported 80 percent of its foodstuffs, with 43 percent of them from the PRC from 1954 to 1963, and 50 percent between 1964 and 1980. They set prices administratively through negotiations between mainland Chinese and Hong Kong officials (Schiffer 1991). Woo (1977) estimated that from 1961 to 1973, Hong Kong's cost of living would have risen by 12.5 to 15 percent without PRC imports. Since the typical blue-collar worker in the 1950s and 1960s spent about 70 percent of household expenditures on food and housing, the subsidies on rent and food substantially reduced their living costs.

The government intervened into agriculture by monopolizing vegetable wholesaling through marketing co-operatives under the Agricultural Department (Chiu and Hung 1997). Since 1946, the government used low-interest loans and cheap fertilizer to lure farmers to join co-operatives thus controlling the supply of vegetables. To protect local produce, the government negotiated with China to keep vegetable and meat imports from China at a low level. Agricultural protection and subsidies allowed the government to influence rural groups, contributing to rural stability amidst rapid urbanization (Chiu and Hung 1997; 1999).

The government also played an important role in negotiating tariffs and quotas with other governments. The quotas, as a form of an exclusive right to export, became benefits that the Industrial Department distributed among local producers through negotiation (Goodstadt 2005, 128). The Interest Rate Committee of the Association of Banks, controlled by government officials and a cartel of banks (Schiffer 1991) set interest rates. Fiscal conservatism during colonial times operated as a conscious strategy to maintain a strong reserve and a fiscal surplus, enabled the government to keep interest rates low along with a cheap currency to maintain export competitiveness.

A third image viewed the Hong Kong state as corporatist. The sociologists Lau (1984) and King (1975) shaped the dominant paradigm on Hong Kong's state-society relations. Lau's famous concept of a "minimally-integrated socio-political system" postulated that the Chinese society and the bureaucratic polity of Hong Kong shared a "boundary consciousness". In this view, a refugee mentality and the political apathy of the Hong Kong Chinese and weak horizontal linkages among social groups brought few social demands, in exchange for low intervention from the state. The state remained autonomous or isolated from society, with the "bureaucratic polity" making most policy decisions with little input from society. King (1975) claimed that appointment to the Executive Council, the Legislative Council and various advisory committees effectively co-opted the Chinese elites. This "synarchy" between Chinese elites and colonial bureaucrats then "administerized" politics. In this sense, colonial regime effectively co-opted possible societal inputs, which led to an "absence" of the confrontational politics common in other developing societies.

Empirically, the state-centred formulations previously discussed overlook the informal politics of the post-war years. Faure (2003) revealed their significance in the early post-war years, in the Urban Council and other venues. Chiu and Hung (1999) have shown how the colonial state intervened repeatedly in the power struggles in Heung Yee Kuk to help the faction that supported government rural development plans come to power. They showed that the colonial government rather unscrupulously intervened directly into society when they considered major interests at stake. Scott (1989) saw the colonial history of Hong Kong as marked by various crises of legitimacy, which the government solved each time by incorporating new elites into the establishment to build a new consensus. The colonial state thus did not function autonomously outside of social demands, but built an increasingly inclusive corporatist network by co-opting major interest groups to legitimize their rule.

The political basis of low intervention

Previous discussions indicated an interventionist colonial government, at least falling short of the dicta of *laissez-faire* or "positive non-interventionism". Compared to other Asian Tigers, however, Hong Kong managed to spur high levels of economic growth with a low-intervention strategy. The state co-opted major interest groups into the administrative structure, along with selective intervention into the economy and the society. This begs a very important political question: on what political basis does this strategy of low plus selective intervention lie?

Earlier scholars attributed Hong Kong's low intervention to Britain's commitment to a free-market ideology (Haggard 1990; Haggard and Cheng 1987; Huang 1997, 101; Lau 1984). This view was clearly problematic, as British colonial governments elsewhere operated in a very interventionist or even predatory manner (Chiu 1996). Studies in the historical archives of post-war Hong Kong showed that the Labour governments in different post-war periods actually pressed Hong Kong to adopt progressive development programmes, only to be fought off by an alliance of Hong Kong's big businesses and colonial bureaucrats (Chiu 1996; Goodstadt 2005; 2007, 71; Bickers and Yep 2009).

The low-intervention strategy stemmed from the colonial nature of Hong Kong as well as the overall strategy of Britain. Before 1958, Hong Kong's budget required approval from London, while the Colonial Office placed a high priority on the financial self-sufficiency of the colony. Britain had always seen Hong Kong's *raison d'être* as entrepôt trade with China. With an uncertain political future in Hong Kong and a turbulent environment in China, Britain, which also feared the competition of Hong Kong products against its industries, deemed any significant investments in Hong Kong risky (Ngo 1997; Chiu 1994; 1996). Chan (1998) argues that Hong Kong's fiscal conservatism chiefly sought to stack up fiscal reserves in the form of a Foreign Exchange Fund in the Bank of England, which the Bank could, in turn, use it to back up the sterling pound. By the time the sterling crisis occurred in 1967, Hong Kong had accumulated a surplus equal to 350 million pounds, about one-third of the reserves of Britain, and 15 percent of the balance of the Sterling Area (Chan 1998, 14; Goodstadt 2005, 61).

Low intervention resulted from the political configuration of the colonial state (Chan 1998; Chiu 1996). Before the 1980s, the British trading firms (*Hongs*), who favoured a low-tax, no-tariff, low-expense government, assimilated political power in Hong Kong. The British merchants and their chief compradors, well represented in the Executive Council and the Legislative Council through appointment, claimed to represent local opinion and in general opposed more welfare or social investment. Chinese industrialists could not access the power centre until late 1970s (Chiu 1996). With most financial institutions in private hands, the colonial government did not have a great deal of leverage to finance industries even had it so desired (Chiu 1994).

Both Ngo (2000) and Goodstadt (2005) see low-intervention as part of a legitimation strategy of the colonial government. The British trading firms actually lobbied hard to seek rents and demanded control over policy-making and government finance (Goodstadt 2005, 164–68). The colonial government found itself torn between granting privileges to the politically dominant trading firms and keeping the underdogs (Chinese industrialists) happy. They solved the dilemma by refusing sectoral intervention. Ngo (1998; 2000) and Goodstadt (2005) agree that since the colonial government did not possess a sound basis of legitimacy on which to adjudicate competing demands from society, it preferred to stay aloof from using public resources to help individual enterprises or sectors, drawing a line between public interests and private profit.

Low intervention also took place partly due to the incremental decision-making style of the bureaucratic polity. In his study of banking policy since the 1930s, Goodstadt (2007) showed that colonial bureaucrats did not have the professional expertise, basic economic statistics or operational knowledge to regulate problematic high-risk banks, and did not draw up an effective banking and monetary policy before the 1980s. Lee and Yue (2001) dismissed non-interventionism, positive or not, as the rhetoric of colonial officials and as an expedient legitimacy tool that allowed pragmatic adaptation. To them, the generalists in the bureaucracy did not have the technical know-how to intervene into industries, even if they wanted to. As a result, the ideological catch-phrase of *laissez-faire* or positive non-interventionism became a convenient tool to fend off socio-economic demands.

The previous discussions showed that the low-intervention strategy of Hong Kong resulted from a combination of its peculiar political configuration and the economic imperatives of the post-war years. It follows that when the political configuration, regime nature and economic environment changed rapidly in the 1980s, the nature of the Hong Kong state would change accordingly.

The changing nature of the state

The images described earlier of the Hong Kong state mostly refer to the political and economic climate before the 1980s. Entering the 1980s, political and economic transformations brought changes in the political configuration, governance needs and development imperatives of the Hong Kong state. The riots in 1966–67 drove the colonial government to improve the living conditions of the lower class in order to maintain social stability, bringing about labour and welfare reforms in the 1970s leading to a gradual expansion of the colonial state (Cheung 2001; Scott 1989). Changes in the economic environment in the 1970s also dictated changes in economic strategy. With the rise of other industrializing Asian economies and rising labour costs at home, Hong Kong gradually lost its edge in labour-intensive manufacturing. International protectionism and slower immigration from the Mainland drove the Hong Kong government to contemplate economic restructuring and industrial deepening (So 1986; Lee 1998). However, with the open-door policy of China, Hong Kong industrialists quickly moved north to take advantage of cheap labour and land, while considering major government investments or subsidies unsafe in the early 1980s with the uncertainty surrounding Hong Kong's future. By the time of the settlement of the sovereignty issue in 1984, Hong Kong had transformed to rely on service industries and re-emerged as an entrepôt and regional financial centre, feeding on the phenomenal growth of China. Economic restructuring toward a service economy meant that Hong Kong must invest more on reproduction of labour, including education, medical and other services.

The Sino-British talks about Hong Kong's future from 1982 to 1984 started a process of politicization and gradual democratization in Hong Kong. With a history dating back to the social movements during the 1970s, the democratic movement in the 1980s had strong support from the grassroots. The introduction of partial elections allowed grassroots groups to seize more institutional resources in order to place social and welfare demands on the political agenda. At the same time, the start of the political transition period saw Beijing step up its co-optation of the local capitalists. With the gradual exodus of British capital, local Chinese capitalists seized the opportunity to launch major investment projects in Hong Kong in the 1980s. Beijing considered this a sign of their confidence that helped pacify Hong Kong society during the transition, and rewarded these tycoons with lucrative mainland and Hong Kong business contracts (Feng 1997). The Chinese Communists believed that if Hong Kong was to remain a thriving capitalist haven after 1997, the capitalists must be given sufficient representation in the new regime. The politically-conservative business sector also offered a natural alliance with Beijing to fend off demands for progressive democratization from the pro-grassroots democrats.

As a result, local businessmen had ample representation in the united front organizations that Beijing created and in the post-1997 political structure. During the drafting of the Basic Law between 1985 and 1990, Beijing supported using the functional constituencies (FCs) to protect business interests after 1997, with the Election Committee (EC) that selects the Chief Executive (CE) heavily weighted in favour of business and professional groups. The EC reserved one-fourth of its membership for representatives from major business groups, with another one-fourth for professional ones. It allocated about one-half of the FCs, or one-fourth of the legislature, for various business sectors, elected by corporations in their respective sectors, with some of them, in fact, reserved for representatives endorsed by the corresponding chambers of commerce or business associations in their respective sectors.

The Basic Law Drafting Committee, also included a large contingent of local Chinese tycoons, who wanted to prevent Hong Kong from turning into a welfare state should future democratic elections put populist politicians in power, and who tried to write the "Hong Kong blend of capitalism" into the Basic Law. Driven by concepts of a "fiscal constitution", the Basic Law included provisions for a low tax policy, a balanced budget, free-port status, a prohibition of foreign exchange controls and a budget whose growth should not exceed that of GDP (Tang 1991).

With a view to the rise of grassroots demands accompanying democratization, the outgoing colonial regime initiated a marketization drive, the Public Sector Reform, in 1989, to try to preserve a neo-liberal economic regime after 1997 Riding the Western tide of New Public Management (NPM), the PSR included marketization, corporatization, hiving off or subcontracting state services and using private management methods in the public sector. The PSR served both as a legitimation device and an adaptation to changing development needs. Lee (1998) and Cheung (1992) both contend that, with full-fledged democratization arrested by China's opposition, the outgoing colonial government needed a new rationale for legitimacy in the transition period. In the face of a politicizing society, it needed to provide more and better government services and enhance managerial efficiency. With fiscal conservatism and a low-tax regime mandated by the Basic Law, the government used marketization as a strategy to economize on, while at the same time, to expand its services in the transition era (Lee 1998). It also hoped to divert public attention from political responsiveness to managerial efficiency, as the divestiture of government organs and functions would lead to more diffused accountability, reducing political pressure on the civil service (Cheung 1992).

In 1995, claiming "positive non-interventionism" had outlived its usefulness, Financial Secretary, Hamish MacLeod, coined the term "consensus capitalism" to describe the government philosophy of the time. It consisted of several major elements: private enterprise and a small government, low taxes, provision of social, physical and regulatory infrastructure to support the market and assistance for the disadvantaged and vulnerable groups in society (Huque 1999). It marked a major departure from the pre-1980s non-interventionist rhetoric: viewing social services to help the underprivileged as necessary and as a support for economic growth. By the 1990s, the Hong Kong government had acknowledged its considerable role in managing the economy and the society, although low taxes and a small government remained paramount principles.

The Hong Kong state, hence, has undergone a major metamorphosis since the 1980s. The PSR represented a pragmatic strategy to cope with changing developmental and political imperatives, moving the outgoing colonial state to a more interventionist stance and to increase social investments. With the political transition and democratization pressure, the state elite was also rapidly restructuring, leading to a new state form after 1997.

The post-1997 state form

The traditional image of the Hong Kong state form has included one of a lean administrative state, governed by a non-partisan civil service autonomous from partisan politics and even social demands. Several major forces of change since the 1980s led to a transformation in state form after 1997. First, the united front built by the Chinese government led to a sizeable corporatist structure, which brought various interests into a large multilateral bargaining framework in the post-1997 state. Secondly, the state expanded its role in social investment and economic regulation, bringing about an expanded state sector and a blurring of the boundary between public and private as well as between state and society. Third, the PSR and other institutional changes led to the rise of quasi-non-governmental organizations (quangos), which in turn led to a weakening of state capacity.

The making of the new state elite

Before the 1980s, British trading firms played the most influential political role in Hong Kong, with Chinese business leaders co-opted by administrative absorption as King depicted (1975). With decolonization, British capital gradually retreated in the 1980s, its leading position taken over by Hong Kong Chinese and mainland capital. The declining authority of the outgoing colonial masters met the expansion of the Chinese government's co-optation network, leading to a gradual exodus by the pro-British figures and business elites in favour of Beijing (Lau 1999). Beijing established a wide variety of "united front" organizations since the mid-1980s, to entice pro-British elites, marginalize local democrats and groom post-colonial elite (Ma 2007, 36–45). Goodstadt (2000) showed that former pro-British elites, local pro-Beijing leaders, and conservative business and professional leaders dominated in these united front bodies.

In the executive-dominant system of Hong Kong, the post-1997 CE held extensive appointment power, ranging from government officials and judges, to policy commissions, public corporations, statutory bodies and advisory bodies. Cheung and Wong (2004) showed that the post-1997 statutory bodies and advisory committees clearly preferred leaders and executives, with ones from the trade, business, finance and industrial sectors, taking up 35 percent of the appointments. Professionals took another 40 percent, with a grossly under-represented labour sector that never exceeded 2 percent of total membership over time. The extensive appointment power of the CE thus allowed him to establish a pro-Beijing business and professional elite stratum in this co-optation network.

The expansion of the political power of the Hong Kong capitalists did not limit itself to the local political scene. Since the transition, the Chinese government gradually increased the size of the Hong Kong delegation to the National People's Congress (NPC) and Chinese People's Political Consultative Committee (CPPCC) in order to co-opt more Hong Kong elites (see Table 3.1). Before the 1990s, these delegates consisted of almost exclusively, long-time pro-Beijing figures who served in PRC-funded enterprises or mass organizations in Hong Kong. In the post-1997 NPC sessions, it extended the network to include professionals and business leaders who did not serve in pro-Beijing organizations. The less influential or less rich would try to gain provincial PC or PPCC membership to improve their mainland connections. With access to central or mainland institutions, these Hong Kong capitalists could wield more influence on Chinese officials, sometimes bypassing the Hong Kong government.

Table 3.1 Number of Hong Kong delegates to the NPC and the CPPCC since 1983

Session	Hong Kong Deputies in the NPC	Hong Kong Deputies in the CPPCC
11th NPC (2008–13)	36	126
10th NPC (2003–08)	37	123
9th NPC (1998–2003)	35	119
8th NPC (1993–98)	28 **	79 **
7th NPC (1988–93)	12 **	
6th NPC (1983–98)	9 **	

** Before 1997, the government included Hong Kong delegates as part of the Guangdong delegation.

Retired civil servants have increasingly become an influential stratum. Hong Kong civil service has set the retirement age at fifty-five;[1] in the modern era, officials at this age remain too young and energetic to truly retire from all work. Table 3.2 shows a list of former civil servants who serve in various public utilities, statutory bodies, public corporations, private enterprises and the like. Their connections with current officials and familiarity with the policy process and information made them a highly valued asset for corporations after "retirement". They have incurred charges of conflicts of interest, as critics doubted that prospective employment after retirement could lure currently-serving officials to favour selected enterprises.[2]

In July 2008, it was revealed that former Director of Building Services, C. M. Leung, would work for a real estate developer, with an annual salary of about US$400,000. The press questioned whether Leung had committed a decision-making "mistake" when he served as Director, which had led to millions of extra profit for his future employer. This led to an outcry against the post-retirement employment of civil servants, which forced the developer to abrogate the contract. Press investigations showed that the committee that approved post-retirement employment applications usually rubber-stamped all of them; in between 2005 and 2007, it had turned down only TWO applications from senior civil servants, out of a total of 212.

Quangos also regarded the former civil servants as favourites for their high-level executive posts, paying them handsomely, at rates exceeding civil service remuneration. The best paid quango jobs have annual salaries ranging from US$600,000 to US$1.2 million, with other lucrative fringe benefits. Government-appointed boards made up of civil servants and business elites invariably decide the pay scales and selection of top personnel. For example, Rafael Hui, Secretary for Financial Services from 1995 to 2000, became Managing Director of the Mandatory Provident Fund Schemes Authority from 2000 to 2003 after "retirement" with an annual salary reaching US$650,000 in 2002–03. However, Hui himself set the employment terms of the post. Joseph Yam, Deputy Secretary for Monetary Affairs in 1991, served as Chief Executive of the Monetary Authority from 1993 to 2009, making US$1.4 million in the year 2007/08, the pay seven times that of the Chairman of the Federal Reserve in the United States and three times

Table 3.2 Former civil servants in public and private employment

Name	Highest Official Rank before Retirement	Major Post-retirement Employment	Nature of Employer
BLAKE Ronald James	Secretary for Works	CEO, Kowloon-Canton Railway Corporation	Public corporation/Railway
CHAN Cho Chak	Secretary for Treasury	Managing Director, Kowloon Motor Bus	Private corporation/Public transportation
CHING Kwok Hoo	Senior Assistant Commissioner, Police Force	Chief Operating Officer, New World Telecom	Private corporation/Telecommunications
CHIU Miranda	Deputy Secretary of Economic Development and Labour	Deputy Chief Executive Officer, Equestrian Events (Hong Kong) of the Games of the XXIX Olympiad Company Limited	Public corporation/Event organization
CHU Patricia	Deputy Director of Social Welfare	Chairperson, Equal Opportunities Commission	Statutory body
CHUNG Lai Kwok	Secretary for Housing	Business Development Director, Hong Kong Ferry (Holdings) Company Limited	Private corporation/Ferries, tourism and exhibition
DILLON Sardara Singh	Assistant Director, Housing Department	Director (Corporate Services), The Link Management Ltd.	Public corporation/Real Estate Investment Trust
FUNG Wing Yip, Wilson	Deputy Secretary for Economic Development and Labour	Executive Director, Hong Kong Productivity Council	Statutory body
HSU Hsung, Adolf	Director of Regional Services	Managing Director, New World First Bus Ltd.	Private corporation/Public transportation

Table 3.2 *(continued)*

HUI Chiu Yin, John	Chief Superintendent of Marine Regional in Hong Kong Police	Director and General Manager, New World First Ferry	Private corporation with public function/Ferry transportation
HUI Ki On, Eddie	Commissioner of Hong Kong Police Force	Consultant, Jardine Securicor Ltd	Private corporation/Security services
JACOBS Piers	Financial Secretary	Vice-president, China Light and Power Ltd.	Public Utilities/Electricity
KWONG Ki Chi	Secretary for Treasury	Chief Executive, Hong Kong Exchanges and Clearing	Public corporation/Financial services
LAM Chung Lun	Deputy Secretary for Monetary Affairs	Managing Director, Urban Renewal Authority	Statutory body
LAM Woon Kwong	Director of the Chief Executive's Office	CEO, Equestrian Events (Hong Kong) of the Games of the XXIX Olympiad Company Limited	Public corporation/Event organization
LAU Yuk Kuen	Deputy Commissioner of Police	General Manager, Sino Group	Private corporation/Real Estate
LEUNG Kwok Sun	Director of Highways	Director, New Railway Projects, Kowloon-Canton Railway Corporation	Public corporation/Railway
LEUNG Sai Wah, Paul	Director of Leisure and Cultural Services	General Manager, Sino Land Company Limited Director of Corporate Communication, Urban Renewal Authority	Private corporation/Real Estate Statutory body

(continued on page 78)

Table 3.2 *(continued)*

LI Kwan Ha	Commissioner of the Royal Hong Kong Police	Consultant, Hutchison Whampoa Group	Private corporation/Real Estate
NG Wing Fui, Nicholas	Secretary for Transport	Chairman, Public Service Commission	Statutory body
PAU Shiu Hung	Director of Architectural Services	Vice-president (projects), Hong Kong Science and Technology Parks Corporation	Public corporation/Technology development
SMITH Bonnie	Assistant Commissioner, Hong Kong Police Force	Deputy Privacy Commissioner for Personal Data	Statutory body
SZE Cho Cheung, Michael	Secretary for Constitutional Affairs	Executive Director, Hong Kong Trade Development Council	Statutory body
TSANG Yam Pui	Commissioner of Police	Executive Director, New World Service Holdings	Private corporation/Real estate
WONG Doon Yee	Assistant Commissioner of Police	Executive Director, Construction Industry Training Authority	Statutory body
YAU Irene	Director of Information Services	General Manager, Corporate Affairs, Kowloon-Canton Railway Corporation Executive Director and Chief Executive, SHKP-Kwoks' Foundation	Public corporation/Railway Social Services

that of the Financial Secretary of Hong Kong to whom Yam reports.[3] These cases smack of corruption, with former civil servants the greatest beneficiaries of the arrangements. The system perpetuates a business-bureaucrat alliance that sees their interests closely related, enabling business to wield further political influence via retired officials.

Eclectic corporatism

Changes in the post-colonial elite structure created new pressures for state intervention. The colonial state had largely refrained from subsidizing individual sectors partly because it did not feel it legitimate to adjudicate competing demands for intervention (Ngo 1997). Their lack made the Hong Kong public believe in a separation between public and private interests (Goodstadt 2005, 118) even without democratic representation. Moreover, the mostly British colonial governor and top officials usually without connections with local business before they came to Hong Kong would commonly leave after retirement. This neutrality of interest, or at least the perception of it, largely perished after 1997. Throughout his CE reign from 1997 to 2005, many in Hong Kong believed that Tung Chee-hwa had given special favours to Li Ka Shing's conglomerate, because he had helped bail out Tung's ailing shipping company in the 1980s. The political changes after 1997 also brought in more private sector elites with greater influence upon the decision-making structure. In 2002, the government introduced the Principal Officials Accountability System (POAS), which replaced civil servants with political appointees as bureau secretaries. In 2008, it extended POAS to include deputy secretaries and political assistants, which became political benefits distributed to nominees from different pro-government parties, business elites and insiders. The post-1997 elite structure thus incorporated a plethora of social, economic and political interests from outside the bureaucracy. Even if the government officials did not seek undue material benefits during their term or after retirement, they faced more demands for intervention and rents after 1997.

This new post-1997 state elite stratum does not constitute a unified "class-for-itself". Members of the new elites shared a general inclination toward political conservatism, loyalty to Beijing, and a pro-business mindset. They would defend the interests of their respective sectors or of the business class in general, but they do not have a common philosophy of economic management. They do not even firmly believe in a free-market ideology. They would invariably use it as a defence, claiming bulwarks of Hong Kong's past success, whenever they faced new government regulation initiatives or increases in social welfare. However, these elites quickly forgot neo-liberal dicta when they asked the government for subsidies or favours to their sectors or enterprises. Unlike European corporatism, these elites seldom serve in policy-making bodies in the executive structure, but dispersed themselves among the various advisory bodies, policy commissions or boards of statutory bodies. This gives them privileged access to power-holders and allows them to lobby for government assistance and intervention, but the decision-making power, in principle, remains in the hands of non-elected bureaucrats. They can sometimes bend government policy in their interest, stage staunch resistance to government initiatives, and demand particularistic favours or subsidies, but cannot really "capture" the state. As a result, neither a clear and consistent economic philosophy, nor coherent state-directed development packages from above after 1997 exists. The state does not operate in a unified, top-down and strongly predatory manner, but utilizes a form of *eclectic corporatism*, with diverse interests seeking their own particularistic rents and favours. This eclectic corporatism brought with it a form of multilateral, *ad hoc*, particularistic bargaining, resulting in *ad hoc*, particularistic and eclectic interventions in various sectors after 1997 with no clear development goals.

Table 3.3 shows a list of major government sectoral subsidies and interventions after 1997. These sectoral interventions ranged from direct subsidies for selected sectors (e.g., tourism and film-making), injection of investments into (partly or wholly) government-owned corporations (e.g., Disney Land and Ocean Park), funds and loans to help enterprises of selected sectors, various funds to assist SMEs or specific projects, to investments in research and development. The levels of subsidies and investments stayed at a relatively low level, because amidst an economic downturn, Hong Kong ran a budget deficit from 1998 to 2005. Nonetheless, the subsidies and interventions listed above naturally attracted increased demands for them, marking a major departure from the pre-1997 governing strategy.

Table 3.3 Major sectoral interventions and subsidies, 1997–2005

Year	Purpose	Nature	Amount (HK$)
1997	Subsidize improvement of service industries	Fund	$50 million
1998	Finance use of innovation and technology in industries and commerce	Fund	$5 billion
	Hong Kong Science Park Corporation development project	Government Investment	$268 million
	Promote tourism by international events	Fund	$100 million
1999	Support community initiatives on sustainable development	Direct subsidy	$100 million
	Disney Land construction	Government Investment	$1.29 billion
	Ocean Park redevelopment project	Government Investment	$500 million
	Loans to fishermen affected by fishing moratorium in South China Sea	Loan Fund	$65 million
2000	Science Park construction	Government Investment	$3.4 billion
2001	Guarantee Loan scheme for Small and Medium Enterprises (SME) for Business Installations and Equipment	Loan Fund	$6.6 billion
	SME Training Fund	Fund	$400 million
	SME Export Marketing Fund	Fund	$300 million
	SME Development Fund	Fund	$200 million
	Enhance professional services	Fund	$100 million
2002	Airport's new exhibition centre construction	Government Investment	$2 billion
2003	Subsidize film-making	Fund	$50 million
	Relaunch Hong Kong's economy following the SARS epidemic	Direct Subsidy	$1 billion
	Promotion for boosting investment	Direct Subsidy	$200 million
	Initiate an integrated-circuit development support centre	Government Investment	$57 million
	Sustainable Development Fund	Fund	$100 million

(continued on page 82)

Table 3.3 *(continued)*

2004	Promotional and training activities in tourism	Direct Subsidy	$95 million
2004	Initiative to nurture design ventures and for training in design and branding	Fund	$250 million
2005	Film Development Fund	Fund	$20 million
	Launch global publicity and promotion programmes	Direct Subsidy	$500 million
	SME Export Marketing Fund (additional)	Fund	$200 million
	SME Development Fund (additional)	Fund	$300 million
	Research and development centre for nanotechnology and advanced materials	Direct Subsidy	$61.4 million
	Research and development for textile and clothing	Direct Subsidy	$60.3 million
	Research and development centre for automotive parts and accessory systems	Direct Subsidy	$100 million
	Research and development centre for logistics and supply chain management enabling technologies	Direct Subsidy	$52.2 million
	Incubation-cum-training centre for digital entertainment development	Direct Subsidy	$30.8 million
	Develop technology and facilities to design and build mechanical watch movements	Direct Subsidy	$54 million
2006	Assist the affected local workers of the live pig farming and pig transport industry	Direct Subsidy	$14.4 million
2007	Assist industries to improve designs and build brand names	Direct Subsidy	$100 million
	Arts and Sport Development Fund and the Arts Development Fund	Fund	$100 million
	Film Development Fund	Fund	$300 million

(continued on page 83)

Table 3.3 *(continued)*

	Assist Hong Kong-owned factories in the Pearl River Delta to adopt clean production technologies	Direct Subsidy	$93 million
2008	Endowment to the West Kowloon Cultural District Authority	Government Investment	$21.6 billion
	Promote Hong Kong as an international convention and tourism capital	Direct Subsidy	$150 million
	Subsidies for energy efficiency projects to building owners	Direct Subsidy	$300 million
	Subsidies to building owners for conducting energy and carbon audits	Direct Subsidy	$150 million
2009	Subsidize arts, culture and sports activities	Direct Subsidy	$100 million
	Subsidize private building owners for energy efficiency improvement projects	Direct Subsidy	$450 million
	Arts and Sport Development Fund	Fund	$150 million
	Sir David Trench Fund for Recreation	Fund	$50 million
	Cantonese Opera Development Fund	Fund	$20 million
	Support research and promotion of Cantonese opera	Direct Subsidy	$33 million
	R&D Cash Rebate Scheme	Direct Subsidy	$200 million
2010	Subsidy scheme for environmentally-friendly commercial vehicles	Direct Subsidy	$540 million
	Science Park Phase III construction	Government Investment	$4.9 billion
	Additional funding for the Cantonese Opera Development Fund	Fund	$69 million
	Additional funding for the Arts and Sport Development Fund	Fund	$3 billion

Eclectic organizational forms

The rise of quangos resulted in a much wider variety of organizational forms for state institutions after 1997. Government figures showed as many as five hundred advisory or statutory bodies of different forms and functions by June 2005 (Table 3.4). These quangos roughly fall into five different types according to their function (Ma 2007, 50 and Appendix One).

1. Policy commissions that shoulder policy-making tasks;
2. Bodies that aid in economic and infrastructural management or in promotion of certain economic sectors;
3. Bodies for regulation and supervision of economic and social activities;
4. Bodies for reflection of public opinion, addressing public grievances, controlling government and protecting civil rights;
5. Agencies that carry out executive and administrative tasks.

Table 3.4 Number of advisory and statutory bodies through June 2005

Type	Statutory	Non-statutory	Total
Advisory Boards and Committee	48	239	287
Non-departmental Public Bodies	14	1	15
Regulatory Boards and Bodies	48	0	48
Appeal Boards	54	5	59
Advisory and Management Boards of Trusts/Funds and Funding Schemes	44	30	74
Public Corporations	5	0	5
Miscellaneous Boards and Committees	16	5	21
Total	229	280	509

NB: Statutory bodies include those set up by enabling legislation. Non-statutory bodies consist of those set up administratively; most of them are advisory bodies.

Source: Legislative Council Paper No. CB(2)2176/04-05(04), Legislative Council Panel on Home Affairs: Review of Advisory and Statutory Bodies, Interim Report No. 14 – Review of the Classification System of Advisory and Statutory Bodies in the Public Sector) http://www.legco.gov.hk/yr04-05/english/panels/ha/papers/ha0708cb2-2176-4e.pdf
Last accessed on 20 February 2008.

In the West, quangos mushroomed because of a widening of government functions, with the belief that they can better handle tasks since they operate more independently, free from government constraints (Wilding 1982). Similarly, the proliferation of quangos in Hong Kong resulted from an expansion of government roles in social investment, labour reproduction, regulation of the financial market, development and management of infrastructure and devising service planning since the 1970s. Democratization since the 1980s introduced popularly-elected legislators, moving the government to be more responsive to public opinion and to open new channels to address public grievances, protect civil rights, enhance accountability and control the government, which, in turn, also partly contributed to more quangos.

The state apparatus links to the quangos in various forms, at arms-length from the core decision-making officials who remained non-elected and non-partisan, most directly or indirectly funded by the Hong Kong government (Scott 2005). Non-governmental bodies using public money (e.g., subvented welfare agencies) provide welfare and education services, with the government controlling the allocation of funds. The government owns majority shares in public corporations, run as profit-maximizing commercial firms that compete with private companies in the market (e.g., the Mass Transit Railway Corporation with other private transport companies). Public utilities usually exist as private monopolies or oligopolies regulated by the government, sometimes headed by former civil servants (e.g., the Kowloon Motor Bus Company). The private-public or state-society boundary has become blurred with many state functions shared by private or public corporations and quangos partially-or fully-funded by government. The state exercises policy, administrative, personnel or financial control over many of these non-governmental bodies, but never completely. The state has its hands in many sectors and policy areas, but the form of societal and economic intervention remains complex. It does not necessarily mean a strong interventionist state, as various factors constrain state capacity.

Constrained state capacity

The aforementioned divestiture of state or quasi-state organizations constrains state capacity, with decision-making power and policy implementation tasks dispersed among different organizations. For example, numerous public bodies and quangos shape housing policy in Hong Kong. By 2008, in principle, the Transport and Housing Bureau is responsible for the making of housing policy. The Hong Kong Housing Authority develops and manages Hong Kong's public housing. The Hong Kong Housing Society serves similar purposes as the Housing Authority, but builds flats for more targeted populations. The Development Bureau handles the government's urban planning, land use, urban renewal, public works and heritage protection policies. The Town Planning Board, a statutory body that monitors draft statutory plans and considers representations, appeals and objections of land use plans oversees statutory planning. The Urban Renewal Authority manages redevelopment of old urban areas, which affects relocation needs, land supply and the stock of new private or public housing. Although, in theory, the Transport and Housing Bureau oversees all policies related to housing, all the bodies mentioned above have a certain degree of autonomy, with many of the quangos having to balance their books from their own income sources, and who may not always agree with the Bureau officials on policy direction.

Scott (2005, 148–53) pointed out several means for the government to control the quangos: (a) by law the CE has the power to direct quangos; (b) by appointment, the government selects board members and chairs with its officials represented on the boards and (c) by legislative scrutiny. However, they have limited effectiveness. After the government has decentralized power and diversified organizations in favour of professional autonomy, market principles or operational flexibility, the government finds it difficult to intervene substantially in daily operations and decisions, without violating the principles of independence. For many quangos, a government-appointed board administers them, with officials usually present on the board. The appointed part-time board members, who invariably belong to the business and professional elite stratum but do not act as practitioners in the field, find it relatively hard to have enough expertise, time or information to monitor the daily operations handled by frontline professionals. The government official(s) present at the board meetings, usually administrative officers as generalists, play the role of a communicator rather than a top-down controller from the state. The state only has a general goal of market-oriented efficiency, but cannot really control or micromanage this bureaucratic complex of hundreds of administrative bodies.

Post-1997 events showed that the quangos had a high degree of autonomy, bringing about weakened state capacity and political accountability. Ma (2004; 2007) showed that during the outbreak of the Severe Acute Respiratory Syndrome (SARS) epidemic in 2003, fragmentation of state structures and decentralization of power hampered any swift responses to the crisis. After the government has decentralized its power over public hospitals and delegated management of them to the non-profit-making Hospital Authority (HA), and it has further dispersed resource allocation to geographical clusters, the Director of Health and the Secretary for Health, Welfare and Food found themselves to hapless to mobilize and to centralize resources to fight the epidemic outbreak. Studying the chaos at the opening of the Chek Lap Kok Airport in 1998, Lee (2000) pointed out that the autonomous Airport Authority had often refused to provide information to the legislature and the government on grounds of commercial confidentiality and organizational autonomy. The government and the legislature could only rely on indirect control that made it difficult for them to detect mistakes beforehand. Even after the fiasco at the opening, it still proved difficult to pin down the responsibility after lengthy investigations, because of the informational asymmetry and diffusion of responsibilities.

Quite contrary to the original goal or rhetoric of efficiency or better management, the quangos did not necessarily demonstrate better financial discipline or efficiency. A large number of quangos, with financial autonomy, follow a pay scale more lucrative than that of the civil service. For example, the HA was always criticized for high staff costs. Its Chief Executive Officer received a raise of 10 percent in 2002, in an age of deflation and widespread pay cuts in the private sector, and with the HA in deficit. The board gave out lucrative bonuses in 2004 despite public criticism of its performance during the 2003 SARS epidemic.[4] In recent years, the Audit Commission has often targeted quangos, criticizing them for overpaying staff, inefficient programmes and lax oversight of expenditures.

This disorganized and fragmented state structure primarily benefits a professional and managerial stratum well-represented in the various quangos. Retired civil servants, well connected to members of this elite stratum and somewhat autonomous from the state and party politics, can benefit the most in monetary and power terms. Members of this elite share a similar outlook in supporting the current capitalist order and (at least) the rhetoric of "managerial efficiency", a limited state role, bureaucratic governance and incrementalism, and showing repugnance for social-democratic ideas. This multifaceted corporatist network would invariably constrain top-down directives from the state, with extensive resources dissipated on various levels of rents and benefits shared by this elite stratum.

The corporatist regime and the new legitimacy crisis

This chapter shows that colonial Hong Kong actually has not adhered strictly to *laissez-faire* or firmly followed free-market capitalism. The low-intervention strategy in colonial Hong Kong did not originate from a free-market ideology, but represented an artefact of the colonial political configuration and pragmatic governance needs adapted to the economic imperatives of the time. The government carefully and consciously made this choice, tailored to enhance the legitimacy of the colonial regime and to promote export-led growth, a strategy contingent upon the regime nature, the elite structure and the development and governance needs of the time. The political changes, which decolonization, democratization and economic restructuring brought about, since the 1980s have changed the state form of Hong Kong. Years of political co-optation have brought about an eclectic corporatist structure that incorporated business and professional elites from various sectors, each bargaining on their own behalf. The diversity and fragmentation of the state structures meant that the business and professional elites did not "capture" the state. It represented a form of "organizational feudalism" that led to more *ad hoc* and particularistic sectoral intervention after 1997, a major departure from the governing strategy before then.

By 2010, the business-dominated and corporatist nature of the regime had led to a new legitimacy crisis for Hong Kong. Heightened income inequality, a market increasingly monopolized by conglomerates and economic dominance by the business class, all led Hong Kong's citizenry to question the legitimacy of the business-dominated regime. The C. M. Leung scandal and the extension of the POAS in 2008, commonly seen as an exercise of rent distribution to various vested interests, gave rise to plummeting popularity for the government. The social movement opposed to the expensive Express Rail Link (XRL) to China in 2009–10 focused public dissatisfaction onto the functional constituency system and alleged business-government collusion. By 2010, the Hong Kong government faced a new legitimacy crisis, with a common perception of government-business collusion, and corporate hegemony seen as the root of the economic plight of the lower class and of the government's inability to respond to public opinion.

Goodstadt (2005) and Ngo (1998) viewed the lack of sectoral intervention as a key part of a legitimation strategy by the colonial regime. In doing so, the non-elected colonial regime maintained an image of fairness, or, at least, of no overt rent-seeking. After 1997, when embeddedness in the multilateral bargaining corporatist structure made it difficult for the post-colonial state to refuse sectoral intervention, its image of neutrality vanished. A government not popularly elected and a business class constitutionally protected within the political structure, made it difficult to legitimize government subsidies or intervention. This brought the legitimacy of the whole regime into question, aggravating pressures for political reform.

Years of political co-optation have brought about a corporatist regime which has yet to build a new legitimacy formula for post-1997 Hong Kong. The government still relies on a non-interventionist philosophy to legitimize its economic policies, but the failure to deliver sustained growth and the government's increased intervention reduced the credibility of this ideology. The eclectic organizational form also led to weakened state capacity, with government development plans invariably constrained and transformed by the multilateral bargaining framework. It is a ship with numerous sailors paddling in an unco-ordinated fashion with faint senses of direction, vulnerable to changing winds and tides in the turmoil of the twenty-first century global capitalism. The lack of a clear direction or a new legitimacy formula will continue to bring governance problems for the post-colonial state of Hong Kong.

4
Governance crisis and changing state-business relations
A political economy perspective

Tai-lok Lui and Stephen Wing-kai Chiu

Post-1997 Hong Kong was in disarray, characterized by emerging social tensions and frequent political rumblings.[1] On 1 July 2003, the sixth anniversary of Hong Kong's return to China, reportedly, about half a million citizens from all walks of life, many of them middle class, joined in a mass protest. It represented an outburst of social, economic and political grievances.[2] It symbolized the public's response to the performance of the government of the Hong Kong Special Administrative Region (SAR) under the leadership of the Chief Executive, Tung Chee-hwa. Similar mass mobilizations, though, on a smaller scale, took place on 1 January and 1 July 2004. Largely a result of increasing discontent, Tung Chee-hwa resigned from the post of Chief Executive of the Hong Kong SAR government in March 2005 before completing his term of office.

The mass protests expressed discontent with diverse origins.[3] Some saw the governance of the Tung administration as a challenge to Hong Kong society's core values.[4] Others concentrated on political and economic issues and criticized Hong Kong SAR government's unpopular initiatives in those policy areas (most notably including Tung's attempt to regulate the housing market and to initiate the legislative process of enacting laws to prohibit any act of subversion against the central government). But the failure of the Tung administration to carry out effective governance really united critical voices from different corners of Hong Kong society. Its policies swung from one extreme to another, compromising and extensively revising policy initiatives in the face of fierce opposition before they had any impact.[5] More interestingly, parties critical of the Hong Kong SAR government did not solely come from the middle class and the grassroots who had suffered from the economic downturn, rising unemployment and the collapse of the property market, but also from the business sector. The government found itself repeatedly in a cross-fire of contentious political activity. It failed to build a consensus and thus experienced great difficulty in taking action. Conflicts continued to haunt the Hong Kong SAR government even after Tung's resignation. The government, by then under the leadership of the new Chief Executive, Donald Tsang, found itself forced to shelve and officially re-launch, the hotly debated West Kowloon Cultural District project (a mega project for building a new Hong Kong landmark that symbolized the city's cultural turn to creative industries) in February 2006 after nearly six long years' planning and discussion. The problem the government faced lies surely not in a matter of an individual political executive's quality or leadership. In fact, the Hong Kong SAR government now sees itself trapped in an impasse.

This chapter analyzes the origins of the present governance crisis in post-1997 Hong Kong. We view the various problems, including those mentioned above, emerging in post-colonial Hong Kong as indicators of more fundamental changes. And, as we shall describe them in the following section, we share an awareness of the impact of broader environmental and institutional challenges on the structuring and restructuring of Hong Kong. Our contribution to this discussion lies in our emphasis on the relevance of class analysis and the critical perspective of the political economy approach. More specifically, in this chapter we shall discuss the changing configuration of capitalist hegemony and its impact on the structuring of government-business relations.

A crisis unforeseen

While sceptical observers of the integration of capitalist Hong Kong into socialist China have always existed, few could have foreseen so many dramatic developments after the handover. Originally, the governments conceived the 1997 handover as nothing more little than a change of flags. It always emphasized continuity—Hong Kong continued to offer a place for making money, whether as compensation for individuals' hard work and/or risky investments or for supporting modernization projects on the Mainland. Despite the fact that the handover represented a major national project symbolizing the end to national humiliation since China's loss to the British in the Opium War, the expectation persisted that ordinary people's life would go on as usual. The government told locals that they could continue to bet on horse racing and to dance in night clubs. The year 1997 was not supposed to bring interruptions to their everyday life. However, as it eventually happened, 1997 turned into a year of significance to most people in Hong Kong. The year marked the end of British colonial rule in Hong Kong since 1842. It also marked the year in which the Asian Financial Crisis impacted the region. Without exception, the sudden change in economic climate and the resultant loss of economic confidence hit Hong Kong. The collapse of the bubble economy, with its dramatic fall in stock and property prices and a sharp rise in unemployment rates, precipitated popular discontents. People became restless and unhappy with the way the newly-established SAR government was handling the situation. Indeed, the evaporation of popular support of the established social and political order represented one of the most striking features of the social and political conditions of Hong Kong society immediately after the 1997 transition. The old magic of Hong Kong seemed to have gone after its return to China.

On the surface, the political settlement reached by the British and Chinese governments in the 1980s concerning Hong Kong's future seemed an ideal political compromise, one that would serve the interests of all the parties concerned. China would resume its sovereignty over Hong Kong, a city long its "window to the world", a source of foreign exchange and overseas investment, a springboard for acquiring an understanding of modern business and management and most importantly, itself the site of a prosperous economy. China expected a significantly important Hong Kong, economically and politically. Britain would maintain its effective governance of Hong Kong before 1997 (in order that the colony would not become a source of political embarrassment). Then it would give up its colonial rule gracefully and in the most dignified manner without really losing its informal influence (ranging from British capital investments to cultural influence) over Hong Kong. Regarding the Hong Kong locals, the Chinese leaders promised that the status quo would remain unchanged for fifty years after the colony's return to China, or until

2047. It would "freeze" (i.e., to keep intact) the institutional setting of the colony, believed to contain all the ingredients of its economic success in the past, and tightly segregate the system of state socialism on the Mainland from capitalist Hong Kong.

However, as it turned out after 1997, such an institutional arrangement became a source of problems for the post-colonial polity. It brought about the subsequent structural and institutional incongruity underlying the Tung Chee-hwa administration's (1997–2004) failure to build its hegemonic rule in the post-colonial environment. The idea of preserving an executive-led, bureaucratic and benevolent authoritarian rule after decolonization, then seen as a continuation of the basic elements of colonial governance which had proved effective and efficient in bringing economic prosperity and social stability to Hong Kong, turned out very problematic. The process of decolonization has restructured the state-society relationship. Contrary to the expectation of the Tung administration to confine Hong Kong as an "economic city" by the practice of depoliticization, the SAR government soon found itself in the cross-fire of contending interests. The economic downturn since late 1997 made the situation even more difficult to handle. The mass demonstration on 1 July 2003, as noted earlier, best summarized the on-going governance crisis of the government.

The Basic Law, the mini-constitution of the Hong Kong SAR, primarily sought to ensure continuity in the social, economic and political system of Hong Kong. On the one hand, it intended such a plan of "deep freezing" Hong Kong to meet the expectations of China—to continue to serve its economic interests without posing new threats (as for example, political challenges to authoritarian rule on the Mainland) and/or triggering undesirable changes to the socialist system through reform. The Basic Law did this by compromising the pace and extent of Hong Kong's democratization before and after 1997. The post-1997 SAR polity, despite the expectation that decolonization would give the locals an opportunity to become the masters of their own society, would not include a fully democratized legislature. Nor would it establish a popularly elected Chief Executive of the SAR government. On the other hand, such an institutional design aimed at easing the concerns of the local population. Continuity in institutional arrangements served to ensure the populace that the Hong Kong way of life would remain unchanged for at least fifty years. However, immediately after 1997, all sectors of society challenged the institutional arrangement of the Hong Kong system. The three pillars of the Hong Kong system— rule of law, personal freedom and an efficient bureaucracy—all came under pressure. First, the controversy concerning the right of abode issue undermined the promise of the continuation of the rule of law. Second, freedom of speech, worship and association touched the nerves of the existing system, with the fear of self-censorship a constant source of anxiety. Controversy concerning the status of Falun Gung continued to politically embarrass the SAR government. Third, in the first year of Tung's administration, the fiasco of the hasty opening of a new international airport and its clumsiness in handling the bird flu fully exposed the bureaucratic sluggishness of the administrative bureaucracy. To further complicate matters, the SAR government itself called for and initiated reforms in the civil service, taking an active part in criticizing the inefficiency and inflexibility of the bureaucracy in dealing with issues arising from the changing social and economic environment. In sum, the once-promised continuity in the institutional arrangement, as an assurance of Hong Kong's stability and prosperity, became a problem of its own.

Falling apart

Observers of Hong Kong politics understand well the environmental and institutional changes the transition period triggered. S. K. Lau has long called for the formation of a strategic governing alliance for the purpose of maintaining effective governance after the 1997 handover. More recently, in his analysis of the institutional foundations of an executive-led polity, Lau again underlined the importance of building such an alliance.[6] He suggested that in order to make it viable, the Chief Executive and his administration must secure meta-constitutional political power and authority and obtain reliable and steady support from a powerful and influential strategic governing alliance. According to Lau, pre-eminent political, economic and social leaders, as well as the groups and organizations under their control compose the strategic governing alliance. This alliance operates as an organized force, with a certain degree of stability and continuity, its members willingly negotiating and possessing the ability to reach compromises. Lau expected this alliance to have the ability to solicit and secure grassroots support. He contends that, in the long run, the absence of support from a powerful strategic governing alliance will not only jeopardize the effectiveness of the governance of the SAR government, but will also undermine the rationale and legitimacy of the entire political system.

The questions Lau raised actually concern the social basis of the political support of the authoritarian and executive-led SAR government. While Lau, of course, correctly stated that the Chief Executive and his administration need to develop mechanisms of interest articulation and political integration vis-à-vis the dominant leaders, he never made it clear how the formation of a strategic governing alliance constitutes a viable political project. Their statuses as local political, economic and social elites do not guarantee that these key players in the political and social arena will necessarily possess the ability to reach compromise and consensus regarding the long-term development of Hong Kong society. We criticize Lau's argument for simply begging the question about the formation of a strategic governing alliance. He fails to recognize the diversity of economic and political interests among the local elites.[7] Without asking questions about class interests, it left us puzzled about the social basis on which the members of the strategic governing alliance come to develop their consensus concerning the long-term development of Hong Kong.

Lee places the issue of the effectiveness of the governance of the SAR government in the post-colonial era within a wider context.[8] She argues that "the governance crisis in Hong Kong is the result of institutional incongruity"[9] More specifically, she suggests that due to changes in the broader socio-economic and political environment, the political and administrative institutions that functioned rather effectively under the colonial setting, which paradoxically enough, served as the blueprint for the institutional arrangements of post-colonial Hong Kong and which the Basic Law deliberately preserved, can no longer meet the needs of the new era. While the bureaucratic colonial state fared reasonably well within an environment of continuous economic growth, the existence of a weak civil society and steady improvements in standards of living, this institutional arrangement is becoming problematic as a result of economic restructuring, the slowing down of economic growth and rising local political demands. Such changes in the socio-economic and political environment call for a different style of governance. The Chief Executive and the SAR government are found incapable of providing the political leadership or maintaining the political legitimacy necessary to pacify rising discontents.

Lee analyzes the governance crisis in post-colonial Hong Kong perceptively and pertinently. While we largely agree that institutional incongruity comprises a critical factor in bringing about the governance crisis in post-colonial Hong Kong, we argue that she could further improve her analysis by developing a more sophisticated explanation of changing state-society relations. In particular, we believe that Lee rather simplistically depicts the evolution of state-society relations in terms of the strength of the civil society. Whereas analysts quite rightly say that Hong Kong has witnessed rising popular demands for policy outputs and participation since the 1970s, the problem encountered by the SAR government by no means simply consists of overloading by claims from below. As we shall argue in a later section, and as the controversies arising from the Cyberport project and the housing strategy announced by Tung Chee-hwa in his first policy speech demonstrated that the SAR government remained quite incapable of maintaining its hegemony over both the dominant class and the dominated classes. Actually, the process of decolonization has posed more problems to the SAR government than the ones envisaged by those who drafted the Basic Law. Lee has rightly pointed to the institutional incongruity in the design of "one country, two systems". However, in our view, the problem does not confine itself to the incompatibility between institutional arrangements and environmental changes; it also includes the equally significant political restructuring triggered by the longer-term emergence of local Chinese capitalists and the more short-term process of decolonization. The resultant constitution and re-constitution of the dominant class has wider implications for state-society relations and the SAR government's capacity for governance. A failure to take note of how the Tung administration had not successfully developed its hegemonic dominance on the basis of a new alliance with the various capitalist factions would significantly weaken our analysis of the origins of the governance crisis in post-colonial Hong Kong. Indeed, not only did popular demands from below challenge the

SAR government, but resourceful and influential capitalists remained uncertain of their stake in the post-colonial era also questioned it. As noted by Lau,[10] the new government still failed to form a strategic governing alliance. In addition, the inability to build a hegemonic bloc weakened its basis of political support as well as its ruling capacity.

Cheung[11] and Tang[12] relate changing state-society and government-business relationships to a discussion about whether the political transition has brought about a change in the philosophy and practice of non-interventionist management of the economy by the SAR government. Both criticize the description of the colonial state (as for example, by Friedman and Friedman[13] and Rabushka[14]) as a minimalist and *laissez-faire* non-interventionist state. They pointed out that the colonial state had long actively regulated its economy and that the scope of its management ranged from the provision of public housing, education and medical services, to regulation of the financial and banking sector. Hamish MacLeod, the former Financial Secretary, in the description of his approach as "consensus capitalism" best summed up the self-awareness of the changing role of the government in the economy.[15] In this regard, the involvement of the SAR government in economic affairs does not break from the mythical past of a *laissez-faire* government. Given the institutional changes brought about by the political transition in both pre-and post-1997 days (including the introduction of popular elections to the legislature and the newly appointed Chief Executive's need of securing public support by delivering policy initiatives and outputs), the SAR government has a tendency to deepen its engagement in the management and regulation of economic affairs despite its vow of a continuation of a free-market economy.

The major contributions of Cheung and Tang lie in their balanced account of state involvement in the broader social and economic affairs of Hong Kong, rectifying the widely held but misleading view of the SAR government as a minimalist state.[16] However, in their analysis of growing institutional pressures on state intervention after the political transition in 1997, they scarcely discuss the content of interventionism. That the two authors have avoided this question reflects a weakness in their analysis—the question that concerns us deals more with state interventionism or otherwise than the equally important issue of the direction of state action. In order to answer this question, we need to ask: what constitutes the social bases supporting or deterring the state from a certain course of action? The housing project of the Tung administration met with opposition not only from those property owners who suffered from a drastic collapse of the estate market, but also from the major property developers. Our question about the social basis of state policy leads us to raise doubts about the under-theorization of state autonomy (or the lack of it after 1997) in Cheung's and Tang's research. Indeed, Tang has succinctly pointed out that "The once intimate government-business alliance has become fragile in post-colonial Hong Kong. The conditions for the old colonial model of economic governance no longer exist."[17] Instead, Tang fails to move on or account for the social foundations of evolving government-business relations. We contend that in order to explain for the changing orientation and involvement of the post-colonial state in economic and social affairs, we need to examine the political economy of government-business relations. A political economy analysis of the dominant class and the changing configuration of the hegemonic ruling bloc is in order.

The previously discussed commentaries on post-colonial politics in Hong Kong share the same tendency of neglecting the need of buttressing their political analysis with a political economy approach.[18] Their analyses all imply certain interpretations (largely similar, though) of government-business relations. Yet, few have made efforts to spell out clearly the composition of the dominant class and how different factions within that class may pose problems for the articulation of a hegemonic class project. The dominant class forms, constitutes and constantly negotiates hegemony, although its existence does not necessarily lead to the formation of political hegemony. All the earlier analyses share a kind of taken-for-grantedness in their understanding and analysis of the dominant class. We argue that we simply cannot assume unity within the dominant class as a fact that does not requires further investigation. Our studies take the formation of the dominant class as our starting point and proceed to investigate how this formation process impacts government-business and state-society relations.

The political order under colonial rule

As noted above, preserving the proven stable political order under British colonial rule for Hong Kong after 1997 became one of the major considerations underlying the political strategy behind drafting the Basic Law. Through the institutional arrangements of including an executive-led polity, emphasizing the administrative strength of the politically neutral civil service, and democratizing the legislature, they hoped that Hong Kong could maintain the key feature of the colonial system conducive to political stability and effective governance—a highly autonomous state which can command respect and compliance from various social sectors, play the role of a referee in regulating competition among different interests as well as concerned parties and confine political contention within acceptable limits. We must note that the cause of the colonial government's ability to do so bears no relation to the complacency of the capitalists of older generations. Indeed, historians have amply documented British merchants' arrogance and their attempts to undermine the authority of the governors.[19] Also, as succinctly put by Ng, "the colonial system was maintained by the painstaking upholding of a delicate policy consent among the ruling elite. Like the SAR government, the colonial government was torn between the contradictory tasks of offering privileges to business in exchange for political support, assuming an arbiter role among competing business interests, and acting as a watchdog against rent seeking to prevent widespread discontent".[20]

The colonial system worked under certain premises. First, the inclusion of major business interests into a political oligarchy. From the very first day of the British colonization of Hong Kong, business interests comprised an important part of political life in the colony— "the colony existed primarily to magnify the profits of the British trading companies and to promote British influence in China".[21] Indeed, the popular saying that "Power in Hong Kong . . . resides in the Jockey Club, Jardine and Matheson, the Hong Kong and Shanghai Bank, and the Governor—in that order" best captured the dominance of business interests in Hong Kong politics.[22] Looking at the representation of socio-economic interests in the major channels of political participation in the 1960s, Rear argues that:

. . . all the evidence suggests that the persons appointed by the Governor do in practice represent only limited interests and that (inevitably, given the system) they are not fully capable of representing the points of view of those whose interests conflict with their own or whose experience of life in the Colony is quite different from their own . . . 99% of the population of Hong Kong is Chinese but only fourteen of the twenty-one unofficials on the two central Councils are Chinese. These twenty-one are with very few exceptions the representatives of big business and banking and, without exception, the representatives of wealth. Thus in a system where the chief policy-makers are chosen from a narrow social class, so also their advisers.[23]

Rear raised his criticism of the narrow social basis of colonial governance in the days of an essentially closed and undemocratic colonial political system. The colonial government justified such undemocratic governance by its claim of being a government by consent,[24] able to maintain effective governance through its responsiveness to public opinion. During the colonial era, before the institutionalization of political representation in the 1980s, an elite basically governed Hong Kong. Based upon a study of the social background of top government officials and the councillors of the Executive and Legislative Councils, Davies elaborates on Rear's notion of "one brand of politics in Hong Kong".[25] He suggests that "there is a relatively small and homogenous elite, that this elite is socially and economically isolated from the lives of the ordinary people of Hong Kong, and that it has a commanding voice in the government of Hong Kong".[26]

People given their positions and roles to play in the Executive and Legislative Councils and other less important advisory bodies within the colonial administrative machinery primarily came from a restricted socio-economic circle, most of them from the business community. Davies' empirical study of the power elite in Hong Kong suggests that "there are some one hundred to two hundred people who can be found with a dominant voice in all parts of the policy process".[27] He explains the dominance of the elite not only by its restricted entry into the key decision-making process, but also in terms of the dominance of certain business groups and networks in the economy. Davies observes that "the commanding heights of the Hong Kong economy are controlled by remarkably few interests. Although the total number of directorships is quite large, many of the directors are members of the families which in effect own the largest Chinese concerns . . ."[28] He further elaborates that:

> The business community in Hong Kong is dominated by relatively few large concerns with which its larger and wealthier members have directorial and financial links. These same few large concerns also dominate the banking system of Hong Kong and the essential public utilities. The concerns themselves are closely linked at the directorial level. However, these links are not only links of the boardroom. The directors meet also in two other places. First, there is the common round of clubs, major and minor, to which so many of them belong. They may not be close personal friends but they share an atmosphere, an ambience, a social nexus. Secondly, there is the shared membership of government councils, committees and boards as well as membership of many of the charitable organisations. The same major names recur in the patrons and boards of directors of these organisations as recur in the commercial directorships and the government committees . . . The sense of separateness that such predominance must inculcate over a period of time is important, for, given, that these are the people who have to make the decisions for the lesser mortals, how much of the life of the lesser mortals can they understand and who is beside them to tell them of it?[29]

Based upon company profiles and directorship data, Leung observes that a handful of key players continued to dominate the business community in the early 1980s:

> In 1982, there were 456 people who held one directorship in the top 100 public companies. Five percent of them were co-opted into the above-mentioned Councils and public interest bodies. Ninety-four people held two directorships, 19 percent of whom were co-opted. Eighty people held three or more directorships, 35 percent of whom were co-opted.[30]

And the colonial bureaucratic administration took good care of business interests in the political domain:

> In 1982, the Hong Kong Bank was linked to 22 of the top 50 public companies in Hong Kong through interlocking directorships. Thus nearly half of the top 50 public companies had, via the board of directors of the Hong Kong Bank, an official channel through which to communicate their views. If we confine our investigation to the top ten public companies, the data show that the Hong

Kong Bank had interlocks with seven of the remaining nine, six of which had their chairman on the Hong Kong Bank's board of directors . . . The Hong Kong Bank alone accounted for two of the nine Unofficials [of the Executive Council in 1982], while the eight interlocking companies among the top ten together had four Unofficial seats. If private companies and the smaller public companies are included, then the total number of directorships in the Executive Council amounted to an impressive 71. In this light, the highest policy-making body in Hong Kong appeared like a meeting ground between top government bureaucrats and the major resource controllers.[31]

In short, until the early 1980s, prior to the introduction of the idea of political representation into the major decision-making bodies, politics in Hong Kong remained largely in the hands of the government bureaucrats and a powerful economic elite.[32]

These quotations should give us a sense of the composition of the ruling elite in the colonial system before its gradual move toward partial democratization in the 1980s. We do not find economic and political elitism as such intriguing. The rather selectively inclusive ruling strategy itself does not guarantee consensus building. The formation of a ruling elite that mirrors the power structure in the economy interests us more. In this regard, Wong's study of interlocking directorates in Hong Kong serves to enhance our understanding of the economic power structure of the colony.[33] The sample of his study of business groups includes "the top 100 largest publicly listed non-financial companies ranked by annual turnover and the top 25 largest local banks . . . ranked by their assets in the 1976, 1981, and 1986".[34] He identifies business groups by detecting "a minimum of three companies linked together with each other directly or indirectly by 3-graphs or 4-graphs".[35] Wong observes that from 1976 to 1986, a shift had taken place from the dominance of the British *hongs* to the emergence of Chinese business groups:

In the 1976 network, except for two small groups, the major business groups are made up of and controlled by non-Chinese business families or organizations. Most of the groups are controlled by a single business family . . . The network is clearly dominated by the Jardine groups of companies.[36]

In terms of centrality, Hong Kong Bank was still dominant [in 1981] . . . The Bank together with the Cantonese group constituted the center of the network in 1981. The 1976 network center based on the Jardine group had disappeared . . . A new feature in the network is the rise of new multi-company Chinese business groups.[37]

The network in 1986 is much more differentiated into separate business groups . . . The rise of separate multi-company Chinese business groups has become much more prominent. This was coupled with a corresponding decrease in the number of non-Chinese business groups. The importance of the Jardine group further declined . . . Compared with the relatively high group centralities of the 1976 and 1981 business groups, the inter-connections among the business groups had decreased. As a whole, we can describe the network as loosely connected and multi-centered.[38]

Cheung offers a more updated analysis of the interlocking directorship of the large corporations in Hong Kong in 1990. Based upon data on thirty-three listed corporations that the Hang Seng Index selected as its constituent stocks, Cheung probes Hong Kong's economic power structure through interlocking directorate analysis.[39] He observes six significant clusters among his sampled corporations, three of them well-known British families and the other three prominent Chinese family groups with substantial control. The Jardine group under the Keswick family, in terms of centrality scores, continued to exert its strategic influence in Hong Kong's business world in 1990, though Chinese family groups have emerged and become prominent.

In short, until the late 1980s, the British *hongs* continued to assume a dominant position in the economic structure. Not only did they occupy a central position among the major business groups, but some of them, particularly the Hongkong and Shanghai Banking Corporation, played the role of "play makers", serving as intermediaries among clusters of business interests. Equally important, each of these major business groups had their own turf, carving out specific domains of business interests under their control. While competition remained inevitable, they built a delicate equilibrium of competing interests, with the overarching colonial government overseeing the entire enterprise. In other words, the economic power structure and its corresponding representation of interests in the formal political structure allowed the colonial government to maintain its effective control over the co-ordination of action and regulation of conflict among the major parties of vested interests.

On this basis, the colonial government could forge a "substantive consent" among the ruling elite.[40] Ngo argues that:

> This substantive consent involved the inseparable components of allowing business domination in the power oligarchy while upholding a policy against preferential treatment for selected business interests. Under this consent, besides the privilege of sharing policy-making power, the oligarchical interests were guaranteed that their profit making would be protected and facilitated by the government. This was realized by a range of pro-business policy measures, including low profits tax, limited social welfare provisions, minimal labour protection, free enterprise, and free capital inflow and outflow. All worked to facilitate profit maximization—a policy goal that was proudly admitted by the government. At the same time, the ruling elite agreed to constrain their privileges by accepting a policy of non-intervention. This meant that the government refrained from using public resources to assist or protect individual business sectors and enterprises. This avoided rent-seeking by individual elite groups, ensuring that policy outcomes were acceptable to the less powerful and to the wider population of players.[41]

The so-called positive non-interventionism the colonial government practised represented an outcome of such a compromise between the economically powerful and the colonial state with both sides accepting certain limits of their actions.[42] As long as both parties found the economic outcomes pleasing, this pact would allow the colonial state to enjoy a high degree of autonomy in its management of social, economic and political affairs.

Changing state-business relations

The earlier studies of business groups by Wong and Cheung hinted that signs of a change within the economic power structure in the 1980s existed. The rise of local Chinese business groups since the 1970s and the consolidation of their economic power in the 1980s through various attempts to take over or merge with declining British companies began to upset the status quo, create a new balance of power and gradually restructure intergroup relations among the economically powerful. Informed by Wong and Cheung, we have carried out an interlocking directorate analysis of the top 250 listed corporations (banks inclusive) in 1983, 1998 and 2004. Strictly speaking, our sample differs from theirs as we utilize a much larger sample size. Nor does our interlocking directorate analysis replicate theirs.[43] In other words, the similarities do not warrant a rigorous comparison of our findings with theirs. In this regard, one should note that we intend to describe the evolving configuration of the economic power structure in Hong Kong with the previously discussed studies as relevant backdrops for a rough understanding of the direction of change since the 1970s. According to Wong, British business groups, with the Jardine group assuming a dominating status, occupied a strategic and commanding position in 1976. Since then, as a result of various business mergers, the balance of power between British and Chinese business groups has begun to shift in the latter's favour.

Table 4.1 Number of interlocks per company

Number of Interlocks per Company	Number of Companies			% of Companies		
	1982	1997	2004	1982	1997	2004
50 or more	8	0	1	3.20	0.00	0.40
40–49	17	1	4	6.80	0.40	1.60
30–39	20	9	4	8.00	3.60	1.60
20–29	27	22	18	10.80	8.80	7.20
15–19	27	16	30	10.80	6.40	12.00
10–14	29	42	31	11.60	16.80	12.40
5–9	31	62	49	12.40	24.80	19.60
3–4	27	35	42	10.80	14.00	16.80
1–2	29	32	31	11.60	12.80	12.40
Total of Companies with Interlocks	215	219	210	86.00	87.60	84.00
No Interlock	35	31	40	14.00	12.40	16.00

Source: Author research.

Table 4.2 Multiple directorships held by individual directors

	Number of Individuals Holding		
Number of Multiple Directorships	**1982**	**1997**	**2004**
7 or more positions	22	3	2
6 or more positions	30	5	4
5 or more positions	48	9	10
4 or more positions	81	27	19
Most positions individually held	22	7	7

Source: Author research.

Tables 4.1 and 4.2 summarize findings of our interlocking directorate analysis. When we took the company as a unit of analysis, we found that very few firms had no interlocks with other companies in the sample, between thirty-five and forty in the three panels. Eight companies had interlocks with fifty or more companies (e.g. a company who shared one or more common director with two other companies counted as two interlocks), but none in 1997 and 2004. At other levels of multiple interlocks, typically we found that 1982 had the densest interlocking networks, while 1997 and 2004 remained relatively constant. If anything, at the level of five to twenty-nine interlocks, we also found that the percentage of firms dropped slightly between 1997 and 2004. In 1982, one should regard Sun Hung Kai Properties Ltd. as the "executive committee" of the business community, as it had the most interlocks with sixty-seven, while Hongkong and Shanghai Banking Corporation had sixty-four. In 1997, the most interlocked company became Hutchison Whampoa (thirty-two interlocks), and, in 2004, Cheung Kong Infrastructure Holdings (thirty-five interlocks), with both companies, interestingly, members of the Li Ka Shing business empire.

Taking the individual director as a unit of analysis, we detected a similar trend. In 1982, eighty-one directors held four or more positions, dropping significantly to twenty-seven in 1997, and further to nineteen in 2004. In an earlier period, a small group of individual directors linked up a large number of firms but it had clearly dwindled in the new century. For example, in 1982, twenty-two individuals had seven or more board memberships, but only two in 2004. In 1982, Charles Lee Yeh Kwong, the "director of directors", held concurrently twenty-two board memberships. In 2004, Canning Fok Kin Ning and Frank John Sixt led with a relatively "meagre" seven board membership.

Thus, "density" of business networks had clearly dropped as measured by interlocking directorships between the 1980s and the 2000s. A cohesive business elite in the early 1980s had loosened up two decades later as a result of decolonization and deregulation. Following Wong's study, we also analyzed the network by means of components. A component consists of a subset of companies connected by a specific number of common ties, direct or indirect. For example, we regarded two companies as in the same component even though they have no common directors but remain connected by a common director with a third company. A k-component (or component by k-graph) means the presence of k common directors between the companies within the components. Figures 4.1, 4.2 and 4.3 summarize the result of the component analysis. They give us a rough idea of the changing economic power structure in Hong Kong in 1983, 1998 and 2004. In the figure, each circle (with different perimeters) represents a component as measured by a 1 to 4-graph respectively. The letters (A to K) represent the broadest 1-graph component, whereas the two-digit circles consist of 2-graph components within the 1-graph circle. The three-digit and four-digit circles constitute the 3-graph and 4-graph components respectively. We drew the size of the circles roughly in proportion to the capitalization and assets asset of the groups.

In 1982, we found a total of 199 companies in the largest 1-graph component, meaning they connected with one common director directly or indirectly through another company, reflecting the dense inter-corporate network during that period. We discovered only two smaller components (Bank of Communications group and Tak Wing Investment group) outside of it. In 1997, the 1-graph component had already shrunk to 111 firms, and further dwindled to seventy-eight in 2004. We found further evidence of greater cohesion of the 1982 business network in that, within the large 1-graph component, eighty-two companies belonged to a 2-graph component, with HSBC the largest one within it. By 1998, we discovered thirteen companies in the largest

Public Company Components, 1982
(with Interlocks excluding Independent Non-executive Director)

Components	The firm with largest total in market capitalization and assets in the component	No. of Firm in the Component
A1	Hongkong & Shanghai Banking Corporation	199
A21	Hongkong & Shanghai Banking Corporation	82
A311	Hongkong & Shanghai Banking Corporation	31
A4111	Hongkong & Shanghai Banking Corporation	11
A4112	Sun Hung Kai Properties Limited	7
A4113	Swire Pacific Limited	3
A312	World International (Holdings) Limited	9
A4121	World International (Holdings) Limited	3
A4122	China Light & Power Company	3
A4123	Nanyang Cotton Mill Limited	3
A313	Wheelock Marden and Company Limited	8
A4131	Wheelock Marden and Company Limited	8
A314	Eda Investments Limited	5
A4141	Associated Hotels Limited	3
A315	Carrian Investments Limited	3
A4151	Carrian Investments Limited	3
A316	Bank of East Asia	3
A317	Liu Chong Hing Investment Limited	3
A22	Overseas Trust Bank	25
A321	Overseas Trust Bank	7
A4211	Overseas Trust Bank	5
A322	Far East Consortium Limited	5
A4221	Far East Consortium Limited	4
A23	Federal Amalgamated Corporation Limited	5
A331	Federal Amalgamated Corporation Limited	5
A4311	Federal Amalgamated Corporation Limited	3
A24	Wing On (Holdings) Limited	4
A341	Wing On (Holdings) Limited	4
A4411	Wing On (Holdings) Limited	4
A25	Regal Hotels (Holdings) Limited	4
A351	Regal Hotels (Holdings) Limited	3
A4511	Regal Hotels (Holdings) Limited	3
A26	Nan Fung Textiles Consolidated Limited	3
A27	Lee On Reality and Enterprises Limited	3
B1	Bank of Communications	5
C1	Tak Wing Investment (Holdings) Limited	3

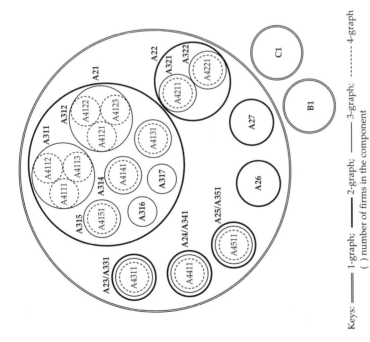

Keys: ——— 1-graph; ——— 2-graph; ——— 3-graph; ------ 4-graph
( ) number of firms in the component

Figure 4.1   The major business groups, 1982

Public Company Components, 1997
(with Interlocks excluding Independent Non-executive Director)

Components	The firm with largest total in market capitalization and assets in the component	No. of Firm in the Component
A1	HSBC Holdings Ltd	111
A21	Hang Seng Bank Ltd	13
A311	Henderson Land Development Co Ltd	8
A4111	Henderson Land Development Co Ltd	5
A22	Hutchison Whampoa Ltd	7
A321	Hutchison Whampoa Ltd	5
A4211	Hutchison Whampoa Ltd	4
A23	Swire Pacific Ltd	5
A331	Swire Pacific Ltd	4
A4311	Swire Pacific Ltd	3
A24	China Resources Enterprise Ltd	10
A341	HKCB Bank Holding Co Ltd	7
A4411	HKCB Bank Holding Co Ltd	3
A342	China Resources Enterprise Ltd	3
A4421	China Resources Enterprise Ltd	3
A25	Hang Lung Development Co Ltd	3
A351	Hang Lung Development Co Ltd	3
A4511	Hang Lung Development Co Ltd	3
A26	Wharf (Holdings) Ltd	9
A361	Wharf (Holdings) Ltd	3
A27	Sun Hung Kai Properties Ltd	5
A371	SmarTone Telecommunications Holdings Ltd	3
A28	Century City International Holdings Ltd	3
A381	Century City International Holdings Ltd	3
A29	Kerry Properties Ltd	3
B1	Guoco Group Ltd	4
B21	Guoco Group Ltd	3
C1	Lai Sun Garment (International) Ltd	7
C21	Lai Sun Garment (International) Ltd	7
C311	Lai Sun Garment (International) Ltd	4
C4111	Lai Sun Garment (International) Ltd	3
D1	Dah Sing Financial Holdings Ltd	3
D21	Dah Sing Financial Holdings Ltd	3
E1	Guangdong Investment Ltd	3
E21	Guangdong Investment Ltd	3
F1	Pacific Concord Holdings Ltd	3
F21	Pacific Concord Holdings Ltd	3
F311	Pacific Concord Holdings Ltd	3
F4111	Pacific Concord Holdings Ltd	3
G1	Tsim Sha Tsui Properties Ltd	3
H1	National Mutual Asia Ltd	4
I1	Wing On International Holdings Ltd	3
I1	China Travel International Investment Hong Kong Ltd	3
K1	Tem Fat Hing Fung (Holdings) Ltd	3

Keys: ——— 1-graph; ——— 2-graph; ——— 3-graph; ------- 4-graph
( ) number of firms in the component

Figure 4.2   The major business group, 1997

Public Company Components, 2004
(with Interlocks excluding Independent Non-executive Director)

Components	The firm with largest total in market capitalization and assets in the component	No. of Firm in the Component
A1	HSBC Holdings plc	78
A21	Hutchison Whampoa Limited	9
A311	Hutchison Whampoa Limited	9
A4111	Hutchison Whampoa Limited	6
A22	Sun Hung Kai Properties Limited	14
A321	Henderson Land Development Company Limited	5
A4211	Henderson Land Development Company Limited	5
A322	Sun Hung Kai Properties Limited	3
A4221	Sun Hung Kai Properties Limited	3
A23	Swire Pacific Limited	6
A331	Swire Pacific Limited	4
A24	China Netcom Group Corporation (Hong Kong) Limited	4
A341	PCCW Limited	3
A4411	PCCW Limited	3
A25	Sino Land Company Limited	3
A351	Sino Land Company Limited	3
A4511	Sino Land Company Limited	3
B1	Wharf (Holdings) Limited	10
B21	Wharf (Holdings) Limited	5
B311	Wharf (Holdings) Limited	3
C1	China Resources Enterprise Limited	4
C21	China Resources Enterprise Limited	5
D1	Guangzhou Investment Company Limited	3
D21	Asia Standard International Group Limited	3
D311	Asia Standard International Group Limited	3
D4111	Asia Standard International Group Limited	3
E1	COFCO International Limited	4
E21	Lippo China Resources Limited	3
E311	Lippo China Resources Limited	3
E4111	Lippo China Resources Limited	3
F1	Regal Hotels International Holdings Limited	3
F21	Regal Hotels International Holdings Limited	3
F311	Regal Hotels International Holdings Limited	3
F4111	Regal Hotels International Holdings Limited	3
G1	BOC Hong Kong (Holdings) Limited	3
H1	Hang Seng Bank Limited	4
I1	Ping An Insurance (Group) Company of China Ltd	4
J1	Guangdong Investment Limited	7
K1	Hopewell Holdings Limited	3

Keys: ——— 1-graph; ——— 2-graph; ——— 3-graph; ------- 4-graph
( ) number of firms in the component

Figure 4.3 The major business groups, 2004

2-graph component, but only nine in 2004. Instead of one large, densely connected network, the 2004 business network had fragmented into a large number of 1-graph components with few connections between them. Interestingly, in 2004, the Hang Seng Bank, which we found within the largest 1 and 2-graph components, had actually become detached from the largest 1-graph component.

Two features stand out in Figures 4.1 to 4.3. First, they clearly show the rise of Chinese business groups and the decline, compared to their previous dominant and central positions, of the British *hongs*. Second, unlike the pattern noted by Wong for the 1970s and for that we found in Figure 4.1, which shows closer interconnectedness among business groups and a certain extent of centrality by the major British *hongs*, the structure has become increasingly nucleated and cellular. Each of the Chinese business group consists of, in fact, a conglomeration of economic activities run by a family. Family-based interests and concerns formed the centre of each of these businesses, growing and evolving around the family interests and concerns. They branched out into different areas of investment and diversified their business without creating inter-familial alliances. To a large extent, each of these family business groups, instead of specializing in certain areas of business, tend to sprawl out and step onto the turf of other groups. The rise of business groups with mainland connections (but not H-shares themselves) also contributed to the fragmentation of the business network. The China Resources group and the Guangzhou Investment group represent prime examples. Interestingly, we further note that these groups with mainland backgrounds also do not connect with each other, each of them forming a 1-graph component of their own.

Thus, while the earlier structure of business groups in Hong Kong gave rise to dominant, central players like the HSBC and the Jardine Group, decentring structure has emerged since the 1980s. The rising Chinese business groups have been working hard to consolidate, and then to expand, their "family kingdoms". Table 4.3 gives an approximate picture of the scope of activity of the Jardine Group in 1961–97. While, sometimes, the numbers can mislead, however, they do reflect a concentration in finance, insurance and real estate, trade and shipping since the corporate restructuring can affect our understanding of activity.

Table 4.3 Jardine Matheson's scope of activity, 1961–97

Resources/Services	No. of Companies			
	1961–71	1972–77	1977–83	1983–97
Agriculture and Forestry	2	3	0	1
Mining		6	6	1
Construction and Engineering	7	10	3	3
Manufacturing	9	75	13	6
Shipping, Transportation	22	92	44	12
Wholesale Trade	18	54	13	20
Retail Trade		5	9	20
Finance, Insurance and Real Estate	19	142	111	87
Business Services	6	50	24	

Source: Adapted from Carol Matheson Connell, *A Business in Risk: Jardine Matheson and the Hong Kong Trading Industry* (Westport, CT: Praeger, 2004), 61–73.

In addition to the fading out of British *hongs* and the rise of Chinese business groups, deregulation also impinged upon the Hong Kong economy during the 1990s. Under the pressure of globalization, Hong Kong gradually relaxed its regulation of certain monopolistic sectors. In particular, new entrants subjected public utilities to increased competition, with telecommunications serving as the prime example. While only one service provider existed before, the 1990s witnessed the introduction of competition in the sector, first, through multiple operators in mobile service and, later, in the provision of fixed-line services. In transport, including ferries and bus services, the government also allowed competitors to enter into hitherto monopolistic sectors. The major groups, eager to enter into the rising telecommunications sector, therefore competed head-to-head with their business rivals, upsetting the previous informal territorial arrangements they each had enjoyed. Table 4.4 presents a rough summary of the major business activities of four leading Hong

Table 4.4 Composition of the four major Hong Kong Chinese business groups

Sector	Li Ka Shing Group	Lee Shau Kee Group	Kwok Family Group	Peter K. C. Woo Group
Property	Cheung Kong (Holdings) Limited (1)	Henderson Land Development Company Limited (12), Henderson Investment Limited (97), Henderson China Holdings Limited	Sun Hung Kai Properties Limited (16)	Wheelock and Company Limited (20), Wharf (Holdings) Limited (4), Wheelock Properties Limited (49), Realty Development Corporation Limited
Telecom	Hutchison Telecommunications International Limited (2332)	–	SmarTone Telecommunications Holdings Limited (315)	New T&T (Hong Kong) Limited
Infrastructure	Cheung Kong Infrastructure Holdings Limited (1038)	–	–	–
Energy	Hongkong Electric Holdings Limited (6)	Hong Kong and China Gas Company Limited (3)	–	–
Transportation	Hutchison Whampoa Limited (13)	Hong Kong Ferry (Holdings) Company Limited (50)	Airport Freight Forwarding Centre Company Limited, River Trade Terminal Co. Ltd., Asia Container Terminals Ltd., Kowloon Motor Bus Holdings Limited (62)	Modern Terminals, Hongkong Air Cargo Terminals Limited, Cross-Harbour (Holdings) Ltd (32), Hongkong Tramways Limited, The "Star" Ferry Co. Ltd.

Table 4.4 (*continued*)

Hotel	Harbour Plaza Hotels & Resorts, Sheraton Hotel	Miramar Hotel & Investment Co. Ltd. (71)	Royal Garden Hotel, Royal Park Hotel, Royal Plaza Hotel	Harbour Centre Development (51), Marco Polo Gateway Hong Kong Hotel, Marco Polo Prince Hotel, Marco Polo Hong Kong Hotel
Finance	Cheung Kong Bond Finance Limited, Cheung Kong Investment Company Ltd.	Henderson International Finance Limited, Henderson Development Limited	–	Beauforte Investors Corporation Ltd (21)
Retail	PARKnSHOP, Watsons, Fortress	–	–	Lane Crawford, Joyce Boutique (647)
Technology	Tom.com (8001)	Henderson Cyber Limited	SUNeVision (8008)	I-Cable Comm (1097)

Source: *Express Weekly*, 8 February 2001. Company annual reports.

Kong Chinese business groups. Overlapping business interests and intergroup competition occur commonly while of course, the business world always, quite truly, functions in such a state of competition. In this regard, fragmentation among business groups by itself does not present an issue of concern. That such fragmentation posed a challenge to the established order that the leading British *hongs* and the colonial government had worked out interests us here.

As we noted earlier, under the colonial regime, the leading British *hongs* and other major business interests had more or less found their own territory and they stayed quite content for the government to leave them on their own to pursue their economic gain in a pro-business environment, with minimal intervention. As long as the government remained "neutral" (i.e., in general, pro-business but without favouring individual groups or sectors) and refrained from becoming intrusive (and therefore with the government acting primarily as a regulator), government-business relations remained largely peaceful and collaborative. Such a government-business alliance worked to secure support from the business sector for launching pro-growth strategies (mainly in terms of infrastructural construction and facilitation of trade and commerce). We found that "The colonial administration converted its non-interventionist precepts into practical protection for the public interests" equally significant.[44] The fortunes of business appeared to depend on market forces rather than on a business-biased environment created by the colonial administration. Positive non-interventionism thus seemed to be an approach to economic management that would guarantee fairness and uphold a competitive spirit. Such a ruling strategy and its ideological components facilitated stability and prosperity. But the decentring, nucleating and cellularizing pattern of the structure of business groups in the 1990s upset such an established order. Growing intergroup, and quite often head-to-head, competition restarted turf-wars in the business world. Here, we find it interesting to note that the consolidation and expansion of Chinese business groups in the 1990s coincided with, partially an outcome of globalization and its resultant push for liberalization, and partially an effect triggered by advances in new technology, the deregulation of major services including telecommunications, energy and public transportation. The opening of new business opportunities intensified competition and created prospects for building a new balance of economic power among the business groups. Our discussion of the pattern of nucleation and fragmentation in Hong Kong's economic power structure implies that once government-business relations (and thus the tacit understanding governing the claims and allocation of economic interests) require restructuring, the state will soon find itself swamped by new claims made by different players within the business world.

Breakdown of the established order

The decolonization process also constituted a process whereby the state re-embedded itself within the socio-economic structure. For ordinary persons, the question of political legitimacy, once an issue rarely questioned, became contentious. When the government failed to ensure economic prosperity and the populace found its performance unsatisfactory, political authority came under constant attack. For the capitalists, the state's need to rebuild its relationship with the business sector kick-started a competition to stake their claims. Previously, the colonial administration took the prevalence of British business interests as a given. Furthermore, the colonial state possessed the ability to rise above diverse interests, maintaining its autonomy and thus effective governance. In a way, decolonization brought the Hong Kong SAR government back to the world of real politics. It had to strike a new deal with the business sector, ensuring capitalists that they would get their fair share.

The Tung administration precisely struggled to achieve this new deal. To do justice to the Tung administration, we must admit that it did not have much room for political manoeuvring. The growth of Chinese business groups and the fragmentation of the economic power structure had restructured the established order, preventing the Tung administration from simply repeating the winning formula the colonial state adopted. Growing intergroup competition and the changing balance of economic power meant that the SAR government had to work out its business alliance with a different set of players and within different parameters. In a way, the new environment forced the SAR government to test its relationship with major business interests by a new attempt to work out a novel kind of tacit understanding and collaboration. The Tung administration encountered an almost impossible situation where it had to find its alliance without upsetting other potential candidates.

The Cyberport incident best summarizes why and how the Tung administration found itself trapped in a cross-fire of criticism when it took the first steps to form its business alliance. The government first announced the idea of building a mega Cyberport project in the budget speech in March 1999. The 26-hectare project encompassed office buildings and residential complexes that would serve as a base for the development of new telecommunications and media technology. It would provide space for enterprises of different sizes, for residential development and facilitate new job creation of some sixteen thousand positions. In the aftermath of the 1997 Asian Financial Crisis, it promoted the project as a way to jolt the economy back onto the growth track. Skipping the usual practice of open land auction or invitations for tender, the government assigned the project to the Pacific Century Cyberworks Group (PCCW), owned by Richard Li, the son of Li Ka-shing. It caused an uproar in the business community, with ten major land developers issuing a joint statement to the government offering to buy the residential land at a price higher than that evaluated in the PCCW offer and also to promise to pay the government an additional sum.[45] Local newspapers also reported intense behind-the-scenes lobbying to block, unsuccessfully, government approval of the project.[46] The unprecedented chain of events involving the Cyberport epitomized the underlying changes in the business network and consequently "the attempt of rival business interests to capture the economic rent created by government intervention and to undermine rivals by means of market protection and closure to competition".[47] The example the Cyberport set, therefore, prompted other business groups to push for similar projects involving the public provision of subsidized land in the guise of ones designed to pioneer development in particular strategic sectors: bio-tech, Chinese medicine or even a shipping terminal complex.

The Cyberport Incident deserves attention not because of the claims of government-business collusion[48] but more because of the surfacing of conflicts between competing business groups in Hong Kong. In 2002, another incident also served to illustrate such manifested rivalries, when seven major groups (Sun Hung Kai Properties, Swire Properties, Wharf Holdings, Hongkong Land, Great Eagle Holdings, Hysan Development and Hang Lung Properties) formed a group, Electricity Consumer Concern, to express dissatisfaction over allegedly excessive electricity charges. "The group seeks to urge the government to ensure the efficient production and distribution of electricity and to establish an efficient regulatory system to enforce the scheme of control".[49] This prompted a war of words between the group and the power companies, in particular, Hong Kong Electric (owned by Li Ka-shing), which publicly released a statement countering criticism, claiming that other public utilities such as tram, bus, ferry, taxi and MTR all registered higher increases than electricity since 1983. The actual ownership of the tram, bus and ferry services by members of the Concern group only served to accentuate the point made by Hong Kong Electric. Even Li himself also publicly rebuked the critics.[50]

Conclusion

The colony built its political order on a firm coalition between the government and big businesses in the territory, made possible by a cohesive business community composed of a dense network of major corporations. The consensus of the business community (or at least the dominant segments of it) on major policy issues, positive non-interventionism prominent among them, provided the pillar of colonial governance, making it easier for it to forge social support for its policies. Since the 1990s, however, the degree of cohesion in the business community has declined, firstly, due to the rise of Chinese business groups and, secondly, to the process of deregulation which led to the intrusion of business groups onto each other's turf and intensified competition. While the colonial state could appear impartially arbitrate any conflicts of interest between big businesses, the SAR government did not have such a luxury. Instead, it has been dragged into rivalries among business groups whenever it decided to intervene in the economic sphere.

Accusations of government-business collusions have popped up from time to time in the SAR, because whenever its government chose to support any projects by assisting their development, it has inevitably aided one group to the discomfort of its rivals. The recent debate over the alleged demise of the "positive non-interventionist" approach to economic management perhaps illustrates the double bind that has ensnared the government. While it has tried its best to articulate a viable development strategy and carve out a new direction for Hong Kong's development, it has found itself caught in a cross-fire of conflicting demands and interests. We argue that they do not emanate merely from the process of democratization or the popular demands for participation or welfare, but also symptomize the underlying changes in the power structure. To construct a viable governing coalition that supports the quest for strong governance, the government must seek a way to overcome the fragmentation of business interests and forge more broad-based support and legitimation of its major development policies.

Appendix: Data sources

We analysed two kinds of public companies in our study: companies listed on the Hong Kong Stock Exchange and licensed banks incorporated in Hong Kong, some of which also listed on the Hong Kong Stock Exchange. We confine ourselves to public companies incorporated here. By so doing, we excluded two types of public companies from our study: First, the listed companies which issued H-shares, preference shares or B-shares. Second, the licensed banks incorporated outside Hong Kong. Further, due to data collection problems, we have also excluded those licensed banks incorporated in Hong Kong without available information on its board of directors or its financial record.

In our study, we have examined the board membership of public companies at three different time points—in the years 1982, 1997 and 2004 respectively. We studied only the top 250 public companies at each time point. In 1982, only 238 public companies registered but with an additional thirty-six non-listed ones for which we had available data. By 1997, the total number of listed companies reached 627, increasing to 975 in 2004. We first entered the asset and capitalization for all listed companies and then selected the top 250 according to total "assets" and "market capitalization" in each year. Since we have encountered some non-listed licensed banks, we counted and compared only company assets in our study and we included all of them in our analysis.

We principally used two sources for company information such as company assets, market capitalization and composition of board of directors. For listed companies, we primarily collected their information from published listed company database handbooks that include data on all listed companies on the Hong Kong Stock Exchange at different time points. These comprehensive handbooks contain archived information on company history, company structure, financial data for previous years and share prices. They are available in university libraries. For the licensed banks, we first compiled lists for different years from the relevant Hong Kong Monetary Authority annual reports. Then, we compared licensed banks to the listed-firm database handbooks discussed previously. For those non-listed licensed banks, we traced their information from their company annual reports and official websites. This explains why we could not find information on those licensed banks without official websites or annual reports accessible to the public.

We used the UCINET 5 statistical software to generate the components.

Information sources

For 1982:

DataBase Publishing. 1982. *Data Base Hong Kong 1983 Public Companies. A DataBook of Public Companies Listed on the Four Stock Exchanges in Hong Kong.* Hong Kong: Printrite.

DataBase Publishing. 1982. *Data Base Banks 82/83: A Directory of All Licensed Banks in Hong Kong.* Hong Kong: Printrite.

For 1997:

EFP International. 1999. *The Primasia Guide to the Companies of Hong Kong.* Hong Kong: EFP International.

HSBC. 1999. *NetTraderCards on CD.* September. Hong Kong: HSBC Broking (Data Services).

Hong Kong Monetary Authority. 1998. *Annual Report 1997.* Hong Kong: Hong Kong Monetary Authority. Available at http://www.info.gov.hk/hkma/eng/public/ar97/toc.htm

For 2004:

HSBC. 2006. *NetTraderCards on CD*. February. Hong Kong: HSBC Broking (Data Services).

Hong Kong Monetary Authority. 2005. *Annual Report 2004*. Hong Kong: Hong Kong Monetary Authority. Available at http://www.info.gov.hk/hkma/eng/public/ar04/toc.htm

Various Annual Reports and Official Websites of Various Licensed Banks

5
The development of citizenship in Hong Kong
Governance without democracy

Agnes Shuk-mei Ku

The Hong Kong government has tended to take an increasingly active role in response to the impact of globalization and amid changing state-society relations. It seeks to enhance governance, but, without an effective institutional structure, its efforts have resulted in some unpalatable outcomes. Extending Marshall's threefold scheme of civil, political and social citizenship to include the notion of democratic citizenship, this chapter will show how the government's existing strategy has become increasingly incapable of coping with new tensions and demands. It will also demonstrate how civil society, in response, is looking for and articulating a new mode of state-society relations that outgrows the conventional model of citizenship.

Modern citizenship in Western capitalism: Underlying contradictions and new fissures

T. H. Marshall's classic essay on citizenship, which sheds light on the tensions and agreements between the institutions of citizenship and capitalism as reflecting the intricate relations between the state and the economy, remains controversial (Marshall 1992). The crux of the recent debate hangs on the changing relations among the state, the market and civil society as well as changing ideas of equality and participation. These debates echo strongly recent discussions on state form and governance issues in the wider literature (Evans 1992; Jessop 1990, 1999). In Marshall's historical account, citizenship in England developed in tandem with the rise of capitalism since the late eighteenth century and the formation of the liberal state which provided the institutional contexts in which citizenship developed. In the eighteenth century, the state first granted civil rights to free individuals to protect their freedom and the property that arose out of the market economy. Political rights (electoral democracy) subsequently developed in the nineteenth century, confined at first to the propertied and educated class (mostly males), and finally extended to universal suffrage through several stages. In the twentieth century, the state provided social rights for all citizens to ameliorate the social inequalities the capitalism generated that remained incompletely resolved under political democracy. In this light, citizenship developed as a product of liberal governance by the state in response to the needs and challenges of capitalism.

Much as scholars have criticized it for evolutionism and ethnocentrism (Giddens 1982; Jessop 1978; Mann 1987), the Marshallian account nonetheless captures an important dilemma in modern society that remains relevant. Clearly then, some contradictions exist between formal equality (civil and political citizenships) and the persistence of extensive social and economic inequality under capitalism (Turner 1990). In principle, citizenship offers a basis for social integration based on the idea of equality, yet certain contradictory developments still permeate it. In large measure, the historical development of citizenship bespeaks a dialectical relationship between its underlying contradictions and the drive toward social integration. Marshall's account offers a sociological approach to analyze this dialectical relationship in relation to class.[1] Bottomore further spells out the role of class conflict as a catalyst for citizenship development (Bottomore 1992). Civil citizenship, however, does not remove class inequalities. Rather, it exists side by side and remains harmonious with them, providing "the foundation of equality on which the structure of inequality could be built" (Marshall 1992, 21). The principles of civil rights and social equality conflict: the former stresses individual freedom whereas the latter entails the subordination of freedom to social justice and market forces to the state (Wagner 2004). Marshall thus proposes the extension of citizenship as the principal political means of resolving, or at least containing, those contradictions. It is the extension of citizenship rights—political citizenship in the nineteenth century and social citizenship in the twentieth—that makes capitalism and its markets workable and sustainable.

Marshall's account of citizenship in England reflects a conjoining of liberalism with social democracy. Nevertheless, whether or not formal citizenship rights would necessarily translate into substantive equality remains an open question. Historically, citizenship depended upon the economy and the prevailing ideology as well as class politics. For example, during the nineteenth century, social citizenship on the whole developed only slightly under the reign of the ideology of freedom. Only after the Second World War did it fully extend as many Western European countries moved toward a welfare state regime. The shifts in ideology as well as in the mode of governance in part resulted from the class-based politics associated with socialism, and in part from a social consensus forged out of a strong economy. In the 1970s, however, *new ideas about* state-market relations and citizen participation began to develop, including, privatization, value-for-money and participatory democracy, which pose questions about the limits of the model from both the right and the left.

Contemporary limits of the liberal model of political citizenship

The liberal model indeed has limits from the point of view of democracy. It tends to reduce citizenship to a passive status of rights the state grants that serve to legitimate it within a capitalist framework (Delanty 2000). In sum, it takes democracy as a means to achieve political legitimacy as well as state goals, rather than an end that results in participation. Today, as the state has entrenched new forms of power in ways that often bypass democratic channels, as for example, subcontracting public services to the private sector, it further diminishes the meaning of democracy. In Western societies, cynicism has grown regarding established politics, and the populace identifies less and less with traditional parties. Distrust in parliaments, parties, government and representative democracy results in growing political disengagement among the larger population. This in turn gives rise to two different political responses from two opposite ends of the ideological spectrum.

On the right, the thrust of neo-liberal governance in the developed democracies in recent years has been to reduce the role of politics altogether. In view of the apparent decline in the effectiveness of democratic institutions, the right of the political spectrum has mounted an attack on the idea of the affirmative state, i.e., a state committed to operating under affirmative legislation and obligations. Adherents advocate reducing the scope and depth of the state's activities. Efficiency, value for money and reduction of state spending constitute the new watchwords, rather than participation or more democratic forms of governance. Privatization shifts power and responsibility from the state to the private domain, which withers the public sphere and expands the market sphere, which in turn reduces the terrain of political participation via the state. Policy communities within a socialist framework that conventionally looked to the state as an agent of resource redistribution remain sceptical of the market. They express worries about threats to social cohesion and justice and therefore reject the neo-liberal position. The debate between liberals and statists brings out the tension between freedom and social justice; yet, it leaves out the question of democratic citizenship from the perspective of the new left.

On the left, critics and activists have turned away from both the market and institutional politics to the idea of direct democracy. Since the late 1960s, various social movements have emerged exploring new forms of participation. They make democracy central to their political project and seek to take politics out of the state and into society (Eder 1993). The new social movements have revived civil society and given rise to an alternative paradigm of citizenship. According to Delanty, in participatory democracy, democracy repoliticizes citizenship, allowing us to speak of democratic citizenship. That is, it shifts from passive rights to active participation; it turns consumers into citizens and it redefines and enlarges the scope of politics to include everyday life issues. From this perspective, moreover, citizenship becomes more than a state-led project; "an expression of networks of communication that extend beyond the boundaries of the state linking to different nodal points in heterogeneous civil societies and social movements" (Delanty 2000, 47).

The idea of democratic citizenship underscores a need to re-examine the current political institutional framework and state-society relations from the point of view of democratic governance as well as effective participation by the people. In the context of increased state power and global capitalism (under the ideological influence of neo-liberalism), the liberal model of political citizenship forms a necessary but insufficient basis for such development. In the rest of the chapter, we shall address the issue of governance in relation to citizenship development in the context of Hong Kong from the late-colonial period to the post-handover era. The discussion will focus on how the system of governing negotiates (or fails to negotiate) ways of resolving the tensions bred by the accumulation imperative under capitalism and the problem of legitimation deficit in the absence of (full) democracy, and how in the process of struggle, civil society is articulating a new vision of democratic governance.

Colonial rule: From *laissez-faire* to governance by social consensus

In Hong Kong, during the earlier stages of British colonial rule, the market principle ran rampant in the economy, unchecked by an institution of citizenship (Ho 2004; Jones 1990; McLaughlin 1993). The overall ruling strategy sought to facilitate the growth of the market while incorporating business elites into the political structure by means of selection. While it suppressed citizenship development from above, a strong movement for citizenship rights from below did not appear in sight either. Capitalists enjoyed many privileges under the colonial government, with the trade union movement ideologically split between two antagonistic nationalistic camps, namely, the pro-People's Republic of China and the pro-Kuomintang (Nationalist Party) camps. Among the general populace, who had largely emigrated from mainland China, neither a notion of rights nor a sense of belonging attached to the identity of citizenship took root. In turn, the government often used the transient mentality of the population to justify denying substantive citizenship to its colonial subjects. The absence of citizenship did not at all attenuate the contradictions that permeate a capitalist economy. This bespeaks an extreme form of capitalist development characteristic of colonial rule.

The mass riot in 1966 exposed the contradictions between capitalism and the absence of citizenship. With rapid population growth (in part due to massive influxes of illegal immigrants from the Mainland and in part caused by the baby boom locally), the 1960s brought forth various kinds of social problems with regard to work, housing and living, which became more acute. As a result, social discontents grew and finally ignited due to a tiny incident relating to livelihood—a fare increase for the Star Ferry (another more politically motivated mass riot in 1967, organized by the leftist forces, followed the incident). During the 1970s, in the aftermath of the two riots, the government launched a series of social reforms, administrative changes and civic campaigns to restore legitimacy and promote a sense of belonging to the community (Turner and Ngan 1995).

The new initiatives marked a shift toward a more interventionist strategy of governance by social consensus. In it, the government sought to mobilize public consent to its rule, without opening up political institutions to democratic participation. Under this model, the government collected and channelled the opinions of the people by means of a system of consultation—through mutual aid societies as well as numerous advisory and consultative committees—that aimed at minimizing open dissatisfaction with official policies (Miners 1998). However, it still lacked political citizenship. In part, the people did not ask for it; in part, the colonial government deliberately placed a hold on political development. The society remained just as de-politicized as before while such laws as the Public Order Bill of 1967 even more cautiously controlled it. That type of system equated the people to a mass of subjects under state paternalism rather than a public of autonomous citizens with equal political rights (Ku 1999).

On the whole, during the 1970s, the governance strategy worked to its intended effect. To a large extent: the decade witnessed expansive economic growth, remarkable upward social mobility and growing middle-class affluence. Social inequalities persisted and protests occurred frequently, but the conflicts did not develop into a wider movement for social or political citizenship. Stepping into the 1980s, the rise of the "1997" issue provided a new context for the development of citizenship, especially with regard to political rights.

Political transition: Governance by corporatism and the rise of contested citizenships

Political citizenship remained repressed under British rule, and only after the 1980s and the 1990s did a critical opportunity arise for the development of democracy. Pertinent to the particular political context of Hong Kong, the government offered the opportunity from above in preparation for the decolonization process, rather than driven by the tensions between capitalism and citizenship demands. The British sought to introduce political reform, working toward the goal of representative democracy. The Sino-British Joint Declaration of 1984, which promulgated the "One Country, Two Systems" principle, ushered in a thirteen-year transitional period of disputes over political reform in the society. The issues at stake concerned not only changing from an authoritarian structure to a more democratic one but also aligning the changes before 1997 with developments after 1997 in a smooth process.

The struggles over political reform brought about a changing conception of citizenship through competing discourses. On the one hand, among middle-class and grassroots networks, a pro-democracy movement emerged in response to the new political opportunity. The Joint Declaration, which laid down the principle of a high degree of autonomy for Hong Kong under Chinese sovereignty and ratified international covenants on rights, provided a legitimate basis for the elaboration of a new discourse of citizenship. In the course of its struggle, the pro-democracy movement actors drew on the new discourse to call for universal suffrage and to challenge the authoritarian government (Ku 1999; Sing 2004). In the process, a new conception of the "public" was developing that required a government inclusive of and accountable to ordinary citizens. The 1990s further saw the emergence of diverse agendas of human rights, anti-discrimination, identity and community issues on a broader front tied to the democratic cause. Examples included, among others, the introduction of the Bill of Rights; legislation on anti-discrimination with regard to gender, disability, and family status; the rise of the homosexual rights movement; and women's groups' participation in the pro-democracy movement.

On the other hand, on the side of the establishment, it articulated a hegemonic discourse stressing administrative efficiency (in lieu of democracy) onto a narrative of prosperity and stability. In the face of strong opposition from Beijing and the business elites, the government proceeded with political reform in only a half-hearted manner. As a result, the government drew up a blueprint for political reform that introduced elections into the legislature on an incremental scale, relying chiefly on the principles of the functional constituency and elite-based elections (it first introduced popular elections to the legislative branch in 1991 and limited them to less than one-third of the seats). A functional constituency consists of essentially a corporatist framework skewed toward business and professional interests. It provided a strategy to broaden the political franchise by incorporating a rising social class—middle-class professionals—into the polity without introducing full universal suffrage. Functional constituencies presently constitute half of the legislature's membership. Apparently, the government aimed to govern by institutional consensus within a corporatist structure more inclusive than before, which differed from both the exclusionary corporatist regime of the earlier colonial days and its strategy of governance by social consensus in the 1960s and 1970s. Again, the government achieved this goal at the price of the suppression of political citizenship—the rights of an individual citizen—but unlike in previous decades, it contained political rights even when the people began to demand them.

During the transitional period, bureaucratic dominance still characterized the political structure, although the rise of contested citizenships as well as the introduction of electoral politics began to increase mobilization of societal interests at all levels, creating an environment which required the government increasingly respond to demands from such interests for allocation and intervention. Not insignificantly, this took place at a time when the government's drive for capital accumulation became stronger than ever, which prompted heightened intervention in the socio-economic realm.

Following the export-led growth of the 1960s, the local economy took off, beginning to acquire the status of an important regional and international financial centre. The 1970s witnessed a shift from *laissez-faire* to a more active role by the government geared toward greater capitalist accumulation in the global economy. State expenditure on physical and human capital investment in times of economic crises characterized active state intervention, while the market remained free from intervention only at the micro-level of operation. By the 1980s, the government admitted, in the words of then-Financial Secretary, Philip Haddon-Cave (1984 [1980]), that it was adopting an approach of "positive non-interventionism" regarding the economy.

It set the scene for a more managerial state, marking a clear policy departure from the bureaucratic reformism of the past. In the final years of British rule, for example, the Patten administration set up an "Efficiency Unit" and introduced a mandatory provident fund scheme financed by both employer and employee contributions (implemented during the Tung era). Other new initiatives at this time included the implementation of a target-based management process in 1997, followed by an enhanced productivity programme in 1998 and civil service reform in 1999 (Lee 2003).

In the 1980s and the 1990s, both the economic accumulation logic and the legitimation impetus drove the government toward greater state function and regulations. This extension of the state resulted in the growth of quasi-government bodies including statutory authorities, public corporations and non-departmental public bodies established to provide wide-ranging services from export credit insurance and trade promotion to urban land redevelopment and mass transportation. Examples included the Equal Opportunities Commission and the Land Development Corporation (later replaced by the Urban Renewal Authority). However, between accumulation and legitimation lies a structural contradiction that may metamorphose into conflict if the government does not control or manage the balance between them well. Indeed, the existing systems not only offer less than adequate mechanisms to resolve the increasing social and political demands but themselves have proven a source of conflict. As we shall see in the next section, politically, the half-reformed system poses a problem of legitimacy under contested citizenship while providing a highly politicized, but less than effective channel to resolve conflicts through the legislature. Socially and economically, a global ideology of neo-liberalism begins to put in place a new governance strategy by the government that aggravates the tensions between capitalism and citizenship.

Poising for strong governance: Whither citizenship after 1997?

The pre-handover years already saw the Hong Kong government resort to more-conscious accumulation and legitimation strategies. After the handover in 1997, several local and global factors have provided the foundation for the rise of a new practice of interventionism (Cheung 2000). It does not signify a complete break from the past so much as an attempt to strengthen state capacity and enhance performance in changing times (Cheung and Scott 2003) in the face of the mounting challenges of globalization and in the context of the post-handover era as well as an increasingly vocal civil society. The government, even more so under the second chief executive (Donald Tsang) than the first (Tung Chee-hwa), stays ready for stronger governance—in the sense of being more assertive and active—but whether this amounts to effective governance remains open to question. Officials' actions and gestures might seem like the outcome of personal whims, but structural, institutional and ideological forces continued at work leading to increased executive domination and interventionism.

Structurally, capitalism, whether under a *laissez-faire* or a neo-liberal framework, has produced mounting social inequalities.[2] Economic globalization further exacerbates the problem while driving the government to a more active and pro-business role to improve competitiveness. In the post-handover context, moreover, a decolonization syndrome operates, prompting ruling elites to adopt new social and economic policies in order to surpass the achievements of the British (Cheung 2000). Thus, on the one hand, the government of the Hong Kong Special Administrative Region (SAR) focuses on building a brand of its own for the city in an age of increasing urban entrepreneurialism and global competition. On the surface, the new type of interventionism seems at odds with the neo-liberal form of governance (with its emphasis on the market). However, in reality, the latter approach signifies only a shift in the form and focus of governance, but not a diminished will to govern. In fact, neo-liberal rule now takes the form of a new alliance among state, market, individuals and other social institutions in the production of an economically competitive city. The West Kowloon Cultural District (WKCD) project represents one outcome of such initiatives, which we shall discuss in greater detail later.

On the other hand, however, class inequalities have become increasingly severe, as housing and labour manifest. Two examples will suffice to show how the government has wavered between a "commandist" method of intervention and a *laissez-faire* style of inaction, both of which proved ineffective. The Tung administration launched a housing policy that set a target of building eighty-five thousand flats per year. It intended to moderate the effects of socio-economic inequalities resulting from soaring housing prices in an unchecked market economy before the handover. Tung's benevolent paternalistic inclinations perhaps both manifested the decolonization syndrome and resulted from his own personality.

However, under executive domination, good intentions could turn into a style of governance verging on commandism. The government did not undertake any prior consultations with the legislature or the public, and the effort was considered as ill-planned and foolhardy— far from being a practical or sustainable project with a clear vision of social citizenship based on political or social consensus. As a result, the policy aroused much concern among the business sector and the general public alike, especially those who suffered from negative assets in the aftermath of the Asian Financial Crisis in 1997. The government insisted on adopting the policy but actually did not carry it through nor did it give any public explanation for dropping it. It used a commandist process, with no consultation and no sense of accountability, resulting in an ineffective outcome.

On a deeper level, the housing problem symptomized acute class inequalities in production relations. In an age of globalization, capitalism has given rise to class polarization, especially in cities like Hong Kong. In particular, low-skilled workers have increasingly suffered from unemployment, poverty and harsh working conditions including low wages and long working hours. A 2007 International Labour Organization (ILO) report noted that in Hong Kong, unlike in most other countries, workers do not have a guaranteed minimum wage, but they lead the world in the average number of working hours per day.[3] All along, the business community and the free-market economists have expressed a very strong opposition against the legislation on a minimum wage, on the grounds that it would contravene the *laissez-faire* principle and bring about unwelcome intervention by the government in the free market. In the final transitional years under Governor Chris Patten, when the government broadened the franchise for functional constituencies on a more democratic basis, the Legislative Council passed the first legislation that safeguarded workers' rights to collective bargaining. It provided a good example of how a democratically expanded polity (political citizenship) could open up an institutional space for possible amelioration or mediation of class inequalities and conflicts. However, after the handover, as the legislature's democratic base shrank, the provisional legislature under the SAR government quickly repealed the law on collective bargaining. Further, the government in 1999 turned down an attempt to establish a minimum wage.

Over the years, without the full protection of political and social citizenship, an unbridled capitalist economy has created a city with one of the highest rates of inequality worldwide. It has a very high cost of living, with the most expensive housing rents in the world, while low-skilled workers do not earn enough to pay the costs.[4] The 2007 ILO report notes that the main cause of poverty in Hong Kong derives not from unemployment but from low wages. In particular, some labour and student organizations revealed embarrassingly low wages for janitors and security guards, even lower than that of the social security allowance for the unemployed. Measures taken by the government, as for example, the establishment of a Commission on Poverty in early 2005, nonetheless failed to alleviate the inequalities. In 2011, after years of delay and inaction, the government finally passed legislation on the minimum wage. However, problems still abounded as a result of ill-considered planning and conflicting interests. For instance, it is not unusual to find employers turning people into part-time or self-employed workers to reduce costs.

Indeed, ideologically, market competition as well as self-reliance, under a structure of class inequalities, remain the ethos of the day. From the late 1980s, the colonial government had already started to adopt a neo-liberal framework; after the handover, the Asian Financial Crisis as well as the increasing trend of global economic competition has prompted the SAR government to devise more aggressive measures for economic development.[5] Administrative reforms, social services and various development projects epitomize a neo-liberal mode of governance that rests on the principles of privatization and marketization. As a result, it diminishes citizenship as a social right.

The setting up of Link Real Estate Investment Trust (Link REIT) in 2004 offers a telling example of privatization against such a background. It comprises 180 properties (primarily shopping malls and car-parks) formerly owned by the Hong Kong Housing Authority, which now constitute one of the world's largest real estate investment trusts. With privatization of public properties and reduced income for the Housing Authority, the lower classes living in public housing became concerned that they would suffer from increased prices and rents as well as reduced debate about the public good. Likewise, in education, the government has introduced a series of reform initiatives under the ideologies of market efficiency and new managerialism since the late 1980s. It proposed a direct-subsidy scheme in the early 1990s; implemented with a slightly more generous appropriation after the handover, reflecting a quasi-privatization of education that works more favourably for elite schools and the wealthier classes. Educational inequalities reinforce class inequalities and vice-versa.

In addition, institutionally, amid increasing social and economic tensions and demands, the design of the political system has induced greater government intervention in an assertive but ineffective manner. On the one hand, the institutional arrangement of political corporatism has made the government susceptible to increasing pressure for intervention to safeguard the multifarious functional interests. On the other hand, the series of legislative elections that have taken place since the early 1990s (including a certain proportion of popular elections) have driven the government to a defensive position vis-à-vis the many diverse demands in society.

Although the government has sought to contain strong opposition through a skewed political structure—skewed in favour of business and conservative interests—under a system where the Chief Executive lacks the popular mandate accorded by universal suffrage, the executive government inevitably becomes subject to increasing pressure from the elected legislature to listen and to perform in order to gain legitimacy. The executive faces an increasingly assertive legislature (Scott 2000), but under a system of executive domination, the former often reacts by further asserting its power. This can prompt political impasses or impulsiveness followed by public outcry. The scrapping of the WKCD proposal in 2006, as we will see, provides an illuminating example of both. Even when the government finds a way to secure enough support under the skewed political system, it does not mean that existing institution can effectively mediate social tensions and conflicts. A half-reformed polity will cause the contradictions both inside and outside the system to surface.

On the political and civic fronts, the SAR government more inclines to an ideology of law and order, which could pose a threat to citizenship rights (Ku 2004). The SAR government, which consists of a less-than-fully-democratic structure leaning in a conservative direction, abolished the Urban Council and the Regional Council (the only institutions with members elected through universal suffrage in the 1990s during the Patten era) and reintroduced an appointment system for the district boards with the effect of increasing state power and further undermining political citizenship. In regard to civil rights, the government not only retains much of the control system in its colonial form (especially with regard to police power)[6] but also shows signs of deterioration. Immediately after the handover, for example, the provisional legislature amended the civil liberties ordinances in terms, albeit less tough than the pre-1990 legislation, though stricter than those the colonial government had relaxed during the final years of British rule.[7] And in 1999, on the right of abode issue, the government requested a legal interpretation from the Standing Committee of the National People's Congress in order to overturn parts of a ruling by the Court of Final Appeal in Hong Kong; a challenge to the rule of law, the foundation of individual liberty.

On the whole, Tung increased intervention on various fronts. But he provided ineffective leadership, which eventually led to his downfall in 2005. The mass demonstration in the summer of 2003 resulted from manifold causes, including not only the controversy over proposed legislation on national security, or Article 23 of the Basic Law, but also a worsening economy that affected the people's livelihood, the government's disrespect for the rule of law and a lack of public accountability in the time of a governing crisis (Ku and Tsui 2009). The widespread social discontent revealed that deep and real contradictions within the political and socio-economic systems existed not only between capitalism and citizenship but also between citizenship and governance.

If Tung's leadership was considered commandist yet weak, Donald Tsang's accession to the Chief Executive's office in 2005 showed both continuity and change as he created a self-conscious image of strong leadership (Chu 2010). Tsang sought to manage the government using the concept of "strong governance" in order to set out a new style of leadership based on effective execution and public consent. He entitled his first policy address in 2005–06 "Strong Governance for the People". Such a government would have "a clear direction, consistency in policy making, forceful and decisive leadership that is efficient and effective". By "strong," Tsang intended to style himself as a decisive and effective executive, with the connotation that his leadership would depart from the rather faltering and unsuccessful style of his predecessor. When he was campaigning for Chief Executive, Tsang expressed his dissatisfaction with the prominence of horse racing coverage and the Ten Gold Songs Awards programme at the broadcast media station RTHK. As a result, it decided to suspend horse racing coverage, which it had supplied for more than thirty years. From Tsang's perspective, this certainly represented "effective" leadership, yet, it came at the cost of some press freedom. Similar to the housing policy of constructing eighty-five thousand flats a year, the WKCD, which spanned the terms of both Tung and Tsang, did not originate out of any clear or widely consulted plan. The administration adopted a top-down approach in its entire decision-making structure and processes. On the one hand, the Tsang administration exemplified a larger trend that had started earlier; while on the other, his leadership consciously assumed a governing strategy that reinforced it.

Like his predecessor, Tsang does not adhere to democracy. Rising out of a civil service bureaucracy that he had served in for nearly forty years, Tsang considers the civil service "the backbone of the SAR Government, and of effective governance". Under his leadership, the government issued the "Consultation Document on Further Development of the Political Appointment System" to canvass public views on how best to further the political appointment system. It has also restructured the Executive Council to dispense with the role of the Principal Officials in it, which effectively transformed a decision-making body into an advisory body exclusively for the Chief Executive in order to further enhance his control. Although Tsang has broadened the base of public representation in the governance structure by setting up the Commission on Strategic Development to advise the government on policy issues, the Commission serves essentially as an advisory body whose members he appoints. All these initiatives under Tsang's leadership resemble the colonial strategy of consensus building among social elites.

While strong governance suggests an assertive state, rhetorically, Tsang's self-styled profile contains a seemingly paradoxical element: adherence to public opinion. As he said in his maiden policy speech, a strong government "heeds public opinion, adopting the public interest as the guiding principle and accepting wide public participation in policy formulation". It appears that Tsang stayed aware of winning popular consent to his leadership. As compared to his predecessor, his appointments indeed demonstrate a higher degree of open-mindedness—as for example, Andy Ho On-tat as the Chief Executive's information co-ordinator and Wong Yan-lung as the Secretary for Justice, people who have shown a stronger inclination toward democracy and the rule of law. However, under a political structure where power remains highly concentrated in the hands of a chief executive "elected" by only a tiny minority of elites, citizenship has become neither fully institutionalized nor duly respected. In this light, the strategy seems one of seeking popularity via public relations rather than cultivating political consensus through deep and open dialogue with diverse voices in society.

In a nutshell, the new mode of governance shows a trend of privatization/marketization under an increasingly directive state, which builds upon a political institution, as well as a style of leadership, characterized by assertive authoritarianism and selective inclusion with an emphasis on public relations and image-making. Under this new mode of governance, the space for citizenship will likely become commoditized, decomposed and displaced. As in the case of the Link REIT, privatization of public properties not only increases social hardships among the lower classes but also reduces the scope of politics by removing a previously public issue from the jurisdiction of the government, including the legislature. The public relations initiative may appear to work for a while, but the top-down model of governance will become inadequate to cope with the new demands of an increasingly vocal civil society. For example, the high-handed dismantling in 2006 of a beloved architectural icon, the Star Ferry tower in the Central District, showed a government that decides and acts alone. The choices for new appointments of deputy ministers and political assistants under bureau directors in 2008 also demonstrated this mindset.[8] As his popularity rating in July 2008 showed, people's confidence in Tsang fell below 50 percent, which was quite low for a political leader. We will further illustrate our argument by examining below the WKCD project of urban and cultural developments that spanned from Tung's term (during which Tsang took on the WKCD and other important projects) to that of Tsang's, and tease out the implications for an alternative form of governance in the new century.

Assertive but ineffective governance: The early WKCD proposal

The manner in which the government handled the WKCD project exemplified a blend of state entrepreneurialism, neo-liberalism and institutionalized disregard for democratic participation. The government made its decisions using a top-down method for the project in reaction to a global imperative. It exemplified the government's turning to the business sector for a social and cultural development project that could otherwise engage citizen participation. The imperious way in which the government managed it finally led to strong opposition by the legislature and the public alike. During the controversy, civil society began to raise new questions regarding governance and participation.

Following and extending the Metro plan promulgated in 1989, the SAR government envisioned Hong Kong as Asia's world city. It spelled out the concept in an official document entitled "Bringing the Vision to Life: Hong Kong's Long-Term Development Needs and Goals", published in February 2000 in conjunction with the formation in 1998 of the Commission on Strategic Development. Tung's administration put forward the WKCD project as a landmark cultural development to enhance "Hong Kong's position as a world city of culture. It began as a tourist-driven imperative in reaction to some global interest in the 1990s, making its first appearance in official discourse when Tung pledged to build "a new, state of the art performance venue" in the West Kowloon Reclamation area to present world-class cultural events (Hong Kong Special Administrative Region Government 1998).

The idea gained momentum very quickly. In April 2001, the government launched the West Kowloon Reclamation Concept Plan Competition, the results of which it announced in February 2002. Forster and Partner won for a design including a glass canopy encompassing twenty-five hectares of the site as its centrepiece. The government set up a steering committee in September 2002, chaired by then-Chief Secretary, Donald Tsang. A year later, it invited proposals for single-package tenders for the development and management of arts and cultural facilities under a land grant for fifty years.

The WKCD project, however, did not originate from plans with wide consultation. As a report by a Legislative Council subcommittee remarked, the government made its decision about the project in a policy vacuum.[9] The public raised strong doubts and criticisms regarding the absence of a clear cultural vision, the immense maintenance costs for the giant canopy, the single-package development approach (under a public-private partnership framework) and the lack of public participation. When Tsang took office as Chief Executive, promising strong governance in his policy address in October 2005, he still said he hoped the project would proceed as soon as possible.

The government adopted a top-down or centralized approach in the entire decision-making structure and processes (Ku and Tsui 2009). While the Chief Secretary chaired the steering committee, the assessment panel consisted of only senior civil servants. The committee even excluded the Executive Council from involvement in the formulation of plans for the WKCD; and only consulted it regarding the invitation for proposals from property developers before the release of documents to the public. Nor did it conduct such centralized decision-making with input from legislators or the public. The legislature solely possessed the constitutional power and function to approve public expenditures. The executive nonetheless bypassed the body in its preparations for the project, justifying its actions on the grounds that the single-package development approach did not involve public funding. This view reflected the neo-liberal trend of privatizing the arts and culture. It underlay a continuation of the executive's previous approach of centralized decision-making regarding arts and culture, only with the difference that officials would now be passing the onus of responsibility onto the business sector. However, the Executive Council used a disputable rationale since land also represents one form of public resource. The legislature therefore argued that it should subject the disposal of land to the same scrutiny as public expenditures. Members called for an executive accountable to the legislature with open and transparent disposal of land resources. It staked out the central issue of executive accountability to a supposedly representative body.

As it progressed forward with the widespread misgivings in society, a protracted struggle over the project took place. More specifically, the legislature delivered a blow to the plan by passing a motion that called for the elimination of the single-developer approach and the idea of a giant canopy. In October 2005, the executive conceded by demanding HK$30 billion (US$3.85 billion) up front from the winner to operate the site's museums and cultural venues and carving out 50 percent of the commercial and residential areas for open bidding. The revised conditions nonetheless did not attract developers, nor did they please the legislators from various parties who, in a rare show of unity, passed a motion in February 2006 urging the government to radically rethink the WKCD project. Toward the end of the month, the government finally scrapped the proposals and the WKCD project returned to square one. Again, this revealed an unplanned outcome of the self-poised style of strong governance: ineffective.

It opens up the question of what institutional structures does a democratic form of governance require that allows for genuine participation by the citizens, both inside and outside the government, and for effective communication between the government and civil society? Before we discuss this question, we will conclude this section by moving beyond a state-centred framework and bring to light the possible role of civil society as well as the idea of tripartite co-operation in the WKCD project.

The development of the WKCD under-represented the cultural sector and civil society as a whole. The paucity of voices from cultural practitioners outside the government actually resulted in the creation of extra-official bodies seeking to bolster discussion of cultural policies—for example, the People's Panel on West Kowloon, set up in 2003 to re-examine the project and gain "a more solid ground for achieving civil society and developing a cultural think tank for Hong Kong".[10] Furthering the rationale that spawned the panel, the body called for the establishment of a "Metropolis Cultural Think Tank" to enable public participation in WKCD planning, and to discuss "Cultural Vision" and "Urban Planning Vision". Such a think tank would serve as a precursor to a Provisional West Kowloon Authority. The panel viewed the authority as the optimal body to oversee the development and operation of the WKCD, provided that tripartite co-operation existed among the government, property developers and members of civil society. These new ideas and practices from civil society remain not only pertinent to the WKCD case, but point more generally toward alternative forms of participation and citizenship from the perspective of democratic governance.

Concluding remarks: Implications for active citizenship and democratic governance

This chapter began with a discussion of Marshall's threefold conception of citizenship that addressed the connections and tensions between capitalism and participation. In particular, political citizenship, albeit not a panacea for social ills, provides an institutionalized means to contain or mediate the structural contradictions bred by capitalism via parliamentary politics. Political citizenship also offers the modern state a basis for legitimacy. It represents by far the most effective way to ensure political equality and to safeguard against state despotism.

In the past, the government in Hong Kong has relied on a strategy of configuring social or institutional consensus in the absence of (full) political citizenship. This strategy might have succeeded previously, but in recent years, as politics has become more complicated and civil society more diverse, new problems have arisen that appear to outrun the adequacy of this model. The problems manifest themselves in several ways including the challenges of globalization; increased social inequalities; a neo-liberal ideology that expands the market sphere at the expense of public accountability; an imperious government under an executive-led, less-than-fully-democratic system and growing demands for participation from civil society. All these problems underscore a need to redesign political institutions in ways that not only allow for more effective participation by the people but also enhance democratic governance.

Policy implementation research has now become increasingly concerned about the need to improve the system of democratic feedback upon political decisions and to enhance the responsiveness of political institutions to the demands of the people. The potential to aid govern ability in which administrations need more participation to make more effective and more legitimate decisions rather than ideological beliefs motivate the various attempts at deepening democracy. Whether out of ethical beliefs or pragmatic concerns, scholars increasingly point to a need to rethink the question of democratic effectiveness under the challenge of neo-liberalism (Fung and Wright 2001; Eder 2001; Goodin 2003; Jessop 2002), requiring a different conception of citizenship and a new set of institutional configurations regarding governance, accountability and participation.

An interlocking system of accountability

Beyond the state and the market, post-industrial society has seen the emergence of other types of governance that rely more on horizontal networks and co-operation among different sectors (Jessop 2002). Networking, negotiation and partnerships constitute part of the new governance strategies. This model nonetheless has its own potential for failure because it possesses less legitimate authority than an elected government, especially in the case of conflict. Goodin's complementary model of accountability takes us a step further toward resolving the problem. He distinguishes among three accountability regimes: the state sector, the market sector and the non-profit sector (Third Sector), each with its own mechanisms of accountability. Holding each sector liable in different but complementary ways could secure democratic accountability (Goodin 2003, 359–96). For example, elections based on an idea of equal citizen's rights will guarantee accountability in the state; the market under the money principle may serve where the state fails to reach; the non-profit sector will help alleviate the effects of class inequality where state regulations and market prices cannot meet the needs of the people.

Regarding neo-liberalism, privatization may result in shielding private contractors from public scrutiny of its services in the name of commercial autonomy or confidentiality. Introducing competitive market principles in the service delivery process may undermine the spirit of co-operation and mutuality present in the Third Sector. The complementary model therefore suggests that the market principle should not dominate the Third Sector. In cases of conflict between citizen rights and market considerations, the accountability regime of the state sector should prevail so as to ensure democratic accountability. To this end, the government should implement measures to safeguard public interests as much as possible. For example, when contracting out services to the market, the government should insert transparency and political accountability provision in agreements. In sum, the democratic state (with the provision of political citizenship) should retain master accountability status—as a legitimate authority—while the market and the Third Sector may play a partnership role in "an interlocking system of social responsibility" (Goodin 2003, 360).

Participation in a new triangulation of political space

Today, the state no longer has the role of the exclusive reference for democratic politics, which has begun to extend to a broader boundary in civil society, developing new institutional forms that span a wide range of practices including public discussion, voluntary associations, informal networking and social movements. In liberal democracy, a decision by popular vote remains necessary but not sufficient to fulfil the conditions for an ideal deliberative process. In principle, partnership governance can help mobilize more people to develop vital human resources in local communities. However, it may also shrink the scope of politics by transferring more and more services and activities from the state to the market. Partnership governance, therefore, may or may not engage citizens in a proactive way as political agents. To enhance democratic participation, activists from the Left have begun experimenting with alternative institutions designed to tap into the energy and influence of ordinary people. The Empowered Deliberative Democracy (EDD) scheme (Fung and Wright 2001) , for example, puts forward the ideas of negotiated arrangements in specific cases of policy implementation, delegation of welfare competencies to groups and a correlative rise of the Third Sector, associative democracy and frequent use of pluralistic methods of communication.

The above procedures have stayed weakly consolidated and institutionalized, and they have their own legitimacy deficits. In this respect, they cannot entirely replace the state as the master accountability authority. Further, for the purpose of enhancing legitimate and effective governance, they should link to institutional democracy—universal elections—within an interlocking system of accountability. A new form of public space is emerging from the new triangulation of politics that necessitates a different way of thinking:

> The dichotomous world-view characterizing social theorizing since the 19th century is no longer adequate. The opposition of state and market, of state and society, of system and lifeworld, have given place to a triangular situation of co-ordination of functionally differentiated spheres of modern life. This shifts the locus of control away from spaces specific to either the state or the economy, or some shared (corporatist) space between both, toward some new type of space . . . The state is now intervening in civil society, creating institutional arrangements which can be called "post corporatist." . . . The space which is shared by these actors is the public space . . . a space extending beyond the boundaries of institutional politics. (Eder 2001, 220)

The context for governance and citizenship has become much more complicated in present-day politics. It requires us to think beyond the conventional dichotomous worldviews of state versus market, state versus society and institution versus everyday life.

6
Civil society organizations and local governance in Hong Kong

Eliza Wing-yee Lee

In recent years, in many countries throughout the world, attention has increasingly shifted to local governance, as distinguished from local government, implying that decision-making more and more involves multi-agency and multi-level collaborations, partnerships and networks. While elected local authorities remain the leading public actors, new local governance framework places greater emphasis on participatory democracy (Leach and Percy-Smith 2001).

Both practical and normative reasons prompt such changes. Practically, such factors as economic globalization and welfare restructuring have led local authorities to play a more important role in economic development and social provision, especially in collaboration with the business and voluntary sectors. Normatively, the ideal of the community has experienced a revival. For instance, Britain under the leadership of the Labour Government has carried out massive reforms in accordance with the Local Government Act 2000. In the United States, heightened suspicion of the strong executive model of local government that prevailed for almost a century has grown while the idea of community governance gains popularity (Box 1998).

Intellectually, several scholarly trends substantiate the value of participatory democracy. The idea of social capital (Coleman 1986; Putnam 1995) emphasizes that norms of trust and reciprocity as well as networks of civic engagement may improve the quality of governance, while the concept of state-society synergy (Evans 1997) illustrates how an active state and mobilized communities may work to enhance the achievement of developmental ends. The idea of "empowered participatory governance" that Fung and Wright (2003) advance emphasizes the capability of ordinary people to make sensible decisions through reasoned deliberation. Utilising such actual cases as the neighbourhood governance councils in Chicago and the participatory budget of Porto Alegre, Brazil, Fung and Wright revitalize the political value of empowering ordinary people to effectively participate in and influence policies which directly affect their lives. Inspired by all these strands of thought, the World Bank published *State-Society Synergy for Accountability* (2004), in which it discusses seven case studies from developed and developing countries, to illustrate how civil society and the state can work in partnership with each other (i.e., attain synergy) to produce policy outcomes that serve the public interest.

All these areas of thought share a number of common themes. Firstly, participatory democracy requires bottom-up participation, and thus the devolution of power to local units that stay as close to the people as possible as well as the provision of institutional support to empower people with the resources and the expertise to facilitate meaningful participation. Secondly, collaborative governance presumes a non-centralized system in which the formal government and civil society share decision-making responsibilities between them, especially the stakeholders in a particular policy issue.

Returning to Hong Kong, since the 1980s, scholars and the society have paid much attention to democratization, especially the controversy over the direct election of the Chief Executive and the legislature. At the same time, they have relatively neglected the development of participatory democracy, especially at the grassroots level, evident from the lack of research papers written on this subject in the past two decades. They treat grassroots participation as a marginal issue rather than the essential building block of a solid foundation for a democratic system. They equally underplay the significance of grassroots participation for good governance despite the fact that in recent years, many public policy problems, as for example, community economy, urban regeneration, poverty alleviation, social service and municipal service. Their solutions obviously call for a strong local governance capacity. In fact, if anything, Hong Kong has actually suffered from a retrocession in local democracy since the handover, as the government revived the system of appointed members for the District Boards (renamed the District Councils in 2000) and abolished the two Municipal Councils (both fully elected bodies before 1997) in 2000, recentralizing executive power in areas of culture, recreation and municipal services. These attitudes and approaches certainly stand in contrast to the international scholarly and political trends of the past two decades.

In this context, this chapter thus wishes to argue that we have a seriously underdeveloped system of local governance, disconnected from the needs of a pluralistic society. I shall first review the historical development of the local government system under colonial rule, followed with an examination of it in the post-colonial era. Utilising the case of a residents' movement related to urban redevelopment in Wanchai, namely the "H15 Project", I shall illustrate how local residents are collaborating with civil society actors and politicians at various levels to strive for their interests. The case depicts the birth of an autonomous civil society at the community level as well as the efforts of civil society actors and liberal-minded local politicians to experiment with a new form of neighbourhood democracy in response to the deficiency of the state-managed local governance system.

Local governance in Hong Kong: An historical review

Throughout the history of the development of local governance in Hong Kong, except for the last few years of colonial rule during which Governor Chris Patten put in place certain liberalizing measures (though transforming the two tiers of local councils into fully elected bodies, unfortunately, proved too little, too late), the community existed as an arena of state control. Under colonial rule, the mode of control operated as follows: (1) state intervention in and penetration of local communities; (2) state absorption of bottom-up inter-civic association collaboration, that it intended to turn into administrative units for top-down control and (3) confinement of community initiatives to administratively defined arenas to prevent them from turning into increased demands for political participation.

Early Hong Kong: The nascent development of community governance

Recent studies have argued that the colonial state penetrated into society far more than often portrayed, and that there existed complex state-society dynamics in which the state actively shaped social relations while social actors utilized its power to mediate relations among themselves (Ngo 1999, chap. 1). Indeed, the colonial state shaped the development of the community from the early colonial period onward. Minimal integration between the state and society (Lau 1982) only occurred in the very early years of colonial rule, when the British colonial state and Chinese society stayed largely segregated from each other.[1] Under this regime, a vibrant community, self-governing and self-organizing evolved, as the classic studies of Sinn (2003), Tsai (1993), Faure (1997) and Tsang (2004) have shown. As Tsai (1993) states, after 1841, urban Hong Kong represented a new settlement, "a frontier outpost". A rich associational life soon emerged as new Chinese migrants became organized in order to solve their common problems. Bringing with them the community ties and experience of social organization from their homeland, they formed a variety of community organizations including dialect groups, regional associations (*huiguan*), craft and trade guilds, temple committees, neighbourhood-based associations, and others. They built ties and networks that cut across sectors while institutions of community governance gradually emerged; among them the *kaifong* associations (neighbourhood/district associations) led by prominent merchants in the neighbourhood that offered charity to the poor and needy. They also provided public space to discuss community matters and arbitrate disputes. Collaboration among *kaifong* associations in the holding of territory-wide events also occurred commonly. The Man Mo Temple Committee took on responsibility for managing the Man Mo Temple, a territory-wide project involving collaboration among dialect groups, guilds and *kaifong* associations. They also developed electoral systems to select representatives to the Committee. The District Watch Committee organized as a spontaneous effort in community policing in the absence of adequate protection from the colonial police force. Needless to say, the historical establishment of the Tung Wah Hospital and Po Leung Kuk represented the high point of the development of civic associations and community self-governance.

Governance in the early Chinese community largely retained the Confucian and paternalistic mode developed in the Ming and Ching Dynasties and followed by merchant elites in mainland China, with predominantly pro-establishment community leaders (Tsai 1993, chap. 3). Nevertheless, generalising from his study of Taiwan and mainland

China, Weller (1999) argues that informal social sectors in Chinese society carry the potential to generate new forms of political life, in other words, nurturing a democratic civility with Chinese cultural roots. In this sense, we can regard early community governance in Hong Kong as a nascent Chinese civil society.

The colonial power, eager to subject the community's collaborative attempts at "rational administration" met the efforts of the Chinese community at self-governance with hostility and suspicion, as for example, the incorporation of the District Watch Committee, an entirely community-based initiative, under the regulation of the Registrar General by ordinance in 1888 (Sinn 2003, chap. 1; Hayes 1996, 102–3). From the 1880s and afterwards, with the appointment of a Western-trained doctor to the Tung Wah Hospital and the subsequent appointment of the Registrar General and a Chinese legislative councillor to the board of directors of the Po Leung Kuk by the governor, self-organized community groups became the object of management and surveillance by the colonial state. From then on, the Registrar General, and its successor, the Secretariat for Chinese Affairs (or SCA, established in 1913) took up the official role of "communicating" with the Chinese community. As Tsai (1993) states, "the assertion of state power and political integration after the mid-1880s meant the progressive decline in the scope of their management of public affairs" (292).

Post-war years

The approach of penetrating community organizations and subjecting them to rational administration continued on into the post-war period. At that time, state penetration into the community pursued the conflicting objectives of ensuring the adequacy of community self-help efforts and the need to suppress anti-colonial forces, especially Chinese nationalism. Under the SCA, Liaison Officers mainly functioned in order "to keep in touch with the principal Chinese associations . . . especially for the dissemination of information and the collection of public opinion" (Hayes 1996, 88). The initiative to revive *kaifong* associations represented the most prominent example of rational administration. Post-war *kaifongs*, unlike the older ones, did not develop on their own. Instead, the SCA promoted them through "enlisting the active help of prosperous Chinese" to set up the local institutions in new urban areas, and later on in new resettlement areas with acute needs for services in education and health care, among others. The number of "Kaifong Welfare Associations"—its present name—grew to sixty by the mid-1960s with a total membership of over 800,000 (Jones 1990, 168; Wong 1972, 264). At the same time, the SCA wanted to fill the leadership of these associations with pro-establishment figures and to guard against their possible infiltration by "subversive elements" or "undercover political agents" (Wong 1972, 106). These *kaifong* associations thus tended to attract the participation of small-business people, traditionalists looking for avenues to establish social and political connections that might bring about economic gain and higher social status. Liaison Officers thus acted as informal surveillance agents, establishing personal ties with the *kaifong* leaders and playing to their traditionalist orientation while having their good services rewarded through the official honours and awards systems (Hayes 1996, 90). The desire of these leaders to gain government recognition turned the *kaifongs* into a pro-government force. On the other hand, as Wong (1972) states, "the distances between the leaders and the ordinary membership—in terms of social class, personal characteristics, interests and involvement in *kaifong* matters—have prevented the latter from active participation and have resulted in a static leadership" (227).

1970s to 1980s

The district administration reform in the 1970s, beginning with the launching of the City District Office (CDO) scheme in the urban areas following the 1966 and 1967 riots, resembles a project of the colonial state to strengthen its rational administration of the newly developed urban communities. The CDO scheme, launched in 1968 under the Secretariat for Chinese Affairs (later renamed the Secretariat for Home Affairs), divided the urban area of the territory into districts, each headed by a District Officer. It intended for the City District Officer to play the same political officer role as its counterpart in the New Territories. Later, the government formed a City District Committee (CDC) in each district, together with numerous area committees, and in 1973, it introduced the Mutual Aid Committee (MAC) scheme, forming what Leung (1982) referred to as a "three-tier participatory structure supported by the government in every local district" (163). The MAC scheme actually had its earlier roots in a burgeoning residents' association movement in the 1960s, when a growing number of occupants of new high-rises initiated the idea of self-organization to solve problems associated with living in multi-storey buildings. Not surprisingly, this community initiative quickly came under the administration of the SCA. While the MAC scheme carried much potential to become the basis of grassroots democracy, as Leung (1982) states, "[f]rom the very beginning, the government had been very cautious not to turn the movement into a grassroots political force. It is comparatively a more democratic and representative institution and can penetrate the silent majority more than most of the other forms of local organizations" (165). The practice of awarding honours and status also soon turned the MAC into a pro-establishment organization.

The efforts of the colonial state at community building from above collided with a similar effort from below, led mainly by social workers. In the early 1970s, the colonial state expanded its financing of social services through the incorporation of non-profit organizations (NPOs), including the old church organizations, indigenized voluntary agencies and Chinese voluntary associations within its funding regime (Lee 2005). The colonial state intended for these state-sponsored social programmes to satisfy the public demand for services and to facilitate the orderly functioning of society. This expansion of funding for the non-profit sector occurred at a time when the role of service provision no longer satisfied the NPOs, who looked, instead, to social activism as a way to achieve societal reform, an attitude especially prominent among church groups. Until then, the colonial state regarded church-related NPOs as its trusted partners (unlike the Chinese ethnic associations which it treated with suspicion). By the 1970s, worldwide changes in theological thinking in Christian churches had taken place, with a new emphasis on their role as "prophet", i.e., as advocates of social justice and reform (Leung and Chan, chap. 3). At the same time, influenced by the activist philosophy of Saul Alinsky, social workers came to see themselves as agents of empowerment. Thus, in ways quite unintended by the colonial state, community development programmes under its sponsorship became the avenue for social workers to realize their conception of a just society. Through organizing community activism, they empowered the grassroots population to strive for improvements in their livelihood through collective action, and provided an important source of democratic education to the population. At the same time, such issue-based community advocacy did not become the basis for neighbourhood democracy or a strong sense of community ownership. As Leung (1986) rightly observes, these protest movements and examples of community activism had a handful of indigenous leaders and community organizers, but no strong grassroots organizations or networks.

With the setting up of the District Board, the introduction of direct elections for the Legislative Council and the development of political parties, many of the indigenous leaders who emerged from community activism turned themselves into politicians. Chiu and Lui (2000) argue that their move into politics had the immediate effect of "'hollowing out' of political organization at the grass roots level" (12).

Post-colonial era

The political forces that the old colonial power constructed continue to shape the organizational environment of the community. The post-colonial state has continued to rely on the pro-establishment forces its colonial predecessors nurtured as the basis of its support and legitimacy. These include the old *kaifong* associations and state-sponsored community-based organizations (CBOs), groups kept alive by the old reward system. The appointment system of the Area Committees and other local committees (as for example, the District Fight Crime Committee) continues to serve as the avenue through which the state rewards its loyal supporters with status and honour. In addition, the pro-Beijing grassroots associations and their leaders, an object of suppression in the colonial years, also now constitute part of the pro-establishment forces.

New grassroots associations have proliferated as a result of the development of political parties. In recent years, political parties and local politicians (notably District Councillors) have begun setting up their own CBOs, which function as means for politicians to reward their supporters through allocating resources they obtain from the

District Council. As party politics developed at the local level, it has permeated such neighbourhood-based organizations (NBOs) as the MACs and Owners' Corporations. By and large, political parties tend to see the District Council, CBOs and NBOs as places for establishing their power bases and for mobilising voters during elections, rather than as avenues for advancing grassroots democracy.

The institutional framework of the District Council has largely encouraged Hong Kong style pork-barrel politics and log-rolling. The lack of executive power coupled with small geographical constituencies (formed under the single-member district simple majority plurality (SMDP) electoral system) provide huge incentives for District Councils to allocate their annual budget in ways that benefited the constituencies of politicians in order to secure voters' support. The lack of responsibility to *govern* means that political parties and factions found it an easy way to exchange their support for each other's spending proposals. As a result, they spent the allocation on such benefits as banquets, short touring trips as well as recreational and ceremonial activities.

In sum, during the post-colonial era, clientelism largely characterized local governance. The post-colonial state relies on clientelism as a way to maintain the loyalty of its supporters, local elites rely on the clientele network as a way to secure their status and power and politicians rely on clientelism as a way to gain the support of voters. While it benefits those who take part in the system, those excluded from the network cannot see their interests represented or their voices heard. Nor does general environment stay conducive to the nurturing of citizenship. Middle-class residents and young people do not have adequate avenues to participate in community governance. In the case of minority groups and the socio-economically disadvantaged, the state-funded NGOs remain their major advocates. At the same time, the broader environment no longer stays receptive to community activism. In the 1990s, the government decided to stop funding a major community development programme (the Neighbourhood Level Community Development Programme). The change in the funding system coupled with the cutback in appropriations after the Asian Financial Crisis has also subjected NGOs to financial austerity, forcing many of them to reduce the resources they devote to community development.

In these contexts, the "H15 Project" significantly illustrates how inadequately the existing system of local governance provides channels for citizens' participation in issues affecting their lives, and how its failure prompts residents to take collective action to defend their interests. More importantly, the case provides a new model of community activism involving collaboration among residents, urban professionals, local NGOs, activists and local politicians. To the extent that such activism has emerged autonomously from below, and has little, if any, connection to the dominant political forces, one can speak of a renewal of civil society and of a new sense of citizenship in the making at the community level.

The case of the "H15 Project"

In 2003, the Urban Renewal Authority (URA) officially announced the H15 Redevelopment Project, a case of urban renewal located in the Wanchai district. It represented by far the largest one in terms of scale taken up by the URA. Aiming to redevelop the major old areas of Wanchai at Lee Tung Street, McGregor Street and part of Amoy Street, the Project affected 8,220 square metres of land, fifty-two buildings and 1,611 residents.[2] It planned to demolish most of the buildings (with the exception of three small low-rise buildings already officially designated as historic sites for preservation) and to rebuild them as modern high-rises for commercial, leisure and residential purposes. In January 2004, the URA sent acquisition letters to the residents and shop owners of the H15 district, offering them $4,097 per square foot to acquire their premises. It claimed that the acquisition price equalled 2.9 times the market value and equivalent to the price of a seven-year-old property of similar size in a similar area. The ability of residents to purchase a property in the same district and to continue to live in the neighbourhood if they choose to do so comprises the guiding principle of compensation.

The H15 district is an old community with over 35 percent of the apartment owners over sixty years old, 66 percent having owned their properties for over twenty years. It contains numerous street-level shops, many of them family businesses, running a variety of eateries, hardware stores, hair salons, construction material companies, laundries, printing companies, grocery stores and bakeries, among others. It has a street scene and shops, characteristic of the old Hong Kong, comprising one of the few old urban communities that remained intact amidst the rapid development of Hong Kong.

Notably, Hong Kong's printing industry originated on Lee Tung Street. After years of development, it had become famous for printing wedding cards. Twenty-two printing shops located there, among them, seventeen wedding card shops; the street became so well-known that it received the nickname of "Wedding Card Street". Gaining a reputation for good quality, variety and sophisticated designs, for many years, couples printed their wedding cards there. Their shops even attracted overseas customers, including members of a Middle Eastern royal family. Lee Tung Street thus evoked sentimental feelings among the population and constitutes part of their collective memory. For the shop owners, they had earned a brand name inseparable from the location, making them unwilling to move their shops to other places, fearful of losing the clustering effect that brought in customers.

The setting up of the "H15 Concern Group"

The Project immediately aroused major concerns among the residents and businesses within the affected district. In 2004, they established a concern group (the "H15 Concern Group") with the help of a local social service NGO. The core members of the Concern Group consisted of second generation residents or business persons from the redevelopment district. They had grown up in the Wanchai district, where many of them lived as long-time neighbours, some of whom ran small businesses started by their parents. Even though one of the primary concerns of the residents remained the amount of their compensation and the manner in which the URA estimated compensation, yet, from the very beginning, they also felt general dissatisfaction at being uprooted from a community to which they had long been attached.

When the Concern Group started, it focused mainly on disseminating important information to residents related to compensation and channels for communicating with the URA. The activists understood well the magnitude of the impact redevelopment would have on the lives of residents. The residents, many of them elderly people, had little knowledge of or skill in dealing with government officials, and would have a difficult time coping with the loss of their support network and personal linkages with their old communities. If they did move out, they would find adjusting to life difficult in a new, totally unfamiliar community. Others who felt a deep connection to the district decried the way they would be uprooted from their community. Very soon, they discovered that the amount of compensation that the URA offered would not adequately recompense them for an apartment purchased in the neighbourhood. Shop owners, especially those in Lee Tung Street, worried that they would lose business if they moved to other districts. Conveying their demands through the slogan "flat for flat, shop for shop", people called for the URA to make arrangements for them to relocate to other premises in the neighbourhood. They also demanded a voice in the planning process for redeveloping the district. The wedding card shop owners wanted the URA to relocate all shops to a street in the neighbourhood. A central issue developed around the people's desire to maintain the old community network and stay associated with the place. The Concern Group initiated a series of protest actions against the URA, stating their demands, and an organized movement was begun.

Civil society formation

The process of negotiating with the URA soon became a journey of self-discovery for the participants in the movement. They started to question whether the URA needed to demolish all the old buildings and rebuild them from scratch; whether redevelopment should necessarily mean destroying old communities and whether a "people-oriented approach" to development should give more priority to social networks, spiritual needs as well as the preservation of cultural heritage and collective memory. Through sharing their life stories associated with Wanchai, the residents rediscovered the history of their community. For instance, they found out that in Hong Kong, only Lee Tung Street had buildings entirely built in the 1950s and 1960s, in the Hong Kong Chinese tenement housing style distinctive of that period.

This journey of self-discovery resulted in the residents changing their priorities, from defending their own personal interests to the realization of a collective goal. In the process, other social groups began to join the cause. Firstly, the social workers from local NGOs, helped introduce the Concern Group to architects and town planners sympathetic to their cause. From these professionals, they learnt that legally, any citizen could submit a development plan to the Town Planning Board. They set up a workshop to develop their own plan for the redevelopment of the H15 district. This started a process of participatory planning unprecedented for Hong Kong. The residents actively collaborated with the professionals, conveying their ideas to them while the professionals provided expertise in terms of technical advice and skills (including drawing up the architectural plans). In March 2005, they submitted a "people-oriented redevelopment plan" to the TPB for approval. Named the "Dumbbell Plan" for the form of its landscape, it embraced the concept of sustainable development, arguing that the plan could preserve a large portion of the old buildings through renovation. By refurbishing old buildings and improving the facilities, the plan would allow the old residents to remain in the community, maintain the vibrant social and economic networks that have evolved over the course of several decades and preserve an important part of Hong Kong's cultural heritage.

Over time, the actions of the Concern Group began to arouse the attention of people in the cultural sphere. Writers, artists, photographers and film producers began to document the controversy through articles and multimedia. For instance, a cultural group named the Community Museum Project[3] spent six months visually documenting Lee Tung Street, culminating in a public exhibition and the publication of *Street as Museum: Lee Tung Street*. These artists actively engaged the residents to tell their life stories, by inviting them to present old items they have kept. One owner of a printing company even gave a public demonstration on how to use an old-style printing machine. The "visual knowledge" produced presented Lee Tung Street as "a vibrant neighbourhood nurtured by a strong communal spirit" (SCMP 2005a) rather than the run-down and aging neighbourhood portrayed by the URA. These "symbolic analysts" made major contributions in the way they framed issues and articulated meanings; and their discursive constructions helped shape the collective identity of the residents as "Wanchai-ers"—a community identity they could be proud of. The networks and attachments shared by the residents also provided a major source of social capital. One second generation resident set up a gallery in the neighbourhood as a venue for exhibitions related to the local community. She remarked, "I feel it's a moral obligation to be involved in the community" (SCMP 2005a). They also helped arouse public attention and initiated a campaign to raise funds for the residents to fight for their rights.

Local politicians

The Wanchai District Council has also strongly supported the collective action of the H15 residents. To understand the political composition of the Wanchai District Council and its significance, one needs to go back to 2003, an important year for post-colonial Hong Kong. Public dissatisfaction with the performance of the Hong Kong SAR government under the administration of Chief Executive, Tung Chee-hwa, had reached a boiling point when over 500,000 people took to the streets on 1 July (the Establishment Day of the Hong Kong SAR) protesting against a major piece of public security legislation that by Article 23 of the Basic Law mandated, and which they widely perceived as a threat to civil liberties. The protest, regarded as a watershed in Hong Kong's political development, it aroused a renewed sense of citizenship as people developed a local political identity and a new civic consciousness. Shedding the political apathy associated with their colonial subjectivity, people now felt empowered to take action to change their fate.

The District Council elections in November 2003, when many more young and educated candidates with a progressive agenda emerged to contest the old conservative candidates, reflected the development of a new democratic civility. For instance, young people inexperienced in electoral politics formed two new political groups called "Civic Act-Up" and "7.1 People Pile". The electoral platforms of these groups included, among others, the fight for full-fledged democracy, minority rights, gender equality and the development of civil society. At the same time, the election saw a huge increase in the number of registered voters and a record high voter turnout, apparently attributed to the mobilization effect of the 1 July mass rally (SCMP, 2003). In Wanchai, several of these candidates won, including Mary Ann King and Chan Yiu-Fai of Civic Act-Up. The election of these candidates tilted the balance of power within the District Council. As a result, it elected a new chairwoman (Ada Wong) liberally oriented. The new District Council strongly sympathized with the cause of H15. Deviating from the usual window dressing role of District Councils in Hong Kong as powerless forums for empty talk, it actively collaborated with the H15 Concern Group. It set up its own Urban Renewal Task Force to study the matter. In 2004, it commissioned consultants to conduct a questionnaire survey of the residents of H15 to collect data about their backgrounds, their opinions and their needs regarding the redevelopment project. It then published a position paper on Wanchai's urban renewal and submitted it to the government, all unprecedented active participation by a local council in urban planning. Later, it released two more reports in collaboration with a local social service NGO and an environmental NGO. It also conducted a street forum in the open area of Lee Tung Street providing a discursive space for residents to voice their concerns and needs as well as promoting their solidarity.

Outcomes and ramifications

The activism of the H15 residents could not make state officials change their minds. The Town Planning Board rejected the Dumbbell Plan on technical grounds. By the end of June 2005, more than 85 percent of the affected home owners had accepted the compensation the URA offered. In August 2005, the Lands Department gazetted the resumption order allowing it to take over properties from owners if they did not agree to sell to the URA within three months (SCMP 2005b). Meanwhile, the "diehard" activists did not stop fighting. As late as June 2006, ten residents and small businesses still remained in Lee Tung Street and refused to move out. They amended their plan and resubmitted it to the TPB. They next petitioned the Town Planning Appeal Board to re-examine the URA's plan. They held protests, hunger strikes and violent confrontations to resist the URA's takeover of the properties.

The collective actions have so far failed to change the fate of Lee Tung Street. Yet, the battle has not ended in a total loss. Rather, it has aroused a great deal of societal attention concerning heritage preservation and raised people's consciousness of their rights. The Dumbbell Plan has won an award from the Institute of Planners for its people-oriented and sustainable vision (SCMP 2006), a major recognition of its achievement if not a rejection of the government's technocratic approach.

Most importantly, the movement has had significant ramifications in realigning civil society groups of all levels. Professional groups organized by architects, planners and academics have become increasingly vocal in recent years, criticising the government's approach to planning and putting forward alternative proposals. In the case of the H15 Project, these groups have spoken out against the URA plan and have shown their support for the residents' cause.[4] For instance, one member criticized the plan as "a fundamental failure to understand what urban renewal means". Others pointed out the soundness of the buildings in Lee Tung Street and that rather than run down, the street actually remained in good condition and open to revitalization. They regarded the government as mistaken in equating renewal with bulldozing. Instead, they argued for an emphasis on refurbishing and injecting new elements to revitalize the area (SCMP 2004a, 2004b, 2004c).

After the Lee Tung Street battle, the H15 members started to collaborate with residents in other districts affected by redevelopment. They shared their information and experience with them and even helped them set up concern groups. For instance, they have worked with residents in Sham Shui Po, an old district housing the poorest part of the population in Hong Kong. In other districts, as for example, the Central-Western district, young professionals and residents particularly concerned about the preservation of historical buildings in the area have established a Mid-Levels Concern Group. They have also been conducting tours to educate the public about the history of Lee Tung Street (SCMP 2006).

The collective actions of Lee Tung Street residents sparked further waves of social movements related to heritage, conservation and redevelopment. To highlight these briefly, in the Star Ferry and

Queen's Pier case in 2008, some movement participants joined hands with a group of heritage protesters, including artists, tertiary students, journalists and professionals to demand that the government stop the demolition of the piers on the grounds that they constituted an important part of the collective memory of many Hongkongers. In 2009, the government's controversial plan to build an express rail link affected hundreds of villagers of Choi Yuen Tsuen. The case attracted the attention of not only university and secondary school students but also ordinary citizens, culminating in a massive sit-in around the Legislative Council Building and confrontation between protestors and the police.

Conclusion

Analysis of the case of the H15 Project illustrates its significance from three perspectives: civil society formation, local governance and state-society relations. First, the controversy witnessed the birth of an autonomous civil society at the community level. Movement activists provided an alternative view of urban renewal that contrasted sharply with the top-down technocratic approach of the state. They demanded a bottom-up participatory approach involving multiple sectors of the population in the planning process in which the preservation of cultural heritage and vital community networks and the rights of residents remain prime concerns. The case has opened up a new mode of mobilization in community action involving collaboration with civil society actors at various levels. As discussed earlier, in the colonial era, a handful of indigenous leaders and community organizers with a weak grassroots basis often led activism at the community level. In the H15 case, the local residents have exercised much stronger agency while they actively collaborated with local NGOs, public interest professionals, writers, artists, academics, progressive politicians and residents from other districts (previously dislocated by urban renewal or are presently confronting the problem) in the form of coalitions and networks. Evidence exists of the potential for the emergence of what Morris (1998) regards as the "community sector" that has proliferated in many American cities as a result of citizen resistance to market-oriented redevelopment programmes. Networks of specialized CBOs comprise the sector making possible citizen-initiated planning and the forcing of public agencies and private developers to engage them in the process of urban redevelopment (Morris 1998).

The case also illustrates the lack of a concept and indeed a system of local governance commensurate with the needs of Hong Kong society in the twenty-first century. While policy related to urban planning and development is rightfully regarded as the domain of the community, especially of local residents directly affected by the policy, in Hong Kong, the decision-making process for such policy remains in the hands of a centralized bureaucracy. The crux of the problem currently lies in the lack of an effective institutional mechanism at the local level that can allow stakeholders and decision-makers to come together to discuss such matters. The residents' movement transcends the limits of state-regulated local communities. The synergistic relations formed between civil society activists and local politicians might form the basis of neighbourhood democracy.

Last but not the least, the waves of social movements set off by the Lee Tung Street residents movement have constituted a process of post-colonial citizenship formation. As Chan and Chan (2007) argue, the demand of the participants for active participation in public policy-making and an emphasis on post-material values permeates all these movements. Equally important, among the movement's participants, a new sense of civic responsibility toward the betterment of one's community and a sense of efficacy in standing up against the state is emerging.

7
Housing policy at a crossroad?
Re-examining the role of the Hong Kong government in the context of a volatile housing market

James Kin-ching Lee

Politicians rarely indulge in intellectualizing public policy debates. An interesting exception occurred in 2006 during the controversy on the meaning and use of the widely accepted and yet conceptually wobbly concept of "positive non-interventionism" (Cheung 2000; Lee and Yue 2001). In response to media charges that the government has officially given up this long-held economic philosophy of Hong Kong, the Chief Executive, Donald Tsang, in a rare newspaper article titled "Small is Still Beautiful", argued that "the government should not intervene in any sector of the market that the private sector can sustain on its own" (Tsang 2006). The role of the government should confine itself to "provide the legal and regulatory infrastructure which underpins free and fair markets". If it takes this line, the government would certainly find it difficult to explain Hong Kong's large public housing sector, let alone to uphold its philosophy of "big society and small government". Today, Hong Kong still prides itself on managing East Asia's second largest public housing programme, with 45.8 percent of households living in either subsidized public rental or home ownership flats (Table 7.1). The Hong Kong government has been actively pursuing a policy of home ownership since publication of the policy paper *Long Term Housing Strategy 1987* (Hong Kong Housing Authority 1987). As Table 7.1 shows, the government has clearly increased subsidized home ownership steadily (from 7.7 percent of the population in 1991 to 16.3 percent in 2009) while at the same time reducing the number of public rental flats (from 41.9 percent of the population in 1995 to 29.4 percent in 2009). In conjunction with other instruments, the home ownership policy shift has significantly impacted the private housing market since the late 1980s and the early 1990s. It started a decade of rapid expansion in private home ownership with a great deal of buoyancy and speculation in the housing market before the 1997 Asian Financial Crisis. Nonetheless, such a scale of state intervention in housing by any government remains difficult to justify conceptually. What can explain this intervention?

Table 7.1 Distribution of population by type of housing

Distribution of Population by Type of Housing					
	1991	1995	1999	2004	2009
	%	%	%	%	%
Public Housing	45.8	53.0	47.2	47.0	45.8
- Rental Flats (PRH)	38.1	41.9	34.3	30.1	29.4
- Subsidized Sale Flats (HOS)	7.7	11.1	13.0	16.9	16.3
Private Housing (mainly home ownership with a small percentage of private renting)	49.1	44.5	50.7	52.0	53.4
Temporary Housing	5.1	2.5	2.1	1.0	0.9

Source: adapted from *Housing in Figures 1991–2009*, Hong Kong Housing Authority http://www.housingauthority.gov.hk/en/aboutus/resources/figure/0,,,00.html

I will attempt a three-part answer. Part I examines the conceptual basis for housing intervention in Hong Kong. I argue at base that housing policy as a unique branch of social policy has played a special role in Hong Kong's economic development, to the extent that it can justify such high level of state intervention on development grounds. I also observe that this mode of housing intervention does not uniquely apply to Hong Kong. Research findings have shown that in varying degrees and under different institutional arrangements, East Asian governments are pursuing a "developmental housing policy" closely tied to the growth of home ownership (Lee, Forrest and Tam 2003). They have used housing to achieve both economic and social goals. This tells one side of the story. However, evidence has also suggested the extreme volatility of Hong Kong's housing sector in recent decades and that housing policy has seemingly failed to achieve its purpose of meeting the housing needs of low and marginal middle-income groups. The developmental housing model stands at odds with a neo-liberalized mode of urban expansion characterized by uneven housing investment and real estate interests. The emphasis on a free-market home ownership policy has spurred rampant housing price inflation which in turn creates affordability problems by pushing housing costs out of the reach of low and marginal middle-income families. This brings in the key issues and problems relating to housing governance in the context of a volatile real estate market which forms Part II of this chapter. Part III will re-examine the role of government in housing policy in a highly congested, high-growth urban environment. The real controversy concerns the capacity of the state to withstand or to provide a check to the incessant advance of neo-liberal urbanization, now a characteristic of most economically vibrant cities in China.

Housing intervention and development in East Asia

Neoclassical justifications

To begin, one can observe that all governments of Western developed industrial economies (e.g. UK, US, Canada, Netherlands, France and Germany) engage in some form of state intervention in housing, either through direct housing provisions or more recently, home purchase or rental subsidies for low-income groups (Balchin 1996; Angel 2000). East Asian economies adopted similar policies. However, the role of government stands out much more prominently in East Asia than in the West, with Singapore, where the state takes up nearly 90 percent of housing production and distribution, as an extreme example. The traditional neoclassical explanation for state intervention in the housing market emphasizes either, on *efficiency* or *equity* grounds.

(1) On efficiency grounds: The existence of market failures in the form of monopolistic or oligopolistic competition in the housing market justifies state intervention in the absence of institutional regulation such as anti-trust law in the US or the Monopolies and Mergers Commission in the UK (Barr 2004). In Hong Kong, this provides perhaps the single most important rationale for state

intervention. Two factors account for this. First, Hong Kong real estate sector operates within an essentially oligopolistic structure and organization, with approximately seven large developers accounting for nearly 70 percent of all new housing supply (Renaud, Pretorius and Pasidilla 1997). High project costs and a limited supply of land necessitate the need for huge capital outlays. Hence, large and vertically integrated corporations often dominate successful real estate developers. The Consumer Council's important study of competition in the real estate industry in 1996 has also confirmed the existence of unfair practices. "The study found that the market in new residential property in Hong Kong is not highly competitive and not very contestable. It identifies some barriers to competition, in particular the shortage and high cost of land and comparative advantage of those with existing land banks" (Consumer Council 1996). In other words, due to the unique form of project management, many small developers stay competitively disadvantaged and excluded from the market as land sales and land supply mostly worked to favour large developers. Second, observing housing price fluctuations in the last two decades provide a simple way to logically deduce market imperfection. Housing prices fluctuate in the short run as a result of heightened speculative activities within the context of a restrictive land supply policy, a point confirmed by an econometric study of Fannie Mae in 1994 (Peng and Wheaton 1994). An interesting finding revealed that when the government restricts the expansion of new land supply but remains flexible on building density (allowing higher-density living), the shortage of land will only cause higher house prices but not a shortage of housing supply. However, expanded land sales will then reduce the scarcity value of land, decrease its current price and, as a consequence, diminish the investment demand for housing. To maintain it, the government resorts to regulated land supply. This, to some extent, explains why housing supply in the short run responds to the demand for investment rather than the one for space and, hence, accounts for a popular allegation in the media that the Hong Kong government adopts a "high land price" policy (Yau and Chan 2005).

(2)   On equity grounds: With access to both housing and home finance capital the principal concern. Low-income households often encounter greater difficulty in saving enough for a down payment to purchase a home and usually have to pay higher interest as banks find the mortgage business with low-income groups more risky. Some of these poor households may not find any way to obtain a loan at any interest rate. To some extent, the government's provision of home loans through the Home Assistance Loan Scheme (HALS), introduced in January 2003, and, the Home Ownership Scheme (HOS), introduced in the late 1970s, resolved this problem. It granted eligible families an interest-free loan of $530,000 (with a thirteen-year term) or $390,000 (with a twenty-year term) or a monthly mortgage subsidy of $3,800 (payable over forty-eight months).[1] However, due to strong political pressures from real estate developers, the government terminated both the HALS and the long-standing HOS in 2004, which, unfortunately, led to problems of horizontal and vertical equity. On the one hand, households previously eligible for HOS found themselves in a worse position when compared to that of public housing tenants. On the other hand, it now leaves marginal middle-income groups who cannot afford private housing in the market with fewer housing choices. However, one interesting observation on the socio-political front does emerge. Despite the strong efficiency-oriented rationale for state intervention, the government has not released any official statements that the housing market has failed. The doctrine of the free market underpinning the philosophy of positive non-interventionism has proved so powerful that public officials have never dared confront the issue of market failure, though knowing full well the nature of imperfect competition as the real culprit. Cheung (2000) has argued that bureaucrats in the post-colonial regime found themselves mostly caught up with complex exogenous and endogenous problems, which resulted in strengthening state intervention rather than weakening it. This perhaps directs our attention to factors which fall outside the ambit of neoclassical explanations—factors more related to the decolonization process after 1997 as well as institutional changes that took place as a consequence of the change of sovereignty.

Beyond neoclassical explanations

The neoclassical approach explains why the Hong Kong government needs to intervene in the housing sector but not how it does so, or how extensively it should intervene. High rates of home ownership and vibrant real estate sectors characterize all the East Asian economies. Their governments all intervene in the housing sector although they use different modes of governance (Lee, Forrest and Tam 2003). For example, why did Japan in the post-war years set up the Japan Housing Loan Corporation that essentially monopolized the mortgage business? How did the Singapore Housing Development Board manage to develop a housing system that monopolizes the supply of home ownership with a ratio up to 86 percent of the total? Why do the South Koreans, despite being unable to obtain mortgages from commercial banks, still manage to achieve a high rate of home ownership? To understand these various housing schemes, we need first to see the role of housing policy in social policy.[2] Traditional social policy tends to group housing policy under the ambit of unilateral transfers (as for example, public assistance, family service, rehabilitation service and elderly care) where the state involves itself in transferring welfare resources to the needy through welfare institutions. While part of the public housing system does remain welfare in nature (for example, rent subsidies for public rental households), it has now become more and more difficult conceptually and practically to classify public housing as traditional social policy. Modern public housing incurs a great deal of capital investments from the state in terms of planning, land use, building, maintenance and housing management. Housing privatization in recent years through the massive selling-off of state housing to sitting tenants denotes a high degree of commoditization and hence results in many tenants becoming homeowners with investment assets (Forrest and Murie 1988).

In Hong Kong, capitalization of real estate assets and housing investments form both a sizeable portion of the GDP (about 29 percent) and a major source of state revenue. Income from land sales at high prices has allowed the adoption of a comparatively low level of personal and corporate taxation in Hong Kong, something which could not have happened if not for the sizable income derived from land revenue (Renaud, Pretorius and Pasidilla 1991, 69). It is now widely recognized that Hong Kong's highly speculative property market had an enormous impact on the economy in the last three decades, though at the same time rendering Hong Kong much more susceptible to global financial hiccups like the one in 1997. With a primarily residual public housing sector, the government is now taking a much more proactive approach in using housing policy to influence economic development and housing market performance through careful adjustments in land and housing supply strategies. It sees more and more the public housing production targets as a tool to regulate, stimulate or even dampen housing speculation in the private sector. All of these point to the emergence of "a developmental housing policy" that does more than simply meeting housing needs.

Housing policy as social policy: Simple versus complex social policy

Public housing policy has always constituted a delicate part of social policy assessment (Kemeny 2001). Housing provision involves substantial capital investment both by the state and individual households. To qualify for public rental housing, an individual must meet certain income criteria and pay rent as tenant. To access a HOS flat, one must demonstrate the ability to secure a home loan and to pay the monthly mortgage. While the state subsidizes housing rents and HOS flat prices, it also assumes a degree of individual responsibility or stakeholding. Subsidized public rental housing could easily equate to a form of *unilateral transfer*. However, with subsidized home ownership, *asset appreciation* becomes more difficult to account for. Many homeowners benefited from asset appreciation in the 1990s since they bought public flats during periods of rapid housing price inflation. Others benefited from the first-time Home Starter Loan Scheme administered by the Hong Kong Housing Society,[3] whose flats appreciated substantially during a prolonged buoyant housing market. However, since the 1997 Asian Financial Crisis, many households who bought HOS flats have faced problems of negative equity. Selling their flats back to the government at the offer price provided a way for them to extricate themselves. But this has become impossible since the Housing Authority has changed its policies in order to protect the government from financial losses.[4] These and other issues have rendered the housing system more complex and controversial. Should social policy form part of an individual's investment portfolio? Should social policy carry the dual purposes of meeting welfare needs and economic development? Or, should state intervention confine itself only to those at the bottom of the housing ladder? Who should be responsible when HOS flats depreciate rapidly as a result of a property slump—the government, the household or both? The questions relating to tenure choices and investment decisions appear difficult to gauge within traditional social policy literature (Lee 2003/4). When Richard Titmuss, the famous British social policy maestro, conceived his *institutional-redistributive model of welfare*, he had in mind a large-scale institutional redistribution of income through the state as the ideal social policy approach (Titmuss 1968). Many universal welfare benefits fall within this category: for example, family welfare, elderly homes, rehabilitation homes and social assistance, which I term *simple social policy goods*, characterized by the consumption-oriented nature of social goods. In essence, simple social policy goods can range from life-sustaining (for example, CSSA/elderly care) to life-enhancing (for example, youth development and rehabilitation) or life-enriching (for example, marriage counselling). Welfare privatization in the last two decades has made simple social policy goods the most vulnerable part of the budget subject to cuts in welfare expenditure. However, another type of social policy goods exists which I will term *complex social policy goods*. Public housing, particularly HOS flats, offers a unique example. Table 7.2 spells out the basic features of these two different forms of social policies. It identifies four primary elements in the framework: (1) complex social policy often embedded itself in and integrates with economic policies; (2) it is both investment/development-oriented; (3) it aims at helping low-income households build up assets for long term social protection and (4) individual responsibility (in the form of contributions) comprises part of the welfare outcome. Put simply, complex social policy aims at long-term social protection through asset-building by individual households, emphasizing social investment rather than short-term consumption. The framework does not rule out the need for certain residual welfare programmes with specific short-term needs, including temporary housing in the case of urban redevelopment. However, social policy generally aims to help low-income households move out of poverty through long-term asset-building (Lee 2010).

Given this conceptual background, it appears that many East Asian governments continue to use housing policies to fulfil both economic and social goals (Doling 1999; Lee, Forrest and Tam 2003). Housing does demonstrate its versatility as a form of complex social policy going beyond simply meeting the sector's needs. In a study of Japan's post-war housing transformation, Tang (2007) suggested that, instead of direct housing production by the state, the Japanese government focused on the provision of low-interest loans to help households buy homes from the market. The Government Housing Loan Corporation essentially monopolized the mortgage business

Table 7.2 Simple and complex social policy

	Simple Social Policy Goods	**Complex Social Policy Goods**
Nature of Social Policy	Unilateral transfer Consumption-oriented Short-term, immediate alleviation of social ills hoping to have long-lasting effects.	Investment-development-oriented Asset-building-oriented Long-term social protection strategies sensitive to risk and income stability issues.
Purpose of Social Policy	Income redistribution on grounds of needs and justice. Emphasis on social rights and citizenship.	Income redistribution on grounds of needs and justice. Emphasis on rights as well as individual responsibility, participation and stakeholding.
Forms of Social Policy	Income support, elderly care, family services, rehabilitation and social insurance.	Housing, education, health, and all forms of asset-building social welfare.
Relationship with the Economy	Basically seen as a distribution system outside the economy.	Social policies seen as an integral part of economic policy.
Role of the State	Mainly to carry out redistribution function outside the market, based on needs criteria.	Redistribution, investment and social development through asset-building both within and outside the market.

for more than three decades by providing the lowest interest rate for the majority of homebuyers. Through a home ownership policy, the Japanese government successfully boosted the post-war economy through massive home loans up until the early 1990s before the prolonged downturn of the Japanese economy. It exemplifies a policy that served both housing needs and economic development. Both Hong Kong and Singapore offer another example in which they have established a large public housing sector, with a long history of dependence on the housing system as an integral part of their development strategy, albeit each with diametrically opposed social purposes and institutions (Chua 1997; Lee 1999).

Home ownership as strategy for social security and asset-building

One interesting implication of the complex social policy thesis is that, other than making use of home ownership policy to boost the real estate sector, housing policy also forms an integral part of the social security system, best illustrated by the Central Provident Fund (CPF) and Housing Development Board (HDB) in Singapore. Chua (1999), in his analysis of Singapore's intriguing mix of the housing and social security institutions, clearly explained how the integration of the two systems works. Through managing the state-led compulsory CPF savings scheme, the government manages to pool the entire population's savings into a powerful capital reserve. The HDB then uses the fund to build affordable home ownership flats and sell them to Singaporeans. At the same time, the HDB provides low interest mortgage loans to homeowners whom they permit to use their CPF savings to pay mortgage debts. This system creates a self-generating flow of capital among citizens, the housing authority and the social security system, thus enabling more than 80 percent of Singaporeans to become homeowners under a system of coerced saving and managed consumption. The HDB realizes the linkage with the social security system through using the CPF for home purchase and helping a great majority of the citizens accumulate wealth through assets held over a lifelong period, so that when people reach old age, they can draw on their stored home equity values as future income protection. As an ideal consequence, the aging population's demand for welfare would burden the government less, protecting it from the pitfalls of the globalized financial vulnerability of a pooled-risk social insurance system. In 2006, the Index of Economic Freedom ranked Singapore as the world's second freest and most competitive economy after Hong Kong.[5] The two freest economies in the world operate East Asia's two largest public housing systems, something that curiously undercuts the argument that state intervention adversely affects economic freedom. The obvious question remains: how is this done? All this boils down to an issue of institutional arrangements. However, for the Singapore housing system to stay sustainable, it needs two additional elements to work: First, a commitment to "big government" with a development strategy that entails a high level of state intervention. Second, the state must possess sufficient capacity to ensure house-price stability through regulation. By restricting the market only to citizens as well as by capping the number of subsidized home purchases at two, Singapore successfully avoided many of the speculative activities, common to open economies, found in Hong Kong or China. However, large-scale global economic crises, as for example, the 1997 Asian Financial Crisis, have affected even the semi-closed Singaporean housing market, though not as seriously as other East Asian economies. Hong Kong has a much more volatile housing market since the real estate sector has stayed completely open. Other than all the standard endogenous economic factors (for example, income, interest rates, demographic and life cycle changes) which affect housing demand and housing prices, Hong Kong also remains subject to a set of exogenous economic factors, as for example, the size and flow of foreign direct investment as well as the emerging influence of investors from the Mainland. This then brings us to some of the key issues and problems that contemporary housing policies face.

Key issues in contemporary housing policy

Torn between two lovers: Maximization of land revenues or maintaining house-price stability?

Economists have long argued that land policy has always played a crucial role in influencing Hong Kong's housing price movements in the private sector (Peng and Wheaton 1994). Tse (1998) questioned this causal relationship and argued for land supply as a consequence rather than a cause of house-price inflation, though he agreed that Hong Kong included its land price regime as a deliberate part of its overall revenue maximization strategy. For example, the decision to announce a five-year land supply schedule in Hong Kong after 1998 created an immediate negative impact on house prices in the private sector. The government saw it as an effective way to cool off speculative activities in the late 1990s. A similar event occurred in Singapore in 1998 when the government took a firm line to curb speculative activities in the property sector by introducing the Capital Gains Tax. In more concrete terms, in the three decades from 1970 to 2000, Hong Kong's total land revenue amounted to US$71 billion (in 2000 constant US dollars). Adding revenues from both rates and property tax, total land-related revenues amounted to US$96.1 billion (Hong 2003, 160). Thus, house-price inflation in a buoyant real estate sector provided the government with an important source of revenue over a long period. Taking a more recent period, from 1996 to 2000, land revenues more than covered the costs of infrastructure and land development. On average, land revenues accounted for 17 percent of total government income, the second most important source following personal and corporate taxes. Land revenues come generally from four sources: (1) initial land auction, (2) annual land rent, (3) lease modification and (4) lease renewal. During the period from 1970 to 1995, land revenues principally derived from land auction (75 percent) and lease modification (20 percent). Why did these two sources predominate? In analyzing Hong Kong's unique leasehold system to capture land value, Hong (1998, 2003) discovered that its structure has created many unforeseen institutional constraints that prevent the government from taking a more long-term perspective in capturing land value through such other methods as land rent. As a consequence, the government has developed a tendency of favouring land auction as a major instrument to maximize land value with the disadvantage of the serious implications it has in causing housing-cost inflation and over-investment by the real estate sector. In the past three decades, when commercial and residential developments peaked, the government's land premium collection also reached a high point, naturally pushing housing prices up as land costs rose.

The government could only remedy the situation by balancing it with a subsidized public housing programme from the 1960s to the 1980s. However, this method has grown less and less effective as housing prices soared to a level even the middle class found intolerable. When the Tung administration sought to redress the situation by setting a sizable housing production target, developers and homeowners who feared that increased supply would undermine equity value strongly opposed it. Between 1998 and 1999, the government announced a series of rescue packages, amounting to US$7.2 billion, to prevent property prices from falling (Lee 2003). First, it suspended all land auctions and tenders. Second, the Housing Authority (HA) abolished its building target of 38,000 units for the middle-income group. Third, the HA introduced the Home Starter Loan Scheme discussed earlier. However, all these efforts did not seem to affect the depressed market. Only after the end of the SARS outbreak and the subsequent official opening up of the border for individual tourists from China and the boost to internal consumption that followed did the property market see signs of an upturn. Since 2004, the housing price index has again risen sharply, returning in many localities to the pre-1997 level in 2010. Land sales and the leasehold system provided a unique source of revenues, which many Western governments do not enjoy, useful for generous subsidies to public housing programmes and to maintain a low tax regime as well as allowing the government to foot the bills for many social welfare services. However, they do not work risk-free. With a robust economy, the government could balance the trade-off between land sales and the provision of public housing for the masses. But the method will become ineffective when the housing market runs out of control. The strong political lobby for the reinstatement of the HOS scheme in recent months provides an example that illustrates the understanding many politicians have of the impossibility that the government will effectively regulate cycles of rampant housing price inflation. In a small open economy like Hong Kong, no institution can effectively control the property market. In his memoir on Hong Kong, the former governor, Chris Patten, admitted candidly that the colonial government's greatest failing lay in housing (Patten 1998, 51). The following quote readily illustrates the hegemonic influence of the powerful developers: "our ability to apply the radical free market solutions that were required was limited by proximity to the transition. Any convincing attack on the monopoly effectively enjoyed by a few extremely rich property developers in Hong Kong, making grotesquely large profits, could have had a serious effect on market confidence at a sensitive time" (Patten 1998, 51). When the new government attempted to correct it by increasing the land supply, it became a political disaster as developers and homeowners alike strongly opposed it. As Hong (2003) rightly pointed out, the Hong Kong experience exposed one potential dilemma of leasing land, that is, the tension between raising public funds and stabilizing housing costs. This essay addressed the following question: To what extent can a government maximize financial returns on land without affecting its role as a protector of the public interest?

Figure 7.1 Housing affordability 1981–2000

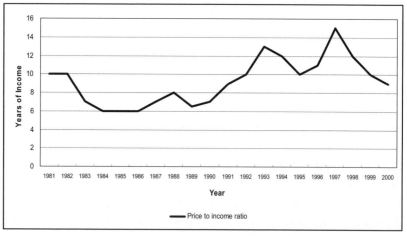

Source: Based on data from Rating and Valuation Department (2001), *Hong Kong Property Review*, and median income data from Census and Statistics Department (2002), *Hong Kong Population Census 2001 Main Tables* (Hong Kong: Government Printing Department).

Inherent instability in the housing system

Housing encompasses two unique characteristics: first, the *use-value*, which suggests that housing provides a household with residence and second, the *exchange-value*, which suggests that housing represents an asset in the capital market capable of being capitalized from time to time. Hence, housing satisfies both a need for space and an aspiration for investment. Unless the state willingly provides housing benefits for everyone, selective housing provision naturally leads to distributional and locational differences for various household sectors. Housing allocation in the public sector therefore always raises questions of equity and distributional justice. I have argued elsewhere that a housing system with a pronounced tendency toward treating housing as an investment good generally entails an unstable housing price regime while one with a strong emphasis on use-value has a more stable price regime (Lee 2000). Its dual nature makes any housing system inherently unstable. While the state maintains an interest in promoting the use-value of housing and, hence, to better achieve market stability, capitalists and real estate developers hold a different view. Fostering the exchange-value of housing for profit maximization interests them more, similar to the logic of leasehold land sale discussed in the last section. In the struggle for domination between consumers and developers, the latter mostly wins. Some argue that the state needs to maintain a certain degree of autonomy in order to strike a balance between the interests of developers and the public in order to maintain stability. But, even then, land scarcity and rapid population growth leave little freedom for the state not to intervene. However, too much intervention contravenes capitalists' interest in profit maximization. The policy pendulum has been swinging uneasily between more state housing and more private housing during different periods of its history. An inherently unstable house price regime can have one adverse consequence—housing becomes highly unaffordable. Using the World Bank definition of housing affordability (the ratio between annual median house price and annual median income), Figure 7.1 shows that for the period from 1981 to 2000, house-price affordability has worsened and fluctuated enormously over a thirty-year period.

Compared to a rough index value of three in most industrial economies, Hong Kong's housing affordability has fluctuated between a low of six to a high of fourteen, which means, in practical terms, that a median income household could take six to fourteen years of total income to afford a median-price flat. Housing prices in the two decades only became relatively affordable at several historical points, for example, immediately after the Tiananmen Incident in 1989 and the period after the Asian Financial Crisis. Housing affordability has represented a fiercely contested political issue in Hong Kong, both before and after 1997. Prior to 1997, the main issue centred on the lack of affordable housing in the market leading to a policy response of building more HOS housing and providing home loans. It resulted in an over-subscribed HOS sector coupled with sluggish loan borrowing—due largely to the fact that loan levels could not catch up with rampant housing price inflation. After 1997, the main issue concerned house-price depreciation and negative equity. Patten (1998) depicted this dilemma succinctly as follows: "a great deal of politics had been channelled into housing activities, and since elected politicians were responsible for so little, from left to right they tended to articulate tenant grievances rather than apply themselves to the fundamental causes of these problems. The construction of public housing has been regarded as substitute for the introduction of democratic politics" (Patten 1998, 52).To sum up, an inherent instability does indeed exist within Hong Kong's housing system, largely stemming from a housing consumption culture and an economy that has come to depend excessively on the benefits of a real estate economy. Although I have also argued elsewhere (Smart and Lee 2003) that the degree of financialization of the real estate sector in a post-Fordist regime like Hong Kong might possess the ability to produce stabilizing effects both in terms of income and employment, nevertheless, such causality still demands greater empirical proof to be conclusive. More importantly, we need to factor in the instability thesis more rigorously than we have in housing policy discourse. We should do so more in good times than in bad.

Figure 7.2 Tenure change in Hong Kong 1971–2001

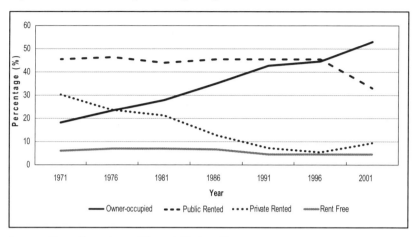

Source: *Hong Kong Annual Report: Various Years*

The risk of home ownership

Home ownership amongst Hong Kong households enjoys unquestionable popularity. Figure 7.2 shows home ownership as the fastest growing type of tenure (from 12 percent in 1971 to just over 50 percent in 2001 and 53 percent in 2005) throughout the last three decades. In 2001, Hong Kong had 1.04 million owner-occupiers, meaning one out of two households could afford their own house. Figure 7.2 also confirms that, other than for cultural reasons, the growth of home ownership has clear roots in policy. While public rental housing has been increasing in absolute terms over the years, in relative terms and within the whole tenure structure, it has remained quite constant (as shown by a relatively flat curve in Figure 7.2). This could not have been achieved without deliberate effort on the part of the government; with the sole purpose of controlling the expansion of rental housing and at the same time to stimulate the growth of home ownership. The government recognized the policy potential as well as the necessity to cater for aspiring young families who wanted to move up the housing ladder when their income and family life cycle position shifted. On the other hand, the government also began to consider public sector reform necessary for the housing sector, particularly in the early 1980s, when the issue of efficiency became a major problem of the then Housing Authority (Wong 1994). The ethos in the late 1980s that the state needed to roll back its involvement and let the market do the job prevailed. With regard to the government-subsidized Home Ownership Scheme, from 1976 to 2000, it managed to account for only 13 percent of all types of tenures. Further, throughout the last twenty-five years, the slow development of HOS had allowed the private market sector an exclusive opportunity to develop Hong Kong's housing market into one of the world's most speculative real estate sectors. State policy had allowed the full commoditization of housing, hoping that the housing market could operate in a perfectly competitive regime with efficient pricing. However, just the opposite happened. Housing prices soared and few could afford to buy in the early 1990s. We know well what happened to the housing market after the Asian Financial Crisis. Other than house prices plummeting more than 70 percent from 1997 to 2004, it left Hong Kong with the severe problem of negative equity. With the market upturn between 2004 and 2006, the problem of negative equity has moderated, but not completely dissipated, since many sub-sectors of the market remain priced below the 1997 level. According to the Hong Kong Monetary Authority's latest survey, the number of residential mortgage loans in negative equity decreased further by some four hundred cases to about 8,800 cases with an aggregate value of HK$15 billion (nearly US$2 billion) in the three months prior to June 2006. Compared to the peak of about 106,000 cases as of June 2003, the number has fallen by 92 percent. While this offers an encouraging sign, policy makers should not stay complacent about it. The existence of negative equity signifies an overstretched banking system. At best, it anticipates automatic correction by the market; at worst, it sends a warning signal of an impending quake in a volatile global financial system. According to the 2001 Census, a little more than one-half million Hong Kong homeowners (537,230) still had an outstanding loan from a bank.

The remaining half million owned their homes outright, figures subject to interpretation in two ways. On the positive side, one can argue that Hong Kong has a mature housing market and that only one out of two homeowners still needs to repay a mortgage. On the down side, the banking sector and half of Hong Kong's homeowners continue subject to the perils and vulnerabilities of a fluctuating local and international economy. Statistics indicate that the share of property-related lending — including for both residential mortgage and property development loans — to total loans for use reached over 50 percent in 2003, compared to less than 30 percent in the mid-1980s. The increase in lending entirely results from a rapid increase in the expansion of residential mortgage business by the banks. Fan and Peng (2003, 131) noted that "the actual financial exposure is likely to be higher than the statistics which do not include corporate loans extended against property collateral". Hence, when another international financial crisis occurs, such a high loan stake held by the banking sector could prove risky for the economy, not to mention its effects on the wealth and consumption of a million households which plan to rely on their stored home equity value for their retirement.

Globally, we also happen to live in a world in which the role of the government in housing changes quickly. Privatization and contraction of the public housing sector everywhere have diminished state capacities to respond as effectively as in the past to shifting housing needs. The rapid expansion of private residential mortgages means that mortgage finance closely links to the global economy, and hence potentially more vulnerable to economic and political disturbances beyond national boundaries. *The Economist* (2005) estimated that the total value of residential property in developed economies rose by more than US$30 trillion over the past five years to over US$70 trillion, an increase equal to 100 percent of those countries' combined GDPs. Wade (2006) suggests that private pension funds and insurance companies' liquidity surge in recent years has a much greater impact on the world economy than the IMF or the World Bank. Insurance companies in the developed world have assets of roughly US$14 trillion and pension funds roughly US$13 trillion, compared with total World Bank lending of less than US$1 trillion. These observations therefore have clear relevance. International asset deflation or inflation; interest rate changes; investment in and out of real estate, occasioned usually by boom and bust in the stock market, tremendously impact the banking sector and individual households. John Quigley (2001), a leading US housing economist, has put forth an interesting argument about the cause of the Asian Financial Crisis. Instead of the common allegation of corrupt banking systems in developing Asian economies, Quigley attributed the crisis to the overblown real estate sectors and the failure of national policy to regulate over-investment in property. His study confirms the much-neglected need for more robust governance structures involving greater scrutiny and regulation of lending practices. In order to contain the risks of excessive concentration in mortgage lending, the Hong Kong Monetary Authority introduced a guideline in 1994 to maintain the ratio of lending to mortgage loans at 40 percent. However, it withdrew the guideline in 1998 when it regarded the housing market then as not overheated. Nonetheless, the government might need to revisit this regulatory measure if the lending-to-loan ratio has consistently exceeded the 50 percent benchmark. Housing policy, as social policy, remains focused on issues of fair rent, access and repair, a visible and tangible part of the discussion of such a new form of governance. However, we must realize that in housing, the business of capitalism actually lies elsewhere—in a world of global financial currents seeking to maximize economic rent while taking little or no consideration of what matters locally.

Concluding remarks: Housing policy at a crossroad?

In Hong Kong, public housing policy still rests heavily on the traditional conception of simple social policy. In other words, officials still regard public housing as one of the maintenance-oriented social programmes that they should terminate one day when the market returns to normal. Following this logic, it should minimize public rental housing and consider HOS a transient social programme, with the idea that one day the market can provide affordable housing for most, if not for all, low-income families when it "finally stabilises". Unfortunately, we now know this will not happen. Worse still, few housing officials adopt an orientation toward a complex social policy approach by viewing housing policy as a long-term development strategy. In terms of comparative housing policy, I have argued earlier on that many East Asian economies demonstrate a tendency to use housing policy to achieve development goals. For Hong Kong, such a generalization can only apply to the earlier stage of its housing history, particularly during the MacLehose era when it built mass public housing to cater for the expansion of the industrial work force (Smart 1986). Nevertheless, since the dawn of housing privatization efforts in the 1980s, housing policy has shifted from a development orientation toward a new set of strategies favouring neo-liberal interests. As a result, the decade from 1986 to 1997 saw one of the most speculative eras in the housing market with the worst housing price inflation recorded in March 1997.[6] The degree of ignorance of officials regarding the pervasiveness of neo-liberal urbanization orchestrated by powerful rent-seeking developers is alarming. The moratorium of the HOS scheme in 2003 exemplifies the policy failure that resulted in financially de-funding the Housing Authority, and which ended up in the establishment of the Link Corporation as the reluctant outcome of a salvage operation to save the Authority from continual budget deficits. Neo-liberal urbanization had successfully destroyed a housing institution that not only provided financial self-sufficiency for the Housing Authority but also demonstrated the possibility of a sustainable use of the duality of housing policy (meeting both housing and asset-building needs of households) as well as the income-generating potential of the HOS scheme when the Housing Authority became one of the key housing suppliers (Lee and Yip 2001).

This chapter seeks to explain the nature, meaning and difficulties of state intervention in housing in the particular context of Hong Kong. By emphasizing the philosophy of positive non-interventionism, the government is in fact creating a "policy trap" for itself, successfully disempowering it from responding effectively to house-price inflation and the incessant advancement of neo-liberal urbanization. Neo-liberalism operates as a powerful bulldozer of destruction and construction in modern capitalism by capitalizing on the processes of urban displacement and segregation through land and real estate is self-evident (Harvey 2005). A trip to any Chinese coastal city would provide one with the best example in the form of new gated communities which socially exclude the urban poor. Scholars have accused modern governance of developing a strong bias in favour of neo-liberal practices in urban development, invariably favouring the rent-seeking behaviour of real estate developers (Lee and Zhu 2006). The media in Hong Kong has never shrunk from similar accusations of the collusion between real estate developers and the government. In various parts of the chapter, I have argued that beneath these charges lies a deep-rooted structural problem in housing policy, which also explains why proactive interventions stay necessary to redress inequalities brought on by the widening wealth gap between homeowners and non-homeowners. Conceptually, I have also explained how housing intervention could become a major part of development strategy through the complex social policy thesis.

Owing to market failures and the prevalence of oligopolistic competition in the real estate sector, homeowners have long been paying high prices for their homes. The emphasis on home ownership and the construction of a consumption culture around owner-occupied housing likewise creates unfair advantages for owners rather than renters, as owners receive a tax allowance for home purchase while renters receive nothing. In fact, rental housing, in both public and private sectors, rapidly declined in the last two decades as a consequence of the home ownership-biased tenure policy. Both policy bias and market response have shaped this decline. Housing policy needs to redress this imbalance within Hong Kong's tenure structure in order that it provides housing consumers with fairer choices.

To conclude, I think housing policy in Hong Kong has reached a crossroad (at present, roughly one half of the population resides in public housing estates with the other half in private housing). In sum, governments need to make a choice between continuing to succumb to a neo-liberal housing policy toward more owner-occupation or a tenure system that seeks to broaden the base of housing policy by redressing the balance between owner-occupation and rental housing. I consider this choice important in that the real estate sector continues subject to excessive volatility from the ebb and flow of global finance. Over-reliance on the efficacy of the market mechanism puts the housing system at risk. A non-tenure-biased housing policy would provide people with a more balanced choice and, hence, in the long run a more stable housing sector.

8

The role of government in managing cross-boundary co-operation between Hong Kong and mainland China

Peter Tsan-yin Cheung

After Hong Kong's return to Chinese sovereignty in 1997, the Hong Kong Special Administrative Region (hereafter the SAR) has developed extensive links with different levels of mainland China's political and economic systems. The phenomenal growth of social and economic interaction between Hong Kong and the Mainland has compelled governments on both sides to cope with the consequences and challenges of such an unprecedented development. The management of many cross-boundary problems requires state authorities to deal with one another since these issues, including infrastructural development, environment and public health, among others, fall into the realm of the responsibilities of the state. During this process, the Hong Kong SAR government has moved away from the *laissez-faire* model of the colonial period to an "activist" model in the post-1997 era.

This chapter explores the role of government in managing cross-boundary co-operation between Hong Kong and mainland China since 1997. My key questions include: What kind of role has the Hong Kong SAR government taken on in managing cross-boundary relations in the post-1997 period? What factors have compelled the Hong Kong SAR government to move in this direction? My discussion will focus more on the role of the Hong Kong SAR government than on its counterparts on the Mainland, and inevitably, its relations with Guangdong province, where most of the cross-boundary interactions take place.[1]

This chapter argues that the imperative of cross-boundary co-operation, amid deepening social and economic interactions between the two areas, has recast the "non-interventionist" state in Hong Kong into an increasingly activist one. It consists of three parts. After the introduction, I will first discuss several issues that provide a context for analysing the role of government in managing cross-boundary issues, including the evolving role of the Hong Kong government in the society and economy before 1997, the framework of the Basic Law, the special features of the Hong Kong-Mainland boundary and the growing social and economic integration between the two areas. Part two looks at cross-boundary intergovernmental relations between Hong Kong and South China and the resultant structural changes in the Hong Kong SAR government since 1997. Part three examines the changing role of the Hong Kong SAR government in managing several key cross-boundary issues, as for example, economic co-operation, infrastructural development and environmental protection as well as public health and food safety. The chapter concludes with a number of preliminary observations about the changing role of government in managing cross-boundary issues in Hong Kong and on the Mainland.

The political and economic context of cross-boundary relations under "One Country, Two Systems"

An evolving local state in Hong Kong: From laissez-faire to positive non-interventionism and beyond

As Anthony Cheung has rightly argued, the colonial government in Hong Kong has gradually evolved in response to both domestic and external challenges even before the city's reunion with China in 1997.[2] The *laissez-faire* form of state intervention in the economy characterized the 1950s and 1960s with minimal interaction between state and society since the administrative absorption of local Chinese elites would sufficiently sustain political stability. In response to challenges to the legitimacy of British colonialism in the aftermath of the 1967 riots and, as a result of rising social expectations and demands, the colonial government resorted to "positive non-interventionism", defined by the rapid growth of social spending and public investment in infrastructure and human capital as well as by government regulation of the financial and banking sectors. The 1980s witnessed even more state expansion, as for example, in the provision of public service through the establishment of quasi-government public corporations and other public bodies.

Since the early 1990s, the colonial state has moved beyond "positive non-interventionism" toward some form of "consensus capitalism" with "widening inclusion of social interests". Cheung hence suggests that "the Hong Kong colonial government was already an active state by highly conscious accumulation and legitimation strategies in response to social, economic and political demands of the 1980s and 1990s".[3] He expects even more state interventionism after 1997 since the institutionalization of functional interests in the post-1997 political system will lead to more demands for state support by them. The absence of electoral legitimacy will compel the new regime to "perform through more state services and goods, and through more active intervention in social and economic development", especially in view of the economic downturn caused by the Asian Financial Crisis. His largely accurate description on the evolution of the state in contemporary Hong Kong provides a useful reminder that while the Hong Kong government often talks about "positive non-interventionism", the colonial state had actually become quite interventionist even on the eve of 1997. The increasing prominence of cross-boundary issues has stimulated even more activism on the part of the Hong Kong SAR government since 1997.

The constitutional framework of the Basic Law

The Hong Kong SAR government operates as a highly autonomous local state. Although sovereignty rests with the central authorities in Beijing, the SAR government enjoys extensive powers in economic, financial and social affairs, including certain areas of international affairs.[4] The Basic Law emphasizes providing guarantees for Hong Kong's high level of autonomy and a relatively clearer delineation of power between the central authorities and the Hong Kong SAR. However, the mini-constitution does not contain elaborate provisions on how the SAR government should conduct its cross-boundary affairs with its mainland counterparts. In fact, widespread anxiety existed in Hong Kong before 1997 that localities and government agencies from the Mainland would interfere in the internal affairs of the territory. Article 22 of Chapter 2 of the Basic Law, which specifically states that the provinces (or departments from the central government) cannot interfere in Hong Kong's own affairs, addressed this concern. If they wanted to establish offices in Hong Kong, they must secure both the consent of the Hong Kong SAR government and the approval of the central government.

Further, while the Basic Law states that the Hong Kong SAR may establish an office in Beijing, it has not specified any guidelines for the creation of similar offices in other localities or the administrative arrangements under which Hong Kong would deal with other mainland provinces or cities. So far, no other provinces have set up official government offices in the Hong Kong SAR, although companies from many coastal provinces and cities, including Guangdong, Shanghai and Beijing, have already established a strong economic presence there. Their offices serve as the *de facto* representatives of local governments while conducting their business and activities in Hong Kong.

Another key provision concerns immigration. While the central government, in consultation with the SAR government, decides the number of mainland people allowed into Hong Kong, the Basic Law has not delegated full power to Hong Kong for controlling emigration from the Mainland and for selecting those who it will allow to enter the territory. In terms of demographic control, the Hong Kong SAR government has taken up the role of "guardian" against a possible mass influx of mainland people, especially in view of the substantial socio-economic gap between the two places. In short, the Basic Law framework principally guards Hong Kong against intervention from the Mainland's local governments, but without specifying clear parameters for the facilitation of such intergovernmental relations. As a result, this ambiguity has given the Hong Kong SAR government a significant amount of room for them to explore various strategies in response to the many challenges arising from cross-boundary activities.

Special features of the Hong Kong-Mainland boundary

The Hong Kong-Mainland boundary, while sharing the characteristics of most borders and border regions elsewhere, exhibits several special features.[5] The current boundary is both material and symbolic. First, while most Hong Kong people, predominantly Cantonese, share similar linguistic, cultural and social traits with their compatriots in

Guangdong province, the divide between the "Two Systems", marked by distinctively different economic, political and legal traditions, still matters. This boundary changed in 1997 from an international border between the United Kingdom and the People's Republic of China to a unique *internal* boundary inside China under the framework of "One Country, Two Systems". The growing socio-economic interactions have, however, made the boundary more permeable and porous.

Second, while culturally and socially similar to their compatriots, many Hong Kong people feel threatened by China's communist political system. Instead, they favour the capitalist economy, free society and British-styled administrative and legal systems in Hong Kong. The close economic ties between Hong Kong and mainland China have not engendered popular demands for closer political and administrative integration. A greater emphasis on symbolic identification with the motherland, especially in the publicity activities sponsored by the Hong Kong SAR government and other pro-Beijing groups, and promotion of national education in schools has become more conspicuous since 2003. Nevertheless, the mass media, business community and the people in Hong Kong continue to show deep concern over corruption, human rights violation, political suppression as well as arbitrary administrative and regulatory practices on the Mainland.

Growing social and economic integration between Hong Kong and the Mainland

The economic interactions between Hong Kong and the Mainland have grown rapidly, in trade in goods and services and investments as well as in demographic and transport movement. Hong Kong has become more reliant on the Mainland trade since 1997. The total merchandise trade between the two has more than doubled from HK$1,116.7 billion in 1997 to HK$2,512.6 billion in 2009. Hong Kong's share of trade with the Mainland has increased from 36.3 percent to 48.7 percent of its total in the same period.[6] Hong Kong's services exports to the Mainland has also jumped from HK$53 billion in 1997 to HK$177.2 billion in 2009, with its share of the total rising from 19 percent in 1997 to 26.9 percent in 2009.[7] Services imports from the Mainland went up only from HK$61 billion in 1997 to HK$90 billion in 2009, while its share of the total actually dropped from 31.2 percent in 1997 to 26.8 percent in 2009.[8] Trade between Hong Kong and the Mainland has increasingly taken place offshore, i.e., outside a physical presence in Hong Kong for the goods involved.[9] The total value of offshore exports increased from HK$34 billion in 2002 to HK$196.6 billion in 2009.[10]

Although its relative importance has declined, Hong Kong still remains the largest source of foreign investment on the Mainland.[11] In 1997, Hong Kong investment (foreign direct investment and other foreign investment) there amounted to US$21.6 billion and rose to approximately US$46.7 billion in 2009.[12] Hong Kong's share in China's total foreign investment has increased from 41.1 percent in 1997 to 50.9 percent in 2009.[13] Starting from HK$20 billion in 1998, foreign direct investment from the Mainland to Hong Kong has increased significantly to HK$192.3 billion in 2009, which made it the highest among all sources of direct inflow of investment.[14] By the end of 2009, the Mainland has already become the largest source of external direct investment in Hong Kong, contributing approximately 47.4 percent of the total.[15] Increasing passenger and vehicular traffic also reflects the growth of cross-boundary social and economic interactions. From 1997 to 2005, cross-boundary passenger and vehicular movement between Hong Kong and the Mainland increased by 9.5 percent and 5.6 percent per year on average respectively.[16] Nonetheless, the growth began to slow down since then. From 2006 to 2010, cross-boundary passenger movement between Hong Kong and the Mainland increased by about 5 percent per year.[17] Over the same period, the growth of cross-boundary vehicular movement grew only around 1.17 percent per annual on average.[18] By 2009, daily cross-boundary vehicular traffic reached 40,400 while the daily passenger flow rose to 530,900.[19]

Cross-boundary relations between Hong Kong and South China

The Hong Kong SAR government has transformed itself from a *laissez-faire* "non-interventionist" state to a more "activist" state in order to foster the economic development of Hong Kong and manage cross-boundary activity. The following section provides an overview of cross-boundary intergovernmental relations between Hong Kong and

South China and the resultant structural changes in the Hong Kong SAR government.

An overview of cross-boundary intergovernmental relations

The Hong Kong SAR government has gradually articulated an economic development strategy since 1997, with a special focus on co-operation and integration with the Mainland. Such a strategy should be best seen as a series of responses to the crisis engendered by the Asian Financial Crisis conditioned by the political transition since 1997. From the beginning, although deeply concerned with Hong Kong's competitiveness and domestic problems, the administration under Tung Chee-hwa, the first Chief Executive (hereafter the CE) of the Hong Kong SAR, did not adopt any master plan. The SAR government aimed to get the best of two worlds as they sought "to establish a framework of arrangements that facilitates seamless interaction within One Country while not in any way compromising the high degree of autonomy we enjoy under Two Systems".[20] With the growth of globalization and the rapid development of mainland China, the mindset of "Fortress Hong Kong", meaning that the city can dictate its own policies without regard to its regional context, no longer remains possible.

The initial phase (1997–2002)

As a key promoter of closer cross-boundary co-operation, Tung Chee-hwa, in his maiden 1997 policy address, announced the establishment of the high level Hong Kong/Guangdong Co-operation Joint Conference (hereafter the HKGDCJC), headed, respectively, by Guangdong's Executive Vice Governor and Hong Kong SAR's Chief Secretary for Administration (hereafter the CS). Nonetheless, the lack of a clear consensus among the political and administrative elite in the initial phase (approximately between 1997 and 2000) partly explains why it has taken much longer for Hong Kong to articulate a strategy on cross-boundary co-operation. Nor was a clear common community consensus on this issue formed at that time. Hence, the government proceeded cautiously toward measures that would facilitate cross-boundary movement (as for example, twenty-four-hour boundary crossing for passengers, which it did not introduce until 2003). During this initial phase, similar to its Guangdong counterparts, the Hong Kong SAR government often defined cross-boundary co-operation primarily as a means to enhance the interests of its own jurisdiction rather than to promote regional prosperity and mutual benefits. The priority of Tung's first term (1997–2002) emphasized expediting the flow of people and goods, especially through improvements of boundary-crossing and infrastructural links, and working closely with Guangdong in handling environmental problems. However, in spite of the initial momentum achieved between 1997 and 1998, it launched few concrete initiatives in 1999 and 2000.

After the onset of the Asian Financial Crisis and China's admission to the World Trade Organization (hereafter the WTO) in 2001, an increasing number of senior Hong Kong officials began to recognize the importance of the Pearl River Delta (hereafter the PRD) to Hong Kong. A clear change took place in the Hong Kong SAR government's approach toward relations with China after May 2001, when the then CS, Anson Chan, stepped down. With the appointment of Donald Tsang as the CS and Antony Leung as the Financial Secretary (hereafter the FS) in May 2001, momentum on cross-boundary co-operation accelerated. Since mid-2001, it has proposed a host of initiatives on cross-boundary matters, as for example, extension of boundary-crossing hours to midnight, increased co-ordination in infrastructural development and facilitation of the inflow of mainland tourists. In order to better co-ordinate the various government bureaus and departments in handling cross-boundary affairs, the governments established the Hong Kong Guangdong Co-operation Co-ordination Unit under the offices of the CS and FS in August 2001 to help these top officials monitor implementation of the initiatives endorsed by the HKGDCJC, review existing policies and arrangements, especially in transportation and boundary-crossing and seek community input on cross-boundary co-operation.[21] The government has now placed a host of new topics on its policy agenda, including, a new express railway linking Hong Kong, Shenzhen and Guangzhou, exploration of cross-boundary co-operation in logistics and finally, the consideration of a bridge-link between Hong Kong and the western part of the PRD. In late 2001, the CE also proposed to the central government the establishment of a Closer Economic Partnership Arrangement (hereafter the CEPA) between Hong Kong and the Mainland.

A new phase of cross-boundary co-operation since 2003

In the first policy address of his second term, delivered in January 2003, Tung Chee-hwa focused for the first time on economic integration between Hong Kong and the PRD.[22] While Guangdong's provincial leaders had already proposed such a direction several years earlier, it marked the first time that the Hong Kong SAR government used the term "economic integration" with the PRD. After much delay, the CE not only introduced twenty-four-hour passenger crossing and clearance at Lok Ma Chau/Huanggang starting from 27 January 2003, but also pledged to improve the other crossings at Lo Wu and Sha Tau Kok and to accelerate the construction of the Shenzhen Western Corridor. Further, Tung revealed that his administration had asked Beijing to support the further relaxation of restrictions in order to expedite mainland residents' visits to Hong Kong, including individuals from Guangdong Province. Hong Kong later relaxed its policy toward the admission of mainland "Quality Migrants", as for example, by eliminating quotas and sectoral restrictions.[23] The SAR government also officially favoured building a bridge between Hong Kong and the western Delta.

The SAR government considered economic integration between Guangdong and Hong Kong a key agenda item and attempted to articulate a more specific *regional* vision based on a clearer division of labour among the various cities. In addition to attracting more foreign capital and talent to the region and encouraging multi-national corporations to set up headquarters in Hong Kong, the CE suggested that the whole region should attract foreign small and medium enterprises to use "Hong Kong as a base to operate businesses in the PRD—with regional offices in Hong Kong, investment, procurement and production in the PRD".[24] Furthermore, PRD enterprises could use Hong Kong as a platform to develop business ties with overseas partners.

The 6th HKGDCJC held on 5 August 2003 took place within a grim political and economic atmosphere since the social and economic repercussions of the outbreak of the Severe Acute Respiratory

Syndrome (hereafter the SARS) deeply affected the region.[25] Nonetheless, Guangdong and Hong Kong government leaders agreed on an unprecedented general division of labour between the two areas: Guangdong to focus on developing into a leading manufacturing base and Hong Kong to strive to develop itself into "an important service centre in finances, business, transportation, logistics and high-value-added services".[26] It would treat more favourably Hong Kong investors in Guangdong's service sectors, as for example, retail and transportation under the CEPA framework.

Since 2003, the central government has taken a more active interest in bringing about closer co-operation between Hong Kong and Guangdong, as for example, boundary-crossing, infrastructure and tourism, in order to boost the Hong Kong economy and assist the Tung administration in the aftermath of the SARS crisis. For instance, the conclusion of CEPA helped both areas to forge closer economic ties, while individual visits by mainland residents to Hong Kong would also stimulate the retail and tourist sectors in Hong Kong. A feasibility study by the National Development and Reform Commission supported the construction of a Hong Kong-Zhuhai-Macau bridge, a project the Hong Kong SAR government favours. In short, the SAR government has clearly taken a far stronger and more active role in a wide range of policy areas, to manage the multifaceted cross-boundary relations and to facilitate economic integration with the Mainland.

Structural changes in the Hong Kong SAR government

The Hong Kong SAR government has introduced profound structural changes in order to better manage the phenomenal growth of cross-boundary interactions since 1997. Apart from previous ad hoc exchanges between individual agencies, liaison procedures between mainland China and Hong Kong mainly involved the management of the boundary, including the annual boundary liaison system and exchanges between law enforcement and other government agencies on the eve of 1997. Since then, the number of intergovernmental contacts between Hong Kong and the Mainland has expanded gradually. In the first three years after 1997, only a few communication channels existed between the two areas, focusing principally on issues that required close co-operation and co-ordination with the Mainland, including public security, water supply, boundary management, marine rescue and a co-operation plan in the event of emergencies at the nuclear power stations on the Mainland.[27]

In the first two years after the formation of the Hong Kong SAR, no officials represented it on the Mainland. The Office of the Hong Kong SAR in Beijing, opened in 1999, stayed the only official unit-in-residence on the Mainland until 2002. Its main tasks include enhancing contacts and communications with the central government and other local authorities, keeping the bureaus and departments of the SAR government informed of the latest developments on the Mainland, conducting "consular" functions, as for example, providing assistance to Hong Kong residents in need on the Mainland and processing visa applications to Hong Kong from foreign nationals on the Mainland.[28] While this Office supplies emergency assistance for Hong Kong people on the Mainland, it does not handle the business disputes of Hong Kong businessmen there. In response to repeated calls from the business sector for the establishment of government offices on the Mainland, the SAR government finally decided to set up, in 2002, the first Economic and Trade Office (hereafter the ETO) on the Mainland, located in Guangzhou, to act as a link between businesses in Hong Kong and their Guangdong counterparts and to organize trade and investment promotion activities in the province.[29]

The HKGDCJC was formed in March 1998 to act as the main channel for intergovernmental contacts and exchanges between Hong Kong and Guangdong. It principally provides a venue for different government departments to finalize and promulgate initiatives reached previously. Only after August 2001 did the Hong Kong SAR government also establish a Guangdong-Hong Kong Co-ordination Co-operation Unit to provide administrative co-ordination for the management of the growing number of cross-boundary affairs.[30] In August 2003, the Hong Kong and Guangdong governments further agreed to expand and enhance the scope and means of communication within the HKGDCJC. The governments upgraded the leading officials of the Conference to the level of the CE and the Governor of Guangdong. They established fifteen expert groups (later expanded to twenty-two) to cover such areas as infrastructure, environmental protection, boundary-crossing, intellectual property rights, education, scientific and cultural co-operation, economic and business co-operation, urban planning and infectious diseases control. Apart from agreeing to conduct working meetings in addition to the annual plenary sessions, both sides created dedicated liaison offices for the management of cross-boundary issues and formed a research group to study long-term measures. The scope and depth of the exchanges between Guangdong and Hong Kong have further widened, encompassing, for instance, the co-location and improvement of cross-boundary checkpoints, joint overseas promotion initiatives, infectious diseases control, and promulgation of a PRD Air Quality Plan as well as co-operation in education, culture and sports.

The Hong Kong SAR government has also upgraded its internal structure for managing cross-boundary affairs. In early 2006, it established a Mainland Affairs Liaison Office under the Constitutional Affairs Bureau, directly led by the Permanent Secretary for Constitutional Affairs. It incorporated the Hong Kong/Guangdong Co-operation Co-ordination Unit into this Office.[31] This restructuring demonstrates the importance that the SAR government attached to the management of its relations with the Mainland. Apart from serving as a liaison unit between the ETOs and the different agencies of the government, the newly-established Mainland Affairs Liaison Office would play a central role in the formulation of overall strategies and directives on co-operation between the Hong Kong SAR and the Mainland.[32] The government also set up a Committee on Economic Development and Economic Co-operation with the Mainland, under the revamped Commission on Strategic Development in November 2005, as a high-level body to advise the government on the formulation of its cross-boundary strategies.[33]

In 2006, the government extended the functions of the Office of the Hong Kong SAR government in Beijing to carry out economic and trade promotions not previously covered by the Office. They include the strengthening of communication and co-operation with provincial governments, exchanging economic information between Hong Kong and Beijing, increasing contacts with Hong Kong businessmen, disseminating information and services on Hong Kong to mainland enterprises and organizing promotion activities for Hong Kong's companies on the Mainland. It opened an Investment Promotion Unit under the Office to strengthen economic ties with the Bohai Bay Area, the north-eastern and north-western regions and to assist mainland enterprises with investing in Hong Kong.[34] The SAR government also emphasized the promotion of Hong Kong on the Mainland through the opening of ETOs to two more cities—Shanghai and Chengdu.[35]

A closer partnership with the business sector in promoting cross-boundary co-operation accompanied the expansion of intergovernmental mechanisms. The Greater PRD Business Council, established in Hong Kong in March 2004, comprises thirty-two prominent businessmen, bankers, scholars as well as legislators and government officials. It provides a platform for the businesses and the government to study various measures and facilitate co-operation between enterprises from Hong Kong and Guangdong.[36] Further, the SAR government has actively participated in the Pan-PRD forum and in trade promotion. Some of these ventures may indicate only symbolic action by Hong Kong officials in order to demonstrate a positive response to central policy, as for example, Donald Tsang's organization of a business delegation to visit the western region of China in 2001 to display his active interest in exploring business opportunities for Hong Kong while contributing to national development. Others, however, involve more substantive trade promotion. For instance, the Hong Kong, Macau and Guangdong delegations at the Pan-Pearl River Delta Regional Co-operation Trade Fair held in June 2006 signed business contracts worth RMB7 billion.[37] The SAR government has clearly taken up the role of a "promoter" in linking together businesses in Hong Kong and on the Mainland.

The role of government in managing cross-boundary interactions

Toward policy co-ordination amid economic integration

In the first two to three years of the post-1997 era, the Hong Kong SAR government primarily followed the "non-interventionist" model, despite the increasing economic transactions between Hong Kong and the Mainland. Collaboration with mainland authorities largely confined itself to the technical or administrative domains. The SAR government focused on maintaining Hong Kong's role as an international finance, trade and services centre, though at the same time, it did not regard seeking economic co-operation with the Mainland as the highest priority. However, in view of the tremendous impact of the Asian Financial Crisis—as for example, a high unemployment rate, deflation and negative economic growth—and the Mainland's entry into the WTO, the SAR government has become much more proactive since 2001 in its approach to the Mainland. The following section details the deepening economic and financial relationships and co-ordination in national and regional development planning between Hong Kong and the Mainland in the last decade.

Forging a closer economic relationship: The Closer Economic Partnership Arrangement (CEPA)

The conclusion of a free-trade arrangement between Hong Kong and the Mainland represents an unprecedented effort by the Hong Kong SAR government to develop closer economic ties between the two places. In order to take advantage of "first-mover" status for Hong Kong's businesses after China's entry into the WTO, the Hong Kong General Chamber of Commerce led in proposing the establishment of a "free trade area" between Hong Kong and the Mainland as early as 2000. Since the idea appealed to Tung Chee-hwa, the SAR government then initiated the negotiations with the relevant ministries on the Mainland in early 2001. After two years of difficult negotiations, both parties signed the formal CEPA Agreement in June 2003, at a time when the Hong Kong economy was suffering from its most serious economic downturn in recent history.

The CEPA Agreement not only allows products of Hong Kong origin into the Mainland without tariffs, it also assists the entrance of Hong Kong service suppliers into the Mainland. Further, it introduces various trade facilitation measures for Hong Kong businesses starting from 1 January 2004, approximately two years before China had to open up its economy in accordance with the WTO schedule. The CEPA Agreement initially expanded further in two stages, January 2005 and January 2006, respectively, by which time it would apply no tariffs to nearly all manufactured products of Hong Kong origin and accord preferential treatment to twenty-seven key service sectors.[38]

As of May 2009, the signatories have agreed upon a total of seven CEPA expansion schemes.[39] The Agreement also covers a number of trade and investment facilitation measures, including customs clearance, e-commerce, transparency in law and regulations, trade and investment promotion, quarantine and inspection of commodities, Chinese medicine and the Individual Visit Scheme.

The Hong Kong SAR government has also exercised greater initiative in attracting overseas and mainland investments. Apart from establishing "Invest Hong Kong", a government agency dedicated to promote marketing and investment, the SAR government has also actively lobbied the central authorities to relax the relevant rules in order to allow mainland enterprises to invest in Hong Kong.[40] After intense pressure by Hong Kong, in August 2004, the central authorities promulgated a series of measures to aid mainland companies' investments there.

Promotion of tourism

The Hong Kong SAR government has played a very active role in seeking the loosening of limits on the number of mainland tourists to Hong Kong since Beijing holds the ultimate authority over this matter. It actually comprised one of the few items discussed in the HKGDCJC from 1998 to 2002, but only after 2003 when Hong Kong suffered from a severe economic crisis did Beijing decide to further relax tourist entry into the region. In order to stimulate the sluggish Hong Kong economy in the aftermath of SARS, the central authorities allowed the residents of four cities in Guangdong province to travel to Hong Kong on an individual basis starting from 28 July 2003 under the Individual Visit Scheme. As a result, tourism between Hong Kong and the Mainland has flourished since then. Currently, the Scheme covers forty-nine cities with a population of 270 million.[41] The number of mainland tourists travelling under the Scheme has increased from 670,000 in 2003 to 5.5 million in 2005 and 14.2 million in 2010.[42] In 1997, some 2.3 million mainland visitors had travelled to Hong Kong, but by 2005, it had multiplied five times over to 12.5 million. In 2010, the number further increased to 22.7 million in 2010.[43] The share of tourists from the Mainland of the total jumped from 20.97 percent in 1997 to 53.7 percent in 2005 and to 63.0 percent in 2010.[44] By 2005, Hong Kong visitors on the Mainland already spent less (approximately HK$24.1 billion) than what mainland tourists did in Hong Kong.[45] The total amount of spending by overnight and same-day mainland tourists more than doubled from HK$38.5 billion in 2004 to HK$83 billion in 2009.[46]

Building Hong Kong into a financial centre for China

The economic growth and opening of the Mainland offer a unique opportunity for Hong Kong to transform itself into a leading financial centre for China. The SAR government has been promoting the financial sector as a key growth engine for Hong Kong. In 1993, the Hong Kong Stock Exchange listed its first ever company from the Mainland. By 1997, their number had increased to 98, and further, by July 2009, to 470.[47] Mainland-affiliated companies on the Hong Kong Stock Exchange held a market capitalization of HK$521.6 billion in 1997, representing 16.3 percent of the total. By the end of 2009, they constituted a combined market capitalization of more than 48 percent of the main board and 61 percent of the total turnover.[48]

Regarding the likelihood of developing the SAR's financial markets, the sector in Hong Kong acknowledged the difficulty of enhancing its role as the financial centre of the Mainland without the direct sponsorship of governments on both sides. Hence, it has collaborated with the relevant authorities in the SAR government, including the Hong Kong Monetary Authority (hereafter the HKMA), to propose further measures to improve Hong Kong's status as a financial centre for the Mainland. As early as September 2000, representatives from both the Hong Kong Association of Banks and the HKMA asked the central government to help Hong Kong banks operate on the Mainland.[49] Such lobbying led to a lowering of the minimum asset requirement for banks from the previous US$20 billion to US$6 billion, under the CEPA Agreement.[50] A memorandum of understanding which allowed Hong Kong banks to take deposits, accept remittances and operate credit card businesses in Renminbi in Hong Kong was finally signed by the People's Bank of China and the Hong Kong Monetary Authority on 19 November 2003.[51] In late 2005, Beijing further expanded the types of Renminbi businesses that Hong Kong banks could perform.[52] In response, the HKMA launched a new Renminbi Settlement System in March 2006 to meet the challenges posed by the growing number of Renminbi transactions.[53] A further breakthrough came in 2007 after continued effort from the SAR government and the Association of Banks requesting mainland approval for financial institutions there to issue Renminbi-denominated bonds in Hong Kong.[54] CEPA IV and VI relaxed restrictions on Hong Kong banks acquiring share in mainland banks, further opening the door for Hong Kong banks to establish sub-branches in Guangdong.[55]

As early as 2000, the HKMA had also put forth proposals to the central government for building a centre for the issuance of bonds in Asia and to allow financial institutions in Hong Kong to issue Renminbi-denominated state bonds.[56] In May 2001, the Hong Kong SAR government recommended series of measures to the central authorities to foster financial co-operation between Hong Kong and the Mainland, including permitting mainland companies listed in Hong Kong to issue Chinese Deposit Receipts on the Mainland and allowing mainland institutional investors to participate in the Hong Kong Stock Exchange under a Qualified Domestic Institutional Investor arrangement (hereafter the QDII).[57] In 2002, banks in Hong Kong called for the development of an offshore Renminbi centre there.[58] In the same year, responding to strong pressure from the SAR government, the mainland authorities promulgated the Qualified Foreign Investor Investment (hereafter the QFII) Scheme, which allows qualified overseas investors, including those from Hong Kong, to invest in stock markets on the Mainland. In April 2006, the central authorities officially promulgated the arrangements for the QDII. In 2007, it further relaxed the restrictions on QDII and issued trial measures for implementation. All the major financial regulators on mainland China have formally begun implementation of the QDII programme since then. The two recent policy planning documents involving Hong Kong and Guangdong (see below) also promise to grant Hong Kong a more important role in developing financial services in the province in order to consolidate its status as an international financial centre.

Co-ordination with regional and national plans

In order to explore the opportunities promised by China's economic growth, the Hong Kong SAR government has stepped up its efforts to seek co-operation with individual provinces and cities on the Mainland. It has signed an increasing number of agreements with other cities and provinces on the Mainland, as for example, a set of economic agreements respectively with Shanghai (October 2003), Beijing (September 2004) and Hainan (November 2004).[59] Areas covered include co-operation in sports, tourism, culture and infrastructure co-ordination and specific projects, as for example, joint management for the Shanghai airport and participation in the 2008 Beijing Olympics for Hong Kong businesses. Other local governments in South China also seized the opportunity to forge a closer economic relationship with Hong Kong. For instance, Shenzhen and the SAR government signed a Memorandum of Co-operation and eight other agreements in June 2004 covering numerous subjects.

Contrary to the suspicion and the public fear articulated in the pre-1997 era regarding closer co-operation with the Mainland, the Hong Kong SAR government has become increasingly active in ensuring that Hong Kong has a role to play in the regional development plans of the Mainland. The government actively participated in the Pan-PRD Regional Co-operation, a regional alliance for the development of economic and social co-operation and co-ordination in nine provinces (Guangdong, Guangxi, Hainan, Fujian, Hunan, Jiangxi, Sichuan, Guizhou and Yunnan) and the two SARs (Hong Kong and Macau). While Guangdong initiated the policy, the SAR government has attempted to use this framework to find a niche for Hong Kong investment in the other relatively less-developed provinces beyond Guangdong.[60]

For the first time after 1997, the Hong Kong SAR government, in 2006, requested that the central authorities incorporate Hong Kong into national development planning. The National 11th Five-Year Plan (hereafter the FYP) stipulated that it supported the development of Hong Kong's financial services, logistics, tourism and information services, and it would maintain Hong Kong's status as a financial, shipping and service centre. Instead of reiterating the opportunities created by China's rise as often occurred previously, senior Hong

Kong officials, including the CS and the Chief Executive of the HKMA, warned in March 2006 that, in view of the rapid development on the Mainland, Hong Kong's economy would be "marginalised".[61] The government organized a high-level Economic Summit in September 2006, attended by thirty-three prominent businessmen, scholars and government officials in order to formulate a host of measures to complement the 11th FYP, including better co-operation in improving maritime, land and air transport linkages between Hong Kong and the cities in the Pan PRD region, air traffic control and the division of labour in port development.[62]

Since late 2008, the central and provincial governments have pledged their commitment to position the PRD as a key economic region in China's development and to improve regional co-ordination and integration. The promulgation of The Outline of the Plan for the Reform and Development of the Pearl River Delta (2008–20) in early 2009 by the National Reform and Development Commission of the central government helped reaffirm the special role played by Guangdong province in reform in the past and potentially in the future.[63] This policy document endorses Guangdong's social, economic and administrative reform initiatives and reiterates the support of the central and provincial governments for promoting a division of labour between Hong Kong and the PRD. Specifically, it highlights Hong Kong's key position as an international finance, trading, shipping, logistics and high value-added service centre. Both sides emphasized closer co-operation in economic development, regional planning and the ongoing cross-boundary infrastructural projects. The National Reform and Development Commission would oversee its implementation by the ministries under the State Council together with the provincial government in order to improve co-ordination. This policy framework has indeed presented an unparalleled opportunity for Hong Kong and Guangdong to foster spatial, social and economic integration by creating more policy space and incentives. Such a major initiative under Beijing's support has ushered in a new era in intergovernmental co-operation within the PRD as well as among the PRD, Hong Kong and Macau. The SAR government also secured another Framework Agreement on Hong Kong/Guangdong Co-operation in early April 2010 to move various items forward within a specific timetable and to seek their incorporation into the 12th FYP.[64] Clearly, both sides have scaled new heights of institutionalized co-operation covering a wide range of policy sectors since 2003.

Co-ordination of infrastructural development

With regard to duplication of infrastructure in the PRD region, the Hong Kong SAR government recognized the urgent need to work with Guangdong and to ask the central authorities to help co-ordinate infrastructure on both sides of the border. Initially, the State Planning Commission and the SAR government established a new entity, the Mainland/Hong Kong SAR Conference on the Co-ordination of Major Infrastructure Projects, in late January 2002 to oversee co-ordination of large scale projects. One of the first major ones included the construction of the Hong Kong-Shenzhen-Guangzhou Express Rail Link, which would improve Hong Kong's link to the rapidly growing economic centres of the PRD.[65] The Guangdong government had already made its own plans for the Shenzhen-Guangzhou section of the Express Rail Link and begun construction in December 2005. In response to such fast-moving developments, the SAR government immediately followed suit with plans for the design and construction of the Hong Kong section of the railway. However, the SAR government did not decide on a detailed plan for the alignment, with a terminus at the West Kowloon Cultural District until April 2008. It secured the funding for the project only in early 2010, after having received strong oppositions from various civil society groups and residents affected by the project.

The keen competition in logistics in the PRD region has compelled the Hong Kong SAR government to take a more active role in exploring coping strategies. Hong Kong's container port is facing stiff competition from ones in the South China region due to their lower handling charges and their growing capacity. The container volume handled by Hong Kong ports increased only slowly from 10.5 million TEUs in 2001 to 11.3 million TEUs in 2007, while Hong Kong's share of container traffic in South China has shrunk from 76 percent in 2001 to 44 percent in 2007.[66] In response to such challenges and to requests the logistics industry has made, the SAR government finally launched the Hong Kong Logistics Development Council in 2002, working with prominent figures in the logistics industries. It commissioned a major study in 2001 to explore long-term measures to enhance the competitiveness of Hong Kong's ports.

Similarly, Hong Kong's airport is beginning to face competition from those in Guangzhou and Shenzhen. The Hong Kong SAR government has put forth proposals to co-operate with the airports of the PRD, particularly the Zhuhai Airport, which has encountered difficulties since its opening. Nonetheless, it made no further progress beyond the formation of an organization for co-operation among the five airports in the PRD, the A5 forum in 2001, and the signing of a number of agreements on technical issues. Eventually, the official meetings of the A5 forum stopped after mid-2003. The central government did not approve the co-operation agreement between Hong Kong and Zhuhai airports until August 2006.[67] On 18 December 2007, the Hong Kong and Shenzhen governments set up a Task Force to accelerate collaboration between their airports.[68] Both sides agreed to commission a preliminary consultancy on the construction of a Hong Kong-Shenzhen Airport Rail Link to connect the two airports.[69] The preliminary consultancy study, completed in late 2008, established the need to construct the railway.[70] At the 12th plenary of the HKGDCJC, both sides agreed to rename the railway, the Hong Kong-Shenzhen Western Express Line, and proposed, in principle, that it would link up western Hong Kong and Shenzhen, the Hong Kong International Airport and the Shenzhen International Airport.[71]

Another key issue concerned construction of the Hong Kong-Zhuhai-Macau Bridge. Originally advocated by the Zhuhai government and some Hong Kong business interests in the 1980s, the Hong Kong SAR government responded indifferently to the idea in the beginning. It denied the immediate need for the bridge in March 2001.[72] Since the SAR government has become increasingly concerned with the lack of cross-boundary linkages between Hong Kong and the western part of the PRD, it has placed the bridge prominently on its agenda again in 2002. However, authorities in Guangdong perceived the project as principally benefiting Hong Kong and having a negative impact on the development of its logistics. As a result, the provincial government no longer continued to be enthusiastic about its construction.[73] The Shenzhen government has even formulated its own plans for the construction of tunnel links between Shenzhen and Zhuhai and between Shenzhen and Zhongshan in recent years. Only after intensive lobbying by the Hong Kong SAR government in Beijing and a change in Guangdong's top leadership in late 2007 would both sides agree to build the bridge in early 2008.

Co-ordination in urban planning

In view of the rapid economic growth in South China, the Hong Kong SAR government has gradually adopted a "regional" perspective in planning that emphasized links with the neighbouring areas on the Mainland.[74] In addition to registering an annual growth rate of 10 percent in the past decade, Guangdong's GDP had already surpassed that of Hong Kong in 2004. In order to strengthen co-ordination of cross-boundary infrastructure, land use, transport and environmental issues, the SAR government consulted the planning authorities in Guangdong province when it carried out the study on its Territorial Development Strategy Plans, the "Hong Kong 2030 Planning Vision and Strategy" in 2001.[75]

Since the various booming cities in the PRD have also been developing without a unified plan, the Guangdong government has promoted the co-ordinated development of the PRD as a whole since 2003. Guangdong has already placed a co-ordinated plan for light rail and highways systems linking the cluster of cities in the PRD on its agenda. Since Hong Kong operates under the framework of "One Country, Two Systems", it remains politically sensitive and administratively problematic for mainland governments to incorporate the Hong Kong SAR into the regional plans of the Mainland. The Guangdong provincial government in August 2005 officially promulgated a Co-ordination and Development Plan of the PRD City Cluster 2004–20.[76] Although the plan mentions Hong Kong and Macau, it excludes them from the planning scheme while the planning departments of the two SARs have minimally participated.[77] In fact, the plan identified two "regional main centres" (Shenzhen and Guangzhou), a subsidiary regional centre (Zhuhai) and six local main centres (Foshan, Jiangmen, Dongguan, Zhongshan, Huizhou and Zhaoqing), without mentioning a clear role for Hong Kong.[78]

In view of such developmental planning by Guangdong and the exclusion of Hong Kong from the process, the Hong Kong SAR government realized that it had to proactively expedite its participation in these planning processes. The HKGDCJC discussed the launching of the Co-ordinated Development of the Greater Pearl River Delta Township plan in May 2004, while it also agreed to upgrade its panel on urban planning to include a dedicated expert group under its aegis.[79] In December 2005, the governments on both sides launched a two-year joint planning study of Hong Kong and Guangdong. Completed in 2009, it examined cross-boundary co-ordination, strategic environmental impact assessment, the protection and utilization of resources and other related issues.[80]

Managing the challenges and consequences of growing social interactions

Boundary crossing

With the increasing growth in cross-boundary movement, there have been calls from different community groups and business associations to improve boundary crossings between Hong Kong and the Mainland, especially the one with Shenzhen. The Hong Kong SAR government has acted rather cautiously on the issue as the boundary symbolizes the "Two Systems". Various concerns surfaced about the negative economic consequences brought about by easier border crossings while the issue proved especially sensitive in the first few years immediately after 1997. For instance, the entertainment and restaurant industries worried that this would mean increased consumption by Hong Kong residents on the Mainland, while the real estate sector became concerned with the negative effects on the price of properties, in particular, those in the New Territories. Politicians and social workers worried about the increase in domestic disputes, as for example, the growth of extra-marital affairs and juvenile crime, as for example, taking drugs in neighbouring Shenzhen.

After repeated calls for a twenty-four-hour cross-boundary checkpoint for passengers, the Hong Kong SAR government answered in May 2000 that it could not feasibly extend the opening hours for the main cross-boundary checkpoint, Lo Wu, during long holidays, but that it would consider the measures for the Lok Ma Chau checkpoints.[81] In October 2001, five major chambers of commerce called upon the SAR government to approve twenty-four-hour cross-boundary checkpoints.[82] In response, it discussed, in 2001, improvements connecting the checkpoints and a new footbridge between the Hong Kong and mainland sides of the Lo Wu checkpoints. The Guangdong and Hong Kong authorities also agreed on the co-location of checkpoints at the Huangguan/Lok Ma Chau boundary crossing in 2002. After negotiations with mainland authorities, the twenty-four-hour Lok Ma Chau boundary checkpoints for passenger traffic finally opened in January 2003.

Further, after repeated requests from Shenzhen, the Hong Kong and Shenzhen governments agreed to study the feasibility of developing the Lok Ma Chau Loop Area and building a new cross-boundary checkpoint at Liantang/Heung Yuen Wai in 2005 and 2006, respectively. After some community discussion, both sides agreed that the use of Lok Ma Chau Loop Area will concentrate on higher education, with complementary hi-tech research and development facilities, as well as the cultural and creative industries. A comprehensive study on the future use of the Loop commenced in June 2009 with an expected completion date at the end of 2011.[83] The governments have signed a co-operation agreement for a joint study of the new cross-boundary checkpoint in Liantang/Heung Yuen Wai in January 2007.[84] After agreeing upon this project in September 2008, the construction has an estimated start-up time of 2013 and with the control point available for use no later than 2018.[85] In September 2006, the SAR government agreed to reduce the size of the boundary region and to explore the feasibility of developing these formerly restricted areas. In January 2008, the government finalized its plan to reduce the size of the Frontier Closed Area to about four hundred hectares.[86] These efforts, promoted by the governments on both sides, will further facilitate cross-boundary traffic.

Environmental protection

The rapid increase in cross-boundary movement in people and businesses between Hong Kong and the Mainland has exacerbated pollution on both sides of the border.[87] Air pollution has emerged as one of the most critical challenges, especially for Hong Kong. Since pollutants do not recognize borders, the growing severity of the problem requires co-ordination and co-operation between different governmental bodies, including the establishment of joint environmental standards and the promulgation of joint studies on the subject and the adoption of anti-pollution measures.

Businesses, political parties and green groups in Hong Kong have called upon the Hong Kong SAR government to negotiate with mainland authorities to adopt joint solutions to contain air pollution. For example, as early as 1999, seventeen chambers of businesses collaborated to form a Business Environmental Council and asked the government to negotiate with mainland authorities, especially the governments in the PRD, in order to reduce air pollution.[88] Foreign business bodies such as the American Chamber of Commerce also petitioned the government to liaise with the mainland authorities to reduce air pollution.[89] The SAR government responded by releasing the PRD Air Quality Development Plan with Guangdong in August 2002, and, subsequently, the setting of targets for reducing air emissions and the publication of a PRD Air Quality Index in late 2005.[90] Nonetheless, the environmental groups argued that these measurements did not effectively contain air pollution. In November 2004, Civic Exchange, a non-government think tank, indicated that the level of volatile compounds in the atmosphere stood at eighty milligrams per square cubic metre in 2002, 30 percent higher than that in twenty European countries.[91] It also called for the creation of a clear, more inclusive process for determining standards and the formulation of a regional energy plan in containing air pollution in the PRD region.[92]

In May 2005, following the request for more direct intervention from various concern groups and the business sector, the central authorities and the Hong Kong SAR government targeted the tackling of air pollution as a policy agenda that they should address. In response, the relevant agencies from Hong Kong and Beijing signed a co-operation agreement on reducing air pollution, which, for the first time, highlighted the involvement of central authorities in resolving the problem.[93] While this shows the determination of the Hong Kong SAR government to deal with cross-boundary air pollution, whether the co-operation agreement between the central authorities and the Hong Kong SAR will prove effective or not remains unclear.

In the planning document for the PRD published in early 2009, one of the key areas concerns jointly building a community with a high quality of life. It will establish joint mechanisms, involving Guangdong, Hong Kong and Macau, to deal with environmental pollution, building cross-border ecological reserves and protecting water resources. The three areas will also develop clean energy and renewable resources, encourage the growth of a regional recycling economy working toward better waste management and gradually adopt unified standards on fuel emission to improve air quality of the region.[94] In the Framework Agreement on Hong Kong/Guangdong Cooperation, signed in early April 2010, one of the major priorities included implementing "a regional ecology and environment protection regime operating at a leading level by the national standards to create a high quality living area". Specific policy commitments include, for instance, jointly exploring the reduction targets and options for the total emission of air pollutants in the PRD region from 2011 to 2020, developing an electric car industry, expanding the Cleaner Production Partnership Programme and building a cross-boundary natural reserve and ecology corridor.[95] As the policy agenda of both governments places high status on environment and quality of life issues, it is clear that they will undertake more sustained, intergovernmental co-operation in the future.

Coping with health and food safety hazards

Confronted by a vigilant media and an alarmed public, necessity clearly dictates the co-ordination and establishment of contingency plans between different state authorities for the management of food safety and public health incidents. The eruption of the SARS in 2003 has compelled the Hong Kong SAR government, in co-operation with mainland authorities, to play a more activist role in detecting and monitoring infectious diseases in order to curb their spread. Despite the establishment of a joint arrangement in June 2002 and before the SARS outbreak in 2003, the notification procedure employed by Hong Kong and the Mainland in the event of infectious disease incidents had not worked effectively, nor had other more elaborate forms of co-operation.

When SARS began to affect South China in February 2003, the general public in Hong Kong only learned about the new diseases from media reports. The SARS outbreak led to the prompt establishment in mid-2003 of new channels for infectious diseases notifications between the Ministry of Health of the Mainland and the Department of Health of the Hong Kong SAR government. Authorities from Hong Kong, Macau and the Mainland agreed to share information and statistics and monitor twenty-eight types of infectious diseases. They established a dedicated expert group in August 2003 as one of the groups under the purview of the HKGDCJC. In October 2005, they signed a co-operation agreement on a response mechanism for public health emergencies that included deployment of a team of experts to respond to cases of public health emergencies and the formation of a co-operation mechanism to handle crises.[96] To facilitate additional co-ordination in containing infectious diseases between Hong Kong and Guangdong, officials signed a similar agreement in June 2006.[97] In June 2007, the Secretary for Health, Welfare and Food of Hong Kong and the Minister of Health signed another memorandum of understanding to strengthen the exchange of health and medical information and the notification and contingency co-operation system on infectious diseases outbreaks and public health emergencies. Both sides also agreed to promote exchanges and co-operation on community health services and hospital management.[98]

The relevant Mainland and Hong Kong SAR government food safety departments have been working closely since July 2003 to establish effective communication channels on food safety as well. In November 2003, the State General Administration of Quality Supervision, Inspection and Quarantine (hereafter the AQSIQ) on the Mainland and the Health, Welfare and Food Bureau of the Hong Kong SAR government signed an agreement to halt the spread of global infectious diseases and to monitor food safety measures.[99]

Although an effective mechanism for the quarantining and monitoring of vegetable supplies to Hong Kong has been adopted since the 1980s, the one for livestock and freshwater fish remains unresolved. The *streptococcus suis* outbreak in pig livestock in June 2005 and the use of malachite green in freshwater fish in August 2005 clearly highlighted these problems. The AQSIQ and Hong Kong's Environmental and Hygiene Department signed another agreement on the new quarantine procedures for chilled ducks and geese exported to Hong Kong in 2005.[100] In April 2006, the Hong Kong SAR and Guangdong also reached agreements on the designation of liaison officers for day-to-day matters and the hosting of urgent high-level meetings in the event of significant food safety incidents.[101] Without an effective method of communications between Hong Kong and the Mainland, the general public would face a serious and immediate risk in food safety.

Many more problems in food safety have emerged since 2005, and, as a result, both sides have had no choice but to further increase co-operation. For instance, in 2006, it was found that Sudan dyes were used in poultry eggs supplied to Hong Kong. In response, the AQSIA announced a series of measures including the issuance of health certificates for eggs, the setting up of a listing regime for egg farms and a requirement to test for Sudan dyes in poultry eggs by the Entry-Exit Inspection and Quarantine Bureaus in various provinces and municipalities prior to their export to Hong Kong.[102] In August 2007, the governments have also signed an agreement for the application of inspection and quarantine seals to the means of transport for freshwater fish supplied to Hong Kong at the 10th Plenary of the HKGDCJC. Under the agreement, the Guangdong side will take responsibility for the sealing, inspection and management of the arrangement.[103] In March 2009, they signed a Supplementary Co-operation Arrangement with the AQSIQ in order to explore methods of inspection and quarantine for food and agricultural products and to combat the illegal importing and exporting of food and agricultural products. It established a liaison officer system between the Food and Environmental Hygiene Department in Hong Kong and the Entry-Exit Inspection and Quarantine Bureau of Guangdong, Shenzhen and Zhuhai, respectively, to enhance communication and co-ordination within the region.[104] In November 2009, the AQSIA introduced new measures to improve the supervision and control of vegetable supplies at source as well as a product-tracing system.[105] In short, these efforts show that cross-boundary intergovernmental co-operation has become much more institutionalized and extensive in order to tackle the emergence of public health and food safety hazards.

Concluding observations

The role of the Hong Kong SAR government: Toward an activist local state

Since 1997, Hong Kong's external environment has experienced profound changes which have stimulated a search for new policy responses by the Hong Kong SAR government. First, Hong Kong's economic restructuring, characterized by the relocation of the manufacturing sector into the Mainland and the rise of the service sector, has brought both risks and opportunities for Hong Kong. With China's opening up to the world, the challenges to Hong Kong's role as an intermediary between the Mainland and the world economy compel the SAR government to devise strategies that allow it to work synergistically within the new economic framework. Second, growing interactions between Hong Kong and the Mainland have engendered a new set of public policy problems, including boundary crossing, infectious diseases, food safety hazards and environmental issues that have compelled the SAR government to co-ordinate and co-operate with the Mainland. Further, the major initiatives taken by Guangdong and other local governments and the ensuing competition in areas including transportation and logistics have triggered more policy responses from the Hong Kong SAR government.

The intensifying cross-boundary interactions between Hong Kong and mainland China have produced conflicting trends and demands. On the one hand, some existing policies and practices on both sides of the boundary present possible obstacles to closer co-operation and integration. Hence, the developmental role of the local state, especially in the case of Hong Kong, will require re-examination as the post-1997 political elite in Hong Kong simply does not consider governmental inaction an option. On the other hand, increasing flows of people, capital and traffic have prompted governments on both sides to work closely together and in some cases, to develop a stronger capacity to cope with cross-boundary problems and regulate intergovernmental interactions (e.g. in public health and environment).

Prospects for cross-boundary co-operation and the role of government

In the following section, the chapter ends with a few more observations on the prospects for cross-boundary co-operation and the future role of government. First, governments in both Hong Kong and the Mainland must respond to community demands for further facilitation of traffic and demographic movements and to manage the newly-emerging problems arising from them. Intergovernmental co-ordination in the region continues to pose a critical challenge because it involves not only the Hong Kong SAR government and the central government, but also different levels of local governments in South China. As more socio-economic issues have emerged as cross-boundary problems, many more government agencies on both sides of the boundary will need to work together in order to resolve them. Hence, the challenges for both intra-governmental as well as intergovernmental co-ordination will likely intensify in the near future.

Second, cross-boundary intergovernmental co-operation has expanded more widely, incorporating social, environmental and public health issues. However, the effectiveness of such interactions varies across policy sectors. For instance, in the aftermath of the SARS outbreak in 2003, leading health officials from Hong Kong, Macau and the Mainland recognized that the possibility of people spreading infectious diseases across the boundary merited special attention and required extensive co-operation. Nonetheless, differences in professional standards as well as competing interests continue to constitute key factors that shape the outcome of such co-operation. Other more complicated problems, as for example, environmental pollution and food safety still remain difficult to resolve. For instance, the deteriorating air quality in the PRD has compelled both sides to reach an agreement on improving air quality in April 2002, although in Hong Kong, it has not improved since then. Achieving effective co-operation stays a daunting challenge.

Third, major differences between Hong Kong and the Mainland regarding the developmental role of government remain evident. While the Hong Kong SAR government has become more proactive in promoting economic integration between Hong Kong and the

Mainland, it will not and cannot follow the example of East Asian developmental states such as Singapore, Taiwan or South Korea. On the contrary, local governments in South China have adopted a much more interventionist approach than the Hong Kong SAR government in steering social and economic development. Such differences in policy approaches remain a key issue in shaping cross-boundary co-operation since their expectations about what government should and can do still diverge.

Fourth, concerns about whether Hong Kong can maintain a high degree of autonomy amid deepening social and economic integration with the Mainland has not vanished. For example, the Hong Kong SAR government (and probably Guangdong as well) has increasingly asked Beijing to balance the different interests and governments in South China, as in the case of CEPA, boundary crossing and infrastructural co-ordination. How intergovernmental co-operation will shape the implementation of "One Country, Two Systems" will stay as a highly contested issue between Hong Kong and the Mainland in the future.

Fifth, the effective management of cross-boundary social and economic flows has become a major challenge to Hong Kong's governance. For instance, in view of the increasing economic integration between both areas, Hong Kong's service sector may further expand into the Mainland while the accompanying outflow of professionals and revenue may have implications for Hong Kong's economy and public finance unless the city's schemes to attract overseas and mainland talent and investment bear fruit. The management of cross-boundary problems demands accomplished political and administrative skills from the Hong Kong SAR government. However, clear signs exist that they often find it necessary to rely upon support from the central authorities. Whether the Hong Kong SAR government can develop the capacity to independently cope with such challenges remains to be seen.

Last but not least, what is often neglected is that societal actors still play a rather important role in cross-boundary matters. The challenge of cross-boundary co-operation has opened up new avenues for society—though predominantly in the business sector so far—to become an active partner in policy initiation and formulation. Many business chambers have acquired particular importance in urging the Hong Kong SAR government to move beyond its self-ordained "non-interventionist" role. For instance, the business sector in Hong Kong has called upon the government to expedite boundary crossing, co-ordinate infrastructural development in the PRD and open up more commercial options for Hong Kong's financial and service sectors on the Mainland. At the same time, such policy think tanks as the Civic Exchange have urged the governments on both sides to improve regional air quality. A new state-society synergy must develop in order to cope with cross-boundary issues as they indeed cover a wide array of policy problems.

The role of the state remains a contested issue in Hong Kong. As shown in the previous analysis, the Hong Kong SAR government has been playing an increasingly pivotal role in steering its social and economic development through co-ordination and integration with the Mainland. The structural changes within the government, the growing numbers of intergovernmental mechanisms as well as many government-driven cross-boundary initiatives aptly reflect the changing role of the SAR government. Under the leadership of Tung Chee-hwa and Donald Tsang, the SAR government has been working actively to formulate strategic plans and co-ordination mechanisms for cross-boundary co-operation, including recent attempts to incorporate the city into regional and national co-operation schemes and development planning. Hence, its growing interactions with its neighbour to the north and the central government in a globalizing world will continue to shape the role and functions of the local state in Hong Kong.

Acknowledgements

I would like to acknowledge the financial support from the University of Hong Kong through the Mrs. Li Ka Shing Fund for the Research Area on the Greater Pearl River Delta and Hong Kong, the Strategic Research Theme in Contemporary China Studies, and the Small Grant Funding. I would also like to thank the research assistance Chan Pui Ki, Anita Chow, Kelvin Sit, Edward Li Xiaoyang and Johnny Yeung provided and the advice from many experts and officials in Hong Kong and Guangdong who shared their insights with me. Any errors remain my sole responsibility.

Notes

Introduction

1. See, among others, Little (1981), Belassa et al. (1982) and Belassa (1988). Also, for a summary of the neoclassical position, see Haggard (1990), Chapter 1.
2. See, for example, Leftwich (1993), de Alcantara (1998) and Jessop (1998).

Chapter 1

1. Ul Haq played a fundamental role in creating the UNDP's Human Development Report with its Human Development Index which translated Sen's concepts into a powerful policy tool.
2. Cf. Negroponte (1996).
3. See Ostrom (1996).
4. See Romer (1986, 1990, 1993a, 1993b, 1994) and Lucas, Jr. (1988). For recent summaries, see Aghion and Howitt (1999) or Easterly (2001a, Chapters 3, 8, 9).
5. Elhanan Helpman (2004) provides one of the best surveys of this evidence. Investment in new knowledge yields private rates of return consistently higher than the rates of return to physical capital with the social rate of return much higher than the private one. Human capital has equally powerful effects. Putting ideas and education together, Jones (2002) argues "between 1950 and 1993 improvements in educational attainments . . . explain 30% of the growth in output per hour. The remaining 70% is attributable to the rise in the stock of ideas . . ."
6. Eighty percent in Solow's original work (1957); 60 percent in more recent work that includes human capital.
7. In their contribution to the *Handbook of Economic Growth,* Acemoglu, Johnson and Robinson (2005), argue unambiguously that institutions are the "fundamental determinants of long-run growth". Dani Rodrik,

in a co-authored paper Rodrik, Subramanian and Trebbi, (2004) entitled "Institutions Rule", contends equally clearly: "the quality of institutions 'trumps' everything else". Easterly and Levine (2003) and Bardhan (2005), among many others, offer further support for the primacy of institutions. See also Evans (2004, 2005).

8.   Among Sen's massive bibliography, *Development as Freedom* (1999a), is, perhaps, the most accessible synthesis

9.   Such as Boozer, et al. (2003).

10.   The literature on the twentieth-century developmental state is vast. For more recent analyses, see Chibber (2003) and Kohli (2004). Likewise, we should not forget Johnson's (1982) pioneering analysis of Japan.

11.   By the 1990s, even the World Bank (1993, 1997) had joined the consensus.

12.   As Amsden particularly emphasized (1989).

13.   The terms derive from Nicolas Negroponte's (1996) observation that economic activities is less and less driven by the rearrangement of atoms (i.e., the physical transformation of goods) and more and more driven by the rearrangement of "bits" that is so say, information, ideas and images.

14.   Opponents of this position will argue that the incentive effects of expected monopoly returns increase the output of new ideas and outweigh the negative effects of subsequent restricted access. How the balance works out in practice depends on specific institutional contexts. In the case of medications, for example, the evidence would seem to support the negative consequences of enforcing monopoly rights. See Angell (2004) for a popular but well-argued exposition.

15.   The term is Robert Reich's (1991).

16.   In this respect, as Chang (2002) underlines, twentieth-century developmental states followed the earlier historical practice of states in the North.

Chapter 3

1.   Civil servants who entered the government after 1987 could choose to set their retirement age at sixty.

2.   The current regulation under the Pensions Ordinance requires that senior government officials not take up any employment in a "sanitization period" of twelve months after retirement. In the second or third year after retirement (length dependent upon rank), any employment requires approval by an Advisory Committee on Post-retirement Employment, appointed by the Chief Executive, and chaired by a judge. It currently consists of officials from Civil Service Bureau, business and professional elites. See the government paper to the Legislative Council, LC Paper No. CB(1)295/05-06(03). Available at: http://www.legco.gov.hk/yr05-06/english/panels/ps/papers/ps1121cb1-295-3e.pdf, last accessed 9 April 2008.

3.   Note that the salary and fringe benefits paid to Hong Kong civil servants are among the highest in the world.

4.   For a glimpse of the financial situation of the Hospital Authority, see Hospital Authority (2007).

Chapter 4

1.   See Siu-kai Lau, "Tung Chee-hwa's Governing Strategy: The Shortfall in Politics", in *The First Tung Chee-hwa Administration: The First Five Years of the Hong Kong Special Administrative Region*, ed. Siu-kai Lau (Hong Kong: The Chinese University Press, 2002), 1–39; M. K. Lee, "Class, Inequality and Conflict", in *Indicators of Social Development: Hong Kong 1999*, ed. Siu-kai Lau et al. (Hong Kong: Hong Kong Institute of Asia-Pacific Studies, The Chinese University of Hong Kong, 2001), 115–35; Po-san Wan and Timothy Ka-ying Wong, "Social Conflicts in Hong Kong 1996–2002", Occasional Paper No. 156 (Hong Kong: Hong Kong Institute of Asia-Pacific Studies, The Chinese University of Hong Kong, 2005). For statistics on the petition and rally, see *Oriental Daily*, 20 January 2001.

2.   Tai-lok Lui, "Under Fire: Hong Kong's Middle Class after 1997", in *The July 1 Protest Rally: Interpreting a Historic Event*, ed. Joseph Y. S. Cheng (Hong Kong: City University of Hong Kong Press, 2005), 277–301.

3.   Lui, "Under Fire".

4.   See, for instance, the "Hong Kong Core Values" campaign launched by local professionals in 2004. For details, consult http://www.hkcorevalues. net.

5.   For a good survey of the performance of the Hong Kong SAR government, see Ming K. Chan and Alvin Y. So, eds., *Crisis and Transformation in China's Hong Kong* (Armonk, NY: M. E. Sharpe, 2002). Also, see Governance Reform Group SynergyNet, *Hong Kong Deserves Better Governance: An Evaluation of Hong Kong's System of Governance and Its Performance* (Hong Kong: SynergyNet, 2003).

6.   Siu-kai Lau, "Xingzheng Zhudaodi Zhengzhi Tizhi" (An executive-led political system), *Xianggang 21 Shiji Lantu* (The 21st century blueprint of Hong Kong) (Hong Kong: The Chinese University Press, 2000), 1–36; Lau, "Tung Chee-hwa's Governing Strategy: The Shortfall in Politics", in *The First Tung Chee-hwa Administration: The First Five Years of the Hong Kong Special Administrative Region*, ed. Siu-kai Lau (Hong Kong: The Chinese University Press, 2002), 1–39.

7.   Lau has not kept himself totally unaware of the issue of diversity of interests. He discusses the impact of the political transition, particularly the emergence of China-centred networks, on the fragmentation of elite politics. See Siu-kai Lau, "Political Order and Democratisation in

Hong Kong: The Separation of Élite and Mass Politics", in *Towards a New Millennium: Building on Hong Kong's Strengths*, ed. Gungwu Wang and Siu-lun Wong (Hong Kong: Centre of Asian Studies, University of Hong Kong, 1999), 68. However, his discussion largely confines itself to the cleavages created by the decolonization process, basically ignoring diversity class interests.

8. Eliza Wing-yee Lee, "Governing Post-colonial Hong Kong: Institutional Incongruity, Governance Crisis, and Authoritarianism", *Asian Survey* 39 (November/December 1999): 940–59.

9. Lee, "Governing Post-colonial Hong Kong", 941.

10. Lau, "Xingzheng Zhudaodi Zhengzhi Tizhi".

11. Anthony B. L. Cheung, "New Interventionism in the Making: Interpreting State Intervention in Hong Kong after the Change of Sovereignty", *Journal of Contemporary China* 9 (July 2000): 291–308.

12. James T. H. Tang, "Business as Usual: The Dynamics of Government-Business Relations in the Hong Kong Special Administrative Region", *Journal of Contemporary China* 8 (July 1999): 275–95.

13. Milton Friedman and Rose Friedman, *Free to Choose: A Personal Statement* (Harmondsworth: Penguin Books, 1980).

14. Alvin Rabushka, *Value for Money: The Hong Kong Budgetary Process* (Stanford, CA: Hoover Institution Press, 1976).

15. Cheung, "New Interventionism", 300.

16. An extended and repeated debate over the nature and practice of the state in Hong Kong has occurred. For early attempts to challenge the view of Hong Kong as the last stronghold of *laissez-faire* capitalism, see A. J. Youngson, *Hong Kong: Economic Growth and Policy* (Hong Kong: Oxford University Press, 1982); Jonathan R. Schiffer , "State Policy and Economic Growth: A Note on the Hong Kong Model", *International Journal of Urban and Regional Research* 15 (March 1991): 180–96; Catherine R. Schenk, *Hong Kong as an International Financial Centre: Emergence and Development 1945–65* (London: Routledge, 2001).

17. Tang, "Business as Usual", 294.

18. Cultural analysis of Hong Kong politics promises to go beyond class analysis of politics. See Agnes S. Ku, "The 'Public' up against the State: Narrative Cracks and Credibility Crisis in Postcolonial Hong Kong", *Theory, Culture & Society*, 18 (February 2001): 121–43. Ku argues that "[in the case of the bird flu crisis in Hong Kong] the challenge was powerfully presented not so much because of capitalist forces or class interests but because *the crisis became a dramatic moment of meaning reconstruction through ironic narration and democratic encoding in the public sphere*" (122, emphasis in the original). Despite reference to Gramsci and his notion of hegemony, nowhere does she make it clear that realpolitik and the contest of meaning and interests carried by political actors with specific interests

in certain courses of development make the widening of narrative cracks and credibility crisis upon which they ground themselves possible. A long-standing bureaucratic and institutionally unaccountable mindset has characterized the civil service. Why and how a narrative displaced to facilitate the rise of a hegemonic discourse on the civil servants and then why and how the same civil service became de-heroized constitute questions left unanswered. As a result, conjunctural analysis becomes free-floating cultural construction of politics.

19. Colin N. Crisswell, *The Taipans: Hong Kong's Merchant Princes* (Hong Kong: Oxford University Press, 1981).

20. Tak-Wing Ngo, "Money, Power, and the Problem of Legitimacy in the Hong Kong Special Administrative Region", in *Politics in China: Moving Frontiers*, ed. Françoise Mengin and Jean-Louis Rocca (New York: Palgrave, 2002), 112.

21. Norman Miners, "Consultation with Business Interests: The Case of Hong Kong", *Asian Journal of Public Administration* 18 (December 1996): 246.

22. Richard Hughes, *Borrowed Place Borrowed Time: Hong Kong and its Many Faces*, 2nd rev. ed. (London: Andre Deutsch, 1976), 23.

23. John Rear, "One Brand of Politics", in *Hong Kong: The Industrial Colony: A Political, Social and Economic Survey*, ed. Keith Hopkins (Hong Kong: Oxford University Press, 1971), 72.

24. G. B. Endacott, *Government and People in Hong Kong 1841–1962: A Constitutional History* (Hong Kong: Hong Kong University Press, 1964).

25. S. N. G. Davies, "One Brand of Politics Rekindled", *Hong Kong Law Journal* 7 (January 1977): 44–80.

26. Davies, "One Brand of Politics", 71.

27. Davies, "One Brand of Politics", 70.

28. Davies, "One Brand of Politics", 66.

29. Davies, "One Brand of Politics", 69.

30. Benjamin K. P. Leung, "Power and Politics: A Critical Analysis", in *Social Issues in Hong Kong*, ed. Benjamin K. P. Leung (Hong Kong: Oxford University Press, 1990), 21.

31. Leung, "Power and Politics", 21–2.

32. The assumption that the colonial government did not make changes in its ruling strategy in dealing with social and political changes in Hong Kong would seem overly simplistic. On the transition from selecting the old rich in Hong Kong to absorbing the younger and emerging professionals and managers since the late 1960s, see Lung-wai Stephen Tang, "The Power Structure in a Colonial Society: A Sociological Study of the Unofficial Members of the Legislative Council in Hong Kong (1948–1971)", BSocSci thesis, Chinese University of Hong Kong, 1973.

33. Gilbert Wong, "Business Groups in a Dynamic Environment: Hong Kong 1976–1986", in *Asian Business Networks*, ed. Gary Hamilton (Berlin: Walter de Gruyter), 87–113.

34. Wong, "Business Groups", 93.

35. Wong, "Business Groups", 94.

36. Wong, "Business Groups", 96–7.

37. Wong, "Business Groups", 103–4.

38. Wong, "Business Groups", 106–8.

39. Mang-King William Cheung, "The Applicability of Four Theoretical Perspectives of Economic Power to the Corporate Market in Hong Kong", PhD diss., University of California, Los Angeles, 1994.

40. Tak-Wing Ngo, "Changing Government-Business Relations and the Governance of Hong Kong," in *Hong Kong in Transition: The Handover Years*, ed. Robert Ash, et al. (Houndmills: Macmillan Press, 2000), 26–41.

41. Ngo, "Changing Government-Business Relations", 32.

42. For a similar argument, see Stephen W. K. Chiu. "Unravelling the Hong Kong Exceptionalism: The Politics of Industrial Takeoff", *Political Power and Social Theory* 10: 229–56.

43. One crucial difference between our analysis and previous ones derives from the appearance, by the late 1990s, of a new type of directors appointed onto the corporate boards, namely, the "independent non-executive directors". As "outsiders" to the management team, an interlock that involves this kind of directors should much less significantly impact the networking relationship between two companies. Under the current listing rules of the Hong Kong Exchange, boards of listed companies must appoint at least three independent non-executive directors to their boards. As the number of this type of directors increased quite dramatically between the three time points, from 0 to 503 in 1997 and 855 in 2004, and they typically occur among the directors with the most multiple memberships, we have decided to exclude them from our analysis of the 1998 and 2004 panels in order to control for their presence over time. For a definition of independent non-executive directors in the context of banking definitions, please refer to HKMA website: http://www.info.gov.hk/hkma/eng/public/index.htm.

44. Leo F. Goodstadt, *Uneasy Partners: The Conflict Between Public Interest and Private Profit in Hong Kong* (Hong Kong: Hong Kong University Press, 2005), 121.

45. See Ngo, "Money, Power", 108–9, there is an account of the series of events in the Cyberport incident.

46. See, for example, "Tycoons Urge Cyberport Tender", *South China Morning Post*, 19 March 1999, A1; "Pressure to Block Cyberport Funding", *South China Morning Post*, 12 May 1999, A2.

47. Ngo, "Money, Power", 109.

48. The claim returned to the political scene in 2005 prompting the government to release twenty-four letters between the government and the PCC Group to prove an absence of collusion with the business

sector. See "Tung Faces Cyberport Pressure", *South China Morning Post,* 3 February 2005, A1.

49. "Developers Step up Campaign over Electricity Charges", *South China Morning Post,* 12 November 2002, A2.

50. "Inside the Business Groups' Ambush of the 'Superman'", *Next Magazine,* 21 November 2002 (in Chinese).

Chapter 5

1. Yet, as Bottomore qualifies, Marshall's principal concern lies more with the impact of citizenship on social classes rather than the reverse (Bottomore 1992).

2. A study by the Census and Statistics Department in June 2007 showed that Hong Kong's Gini coefficient rose from 0.483 in 1996 to 0.500 in 2006, higher than that of developed countries.

3. See Report of the Director-General, International Labor Organization. 2007. *"Equality at Work: Tackling the Challenges,"* presented at the International Labor Conference, Geneva.

4. For instance, in 2007, the wage level of the lower quartile of the overall wage distribution equalled HK$7,147 (around US$920), 29 percent lower than the median wage level of HK$10,123 (around US$1,300). See the Report of the Commission on Poverty on its website.

5. Tung set up such high-level commissions as the Commission on Strategic Development and the Commission on Innovation and Technology, and created a HK$5 billion Innovation and Technology Fund; he also establish a special task force of experts, economists and trade unionists to look into issues of employment and unemployment amid an economic downturn.

6. In June 1997, the government tabled an Independent Police Complaints Council Bill that intended to give statutory power to a police watchdog organization. However, it suddenly withdrew the bill before its third and final reading, leaving the police with minimally monitored power until today.

7. For example, before 1995, the Public Order Ordinance required organizers to get a license for public assembly. In 1995, as part of the liberalization of the law under the Bill of Rights, it relaxed the law to remove the requirement for a licence. Then, in 1997, the provisional legislature amended the law to include a clause that required a notice of non-objection from the police.

8. There has been widespread criticism of several key aspects of the appointments, namely, the nationality and experience of the appointees, their salaries and the transparency of the recruitment process.

9.   See People's Panel on West Kowloon, www.ppwk.org/aboutus.html
10.   Ibid.

Chapter 6

1.   According to Sinn (1986), such segregation occurred in the first four decades of colonial rule.
2.   For details, see the website of the Urban Renewal Authority: http://www.ura.org.hk/html/c800000e23e.html [last visited on 30 April 2010]
3.   For details of the organization, see http://www.hkcmp.org/cmp/c_001.html.
4.   These groups include the Urban Regeneration Taskforce, the Centre for Community Renewal, and Urban Watch.

Chapter 7

1.   Hong Kong Housing Authority webpage: http://www.housingauthority.gov.hk/en/residential/shos/homeloan/0,,,00.html
2.   This chapter defines housing policy at two levels: first, it concerns all policies within the organizational context of the Housing Bureau; second, it also includes government regulatory activities aiming at stabilizing the housing market, discouraging overheated speculative activities and increasing land supply, among others.
3.   The Hong Kong Housing Society, an independent and not-for-profit housing organization established in 1948 and incorporated by ordinance in 1951, provides social housing through a number of innovative schemes. As a partner of the government, it builds self-contained homes for low income families.
4.   Prior to 1997, the Housing Authority was obliged to buy back vacant public flats at cost, but since 1998, they could only buy back flats at market price as a result of enormous asset price depreciation.
5.   2006 Index of Economic Freedom, Heritage Foundation.
6.   In March 1997, house prices had risen more than 30 percent within a month, the highest monthly increase ever recorded.

Chapter 8

1.   This chapter has drawn selectively from some of the data and analysis from my previous works on cross-boundary relations between Hong Kong and South China. See Peter T. Y. Cheung, "Cross-boundary Cooperation in South China: Perspectives, Mechanisms and Challenges", in *Developing a Competitive Pearl River Delta in South China Under One*

Country-Two Systems, ed. Anthony Gar-on Yeh, et al. (Hong Kong: Hong Kong University Press, 2006), 449–79; Peter T. Y. Cheung, "Cross-boundary State-society Interactions in South China", in *Dynamics of Local Governance in China during the Reform Era*, ed. Tse-kang Leng and Yun-han Chu (Lanham, MD: Lexington Books, 2010), 273–306.

2. Anthony B. L. Cheung, "New Interventionism in the Making: Interpreting State Interventions in Hong Kong after the Change of Sovereignty", *Journal of Contemporary China* 9 (July 2000): 291–308.

3. Cheung, "New Interventionism", 307.

4. Peter T. Y. Cheung, "Intergovernmental Relations between Mainland China and the Hong Kong SAR," in *Public Administration in Southeast Asia: Thailand, Philippines, Malaysia, Hong Kong and Macao*, ed. Evan M. Berman (London: CRC Press, 2010), 255–81.

5. James Anderson and Liam O'Dowd, "Borders, Border Regions and Territoriality: Contradictory Meanings, Changing Significance", *Regional Studies* 33 (October 1999): 593–604.

6. Data compiled from *Hong Kong Annual Digest of Statistics*, various years and other statistics from the website of the Census and Statistics Department, the government of the Hong Kong Special Administration Region. See also http://www.censtatd.gov.hk/hong_kong_statistics/statistical_tables/index.jsp?charsetID=1&tableID=060.

7. Census and Statistics Department, *Reports on Hong Kong Trade in Services Statistics*, various years. See also http://www.censtatd.gov.hk/hong_kong_statistics/statistical_tables/index.jsp?tableID=083&ID=&subjectID=3.

8. Census and Statistics Department, *Reports on Hong Kong Trade in Services Statistics*, various years. See also http://www.censtatd.gov.hk/hong_kong_statistics/statistical_tables/index.jsp?charsetID=1&tableID=084.

9. Yun-wing Sung, *The Emergence of Greater China: The Economic Integration of Mainland China, Taiwan and Hong Kong* (Basingstoke: Palgrave Macmillan, 2005), 108.

10. Census and Statistics Department, *Reports on Hong Kong Trade in Services Statistics*, various years. See also http://www.info.gov.hk/gia/general/201102/11/P201102110143.htm.

11. Sung, *Emergence of Greater China*, 109.

12. *China Statistical Yearbook 2010*, chap.17, Foreign Trade and Economic Cooperation.

13. Data compiled from the statistics table available at the National Bureau of Statistics of China website. See http://www.stats.gov.cn/english. See also *China Statistical Yearbook 2010*, chap. 17, Foreign Trade and Economic Cooperation.

14. *External Direct Investment Statistics of Hong Kong 2000* (Hong Kong: Census and Statistics Department, 2002), Table 2, 12–13; and *External*

Direct Investment Statistics of Hong Kong 2008 (Hong Kong: Census and Statistics Department, 2009), Table 2, Charts 2a and 2b, 12–13. See also http://www.censtatd.gov.hk/hong_kong_statistics/statistical_tables/index.jsp?charsetID=1&tableID=048.

15. See http://www.censtatd.gov.hk/hong_kong_statistics/statistical_tables/index.jsp?charsetID=1&tableID=048.

16. See the discussion paper, "Transport Infrastructure Development", for the Transport Infrastructure Development Focus Group at the Economic Summit on "China's 11th Five-Year Plan and the Development of Hong Kong", at http://www.info.gov.hk/info/econ_summit/eng/pdf/paper_7.pdf, 5 and Annex 4, 27. See also *Monthly Traffic and Transport Digest* (February 2010) at http://www.td.gov.hk/filemanager/en/content_4339/table81e.pdf, Table 8.1e.

17. *Hong Kong Monthly Digest of Statistics*, various years.

18. *Monthly Traffic and Transport Statistics, Transport Department*, various years.

19. *Hong Kong 2009*, chap. 13, Transport. Available at http://www.yearbook.gov.hk/2009/en/pdf/C13.pdf.

20. Speech delivered by the Chief Executive at the 140th anniversary celebration of the Hong Kong General Chamber of Commerce, 22 February 2001. Available at http://www.ceo.gov.hk/archive/97/05/speech/cesp.htm.

21. See Legislative Council Panel on Commerce and Industry, "Hong Kong Guangdong Co-operation Co-ordination Unit", at http://www.legco.gov.hk/yr01-02/english/panels/ci/papers/ci-1112-cb1-220-le.pdf.

22. For the full text of the 2003 Policy Address, see http: www.policyaddress.gov.hk/pa03.

23. This scheme came into force on 15 July 2003. See Immigration Department Admission Scheme for Mainland Talents and Professionals at http://www.immd.gov.hk/ehtml/20030715.htm.

24. See http://www.policyaddress.gov.hk/pa03/eng/p37.htm.

25. Details of the agreements reached in this meeting can be found in "Develop New Frontiers in Hong Kong Guangdong Co-operation". Press release of the Hong Kong SAR government, 5 August 2003. See http://www.info.gov.hk/gia/general/200308/05/0805257.htm.

26. Peter T. Y. Cheung, "Cross-boundary Cooperation in South China: Perspectives, Mechanisms and Challenges," in *Developing a Competitive Pearl River Delta in South China under One Country-Two Systems*, eds. A. G. O. Yeh, G. Chen, V. S. Sit and Y. Zhou (Hong Kong: Hong Kong University Press, 2006), 463.

27. See Standing Mechanisms for Co-operation or Notification between the SAR Government and Mainland Authorities. Available at http://www.legco.gov.hk/yr04-05/english/counmtg/hansard/cm0629ti-translate-e.pdf.

28. Constitutional Affairs Bureau, Hong Kong SAR government, "Establishment of the Mainland Affairs Liaison Office". Paper presented to the Panel on Constitutional Affairs of the Legislative Council. Available at http://ww.lego.gov.hk/yr05-06/english/panel/ca/paper/ca1121cb2-396-3e.pdf.

29. Website of the Hong Kong Economic and Trade Office in Guangdong, http://www.gdeto.gov.hk/eng/about/role.htm.

30. An Administrative Officer Staff official (Grade B) with a small support staff of six headed the Unit. The tasks of the Unit include following the initiatives as agreed in the HKGDCJC, through the study of facilitation the flows of goods and people, and the mapping out of an "action agenda" for Hong Kong to benefit from the development in the PRD Region. For details, see Hong Kong/Guangdong Cooperation Coordination Unit, "Work Schedule". Paper presented to the Finance Committee, Establishment Subcommittee at http://www.legco.gov.hk/yr01-02/english/fc/esc/papers/ei01-05e.pdf; and Hong Kong/Guangdong Cooperation Coordination Unit. Paper presented to the Commerce and Industry Committee at http://www.legco.gov.hk/yr01-02/english/panels/ci/papers/ci-1112-cb1-220-1e.pdf. The Hong Kong SAR government actually did not attempt to make the posts in the Group a part of the permanent establishment of the Hong Kong SAR government, in order to avoid possible opposition.

31. Constitutional Affairs Bureau, "Establishment of the Mainland Affairs Liaison Office", par. 19.

32. Constitutional Affairs Bureau, "Establishment of the Mainland Affairs Liaison Office", par. 6.

33. Committee on Economic Development and Economic Cooperation with the Mainland, Commission on Strategic Development. See http://www.cpu.gov.hk/english/csd_edc.htm.

34. Since the Office of the Hong Kong SAR government in Beijing lies under the purview of the newly-established Mainland Affairs Liaison Office, a Directorate 6 (D6) rank official rather than a Bureau Secretary (Directorate 8) official would head the office. See Constitutional Affairs Bureau, "Establishment of the Mainland Affairs Liaison Office", Enclosure one, Current Forecast of Creation/Deletion of Civil Service Permanent Directorate Post in the 2005/06 Legislative Session, 1.

35. See Constitutional Affairs Bureau, "Establishment of the Mainland Affairs Liaison Office", par. 10.

36. "Terms of Reference", in *The Greater Pearl River Delta Business Council, 2004/05 Annual Report,* 21.

37. *Ta Kung Pao,* 7 June 2006, A10.

38. See Legislative Council Secretariat, *Background brief on developments of the Mainland and Hong Kong Closer Economic Partnership Arrangement,* at

http://www.legco.gov.hk/yr05-06/english/panels/ci/papers/ci0718cb1-1977-e.pdf, 2.

39. See "Mainland and Hong Kong Closer Economic Partnership Arrangement" at http://www.tid.gov.hk/english/cepa/further_liberal.html.

40. *The Chief Executive's Policy Address 2001*, "Facilitating Foreign and Mainland Enterprises", par. 82, at http://www.policyaddress.gov.hk/pa01/e82.htm.

41. See http://www.tourism.gov.hk/english/visitors/visitors_ind.html.

42. See http://www.tourism.gov.hk/english/statistics/statistics_perform.html.

43. See http://www.tourism.gov.hk/english/statistics/statistics_perform.html.

44. See http://www.tourism.gov.hk/english/statistics/statistics_perform.html.

45. Census and Statistics Department, "Consumption Expenditure of Hong Kong Residents Travelling to the Mainland of China, 2005", in *Hong Kong Monthly Digest of Statistics May 2006* (Hong Kong: Census and Statistics Department, 2006), FA1–13.

46. *Hong Kong Annual Digest of Statistics 2010* (Hong Kong: Census and Statistics Department, 2010), 226.

47. "Number of Hong Kong-listed Mainland Firms Grow to 470", *People's Daily Online,* 7 May 2010, at http://english.peopledaily.com.cn/90001/90778/90857/6681729.html.

48. "Market Capitalisation of China-Related Stocks (Main Board and GEM)", Statistics and Research, *HK Exchanges and Clearing* at http://www.hkex.com.hk/eng/stat/smstat/chidimen/cd_mc.htm.

49. *Apple Daily,* 11 January 2003, B3.

50. See Trade and Industry Department, *Specific Commitment on Liberalization of Trade in Services,* at http://www.tid.gov.hk/english/cepa/files/annex4.pdf, 30.

51. "Personal RMB service OK'd in HK". *China Daily,* 19 November 2003. Available at http://www.chinadaily.com.cn/en/doc/2003-11/19/content_282646.htm.

52. "HK's RMB business to expand", *People's Daily,* 27 September 2005. Available at http://english.peopledaily.com.cn/200509/27/eng20050927_211099.html.

53. See discussion paper, "Consolidating Hong Kong's Position as an International Financial Centre", for the Financial Services Focus Group at the Economic Summit on "China's 11th Five-Year Plan and the Development of Hong Kong, at http://www.info.gov.hk/info/econ_summit/eng/pdf/paper_5.pdf.

54. *Ta Kung Pao,* 17 January 2007, A2.

55. *China Daily News,* 30 April 2007, A6 and *Nan Fang Daily,* 22 May 2009, ND03.

56. *Wen Wei Po,* 15 October 2003, A16.

57. *Hong Kong Economic Times,* 8 August 2001, A3.

58. *Hong Kong Commercial Daily*, 3 June 2002, A1; and *Hong Kong Economic Journal*, 20 February 2003.

59. See the discussion paper, "The Opportunities and Challenges Presented by the 11th Five-Year Plan and the Outlook for Hong Kong", for the plenary session of the Economic Summit on "China's 11th Five-Year Plan and the Development of Hong Kong", at http://www.info.gov.hk/info/econ_summit/eng/pdf/paper_1.pdf.

60. See the discussion paper, "Innovation, Technology and Information Services", for the Professional Services, Information Technology and Tourism Focus Group at the Economic Summit on "China's 11th Five-Year Plan and the Development of Hong Kong", at http://www.info.gov.hk/info/econ_summit/eng/pdf/paper_9.pdf.

61. *South China Morning Post*, 21 March 2006, EDT 2.

62. "Opportunities and Challenges", Economic Summit.

63. National Development and Reform Commission, "Outline of the Plan for the Reform and Development of the Pearl River Delta". See http://www.china.org.cn/government/scio-press-conferences/2009-01/08/content_17075239.htm.

64. "Signing Ceremony of Framework Agreement on Hong Kong Guangdong Co-operation Held in Beijing". Press Releases of the Hong Kong SAR government, 7 April 2010. See at http://www.info.gov.hk/gia/general/201004/07/P201004070113.htm; http://gia.info.gov.hk/general/201004/07/P201004070113_0113_63622.pdf (in Chinese); and http://gia.info.gov.hk/general/201004/07/P201004070113_0113_63623.pdf (in Chinese).

65. *Ming Pao*, 1 February 2001, A6.

66. See the discussion paper, "Logistics and Maritime Services" for the Maritime, Logistics and Infrastructure Focus Group at the Economic Summit on "China's 11th Five-Year Plan and the Development of Hong Kong", at, http://www.info.gov.hk/info/econ_summit/eng/pdf/paper_6.pdf, 31.
For statistics from 2005 to 2006, see also Transport Branch, Transport and Housing Bureau, *Study on Hong Kong Port Cargo Forecasts 2005/2006, Executive Summary*, at http://www.logisticshk.gov.hk/board/PCF05-06ES.pdf, 4–5. The data for 2007 is an estimate.

67. "Seventh Working Meeting of HK/Guangdong Co-operation Joint Conference Held in HK". Press Release of the Hong Kong SAR government, 5 July 2006. Available at http://www.info.gov.hk/gia/general/200607/05/P200607050254.htm.

68. "Hong Kong/Shenzhen Co-operation Scheme Achieves a Milestone". Press Release of the Hong Kong SAR government, 18 December 2007. Available at http://www.info.gov.hk/gia/general/200712/18/P200712180273.htm

69. *Ming Pao*, 18 January 2008, A17.

70. *Hong Kong Economic Times,* 31 December 2008, A2.

71. "12th Plenary of the Hong Kong/Guangdong Co-operation Joint Conference Held in Hong Kong Today". Press Release of the Hong Kong SAR government, 19 August 2009. Available at http://www.cmab.gov.hk/en/press/press_2148.htm

72. "LCQ2: Bridge Connecting Zhuhai and Hong Kong". Press Release of the Hong Kong SAR government, 7 March 2001. Available at http://www.info.gov.hk/gia/general/200103/07/0307206.htm.

73. *Ta Kung Pao,* 10 April 2002, A8.

74. Press Release of the Hong Kong SAR government, 25 July 2002. Available at http://www.info.gov.hk/gia/general/200207/25/0725173.htm. (in Chinese)

75. See Stage 1 Public Consultation, Planning Objectives and Key Study Areas, Hong Kong 2030 Planning Vision and Strategy, at http://www.pland.gov.hk/pland_en/p_study/comp_s/hk2030/eng/con_digest/pdf/Stage1_planningobjective.pdf

76. "Co-ordination and Development Plan of the Pearl River Delta City Cluster, 2004–2020", in *The Greater Pearl River Delta Business Council, 2005/2006 Annual Report,* 40.

77. Chun Yang, "Multilevel Governance in the Cross-boundary Region of Hong Kong-Pearl River Delta, China", *Environment and Planning A* 37 (December 2005), 2147–68.

78. See Guangdong Provincial Government, *Co-ordination and Development Plan of the Pearl River Delta City Cluster, 2004–2020,* at http://www.gdcic.net/oldweb/zgb/images/guihua.pdf (in Chinese), 7.

79. "Guangdong Co-operation Third Working Meeting Held in Hong Kong". Press Release of the Hong Kong SAR government, 21 May 2004. Available at http://www.info.gov.hk/gia/general/200405/21/0521240.htm.

80. See "Planning Study on the Co-ordinated Development of the Greater Pearl River Delta Townships". Planning Department, Hong Kong SAR government. Available at http://www.pland.gov.hk/pland_en/misc/great_prd/gprd_e.htm.

81. *Ta Kung Pao,* 3 May 2000, A10.

82. The five chambers of commerce are the Hong Kong General Chamber of Commerce, the Hong Kong Chinese Chamber of Commerce, the Hong Kong Federation of Industries, the Hong Kong Chinese Manufacturer's Association and the Real Estate Developers' Association. See *Sing Tao Daily,* 23 October 2001, A2.

83. "Planning and Engineering Study on Development of Lok Ma Chau Loop." Available at http://www.lmcloop.gov.hk/eng/study.html

84. "CS Attends Eighth Working Meeting of Hong Kong /Guangdong Co-operation Joint Conference." Press Release of the Hong Kong SAR government, 29 January 2007. Available at http://www.info.gov.hk/gia/general/200701/29/P200701290210.htm.

85. "Hong Kong-Shenzhen Joint Task Force on Boundary Transit Development Holds Third Meeting". Press Release of the Hong Kong SAR government, 27 April 2009. Available at http://www.info.gov.hk/gia/general/200904/27/P200904270219.htm

86. "Plan Finalised for Reducing Coverage of Frontier Closed Area." Press Release of the Hong Kong SAR government, 11 January 2008. Available at http://www.info.gov.hk/gia/general/200801/11/P200801110129.htm

87. Due to space limitations, this section only discusses the issue of air pollution.

88. *Ming Pao,* 9 June 1999, A12.

89. *Ming Pao,* 19 July 2000, A8.

90. "PRD Regional Air Quality Index to go public from tomorrow." Press release of the Hong Kong SAR government, 29 November 2005. Available at http://www.epd.gov.hk/epd/english/news_events/press/press_051129a.html.

91. *Ming Pao,* 5 November 2004, A15.

92. See "Air Pollution: Air Quality Management Issues in the Hong Kong and the Pearl River Delta", at http://www.civic-exchange.org/wp/wp-content/uploads/2010/12/200411_WhitePaper.pdf.

93. See Standing Mechanisms.

94. "Outline of the Plan for the Reform and Development of the Pearl River Delta" (2008–2020). National Development and Reform Commission. Available at http://en.ndrc.gov.cn/policyrelease/P020090120342179907030.doc; http://gia.info.gov.hk/general/201004/07/P201004070113_0113_63622.pdf; (in Chinese) and http://gia.info.gov.hk/general/201004/07/P201004070113_0113_63623.pdf (in Chinese).

95. "Signing ceremony of Framework Agreement."

96. See Health, Welfare and Food Bureau, *Notification of Infectious Diseases between the Mainland and Hong Kong,* at http://www.legco.gov.hk/yr05-06/english/panels/hs/papers/hs0109cb2-768-3e.pdf, 2–3.

97. "Tripartite meeting on infectious diseases held in Dongguan Press Release of the Hong Kong SAR government." Press Release of the Hong Kong SAR government, 29 June 2006. Available at http://www.info.gov.hk/gia/general/200606/29/P200606290161.htm.

98. "Mainland and Hong Kong SAR sign MOU to enhance health and medical cooperation Press Release of the Hong Kong SAR government." Press Release of the Hong Kong SAR government, 22 June 2007. Available at http://www.fhb.gov.hk/en/press_and_publications/press/2007/press070622.htm.

99. "AQSIQ and HWFB sign Co-operation Arrangement Press Release of the Hong Kong SAR government." Press Release of the Hong Kong SAR government, 17 November 2003. Available at http://www.info.gov.hk/gia/general/200311/17/1117226.htm.

100. *Hong Kong Commercial Daily*, 1 July 2006, B9.
101. "Framework Agreement on Exchanges and Co-operation in Food Safety." Press Release of the Hong Kong SAR government, 11 April 2006. Available at http://www.info.gov.hk/gia/general/200604/11/P200604110145.htm.
102. "Mainland and HK team up to enhance safety of food for supply to HK." Press Release of the Hong Kong SAR government, 28 November 2006. Available at http://www.fhb.gov.hk/en/press_and_publications/press/2006/press061128.htm.
103. "Tenth Plenary of the Hong Kong/Guangdong Co-operation Joint Conference held in Hong Kong today." Press Release of the Hong Kong SAR government, 2 August 2007. Available at http://www.info.gov.hk/gia/general/200708/02/P200708020266.htm.
104. "FHB and AQSIQ sign Supplementary Co-operation Arrangement." Press Release of the Hong Kong SAR government, 26 March 2009. Available at http://www.fhb.gov.hk/en/press_and_publications/press/2009/press090326a.htm.
105. See the information paper for the Legco Panel on Food Safety and Environment Hygiene, "New Administrative Measures for Vegetables Imported from the Mainland" [LC Paper No.CB(2)431/09-10(03)], at http://www.legco.gov.hk/yr09-10/english/panels/fseh/papers/fe1208cb2-431-3-e.pdf.

References

Introduction

Asian Development Bank. 1995. *Governance: Sound Development Management.* n.p.: Asian Development Bank.

Balassa, Bela. 1988. "The Lessons of East Asia Development: An Overview." *Economic Development and Cultural Change* 36 (April): S273–90.

Balassa, Bela et al. 1982. *Development Strategies in Semi-industrial Economies.* Baltimore: Johns Hopkins University Press. de Alcantara, Cynthia Hewitt. 1998. "Uses and Abuses of the Concept of Governance." *International Social Science Journal* 50 (March): 105–13.

Deyo, Frederic C. 1987. "Coalitions, Institutions, and Linkage Sequencing: Toward a Strategic Capacity Model of East Asian Development." In *The Political Economy of the New Asian Industrialism*, edited by Frederic C. Deyo, 227–48. Ithaca, NY: Cornell University Press.

The Economist. 2010. "End of an Experiment: Hong Kong's Economy." 17 July, 73.

Evans, Peter B. 1995. *Embedded Autonomy: States and Industrial Transformation.* Princeton, NJ: Princeton University Press.

Fung, Archon, and Erik Olin Wright. 2001. "Deepening Democracy: Innovations in Empowered Participatory Governance." *Politics & Society* 29 (March): 5–41.

Gerschenkron, Alexander. 1962. *Economic Backwardness in Historical Perspective, Book of Essays.* Cambridge, MA: Harvard University Press.

———. 1967. "The Discipline and I." *Journal of Economic History.* 27 (December): 443–59.

Haggard, Stephan. 1990. *Pathways from the Periphery: The Politics of Growth in the Newly Industrializing Countries.* Ithaca, NY: Cornell University Press.

Held, David, and Anthony McGrew. 2003. "The Great Globalization Debate: An Introduction." In *The Global Transformations Reader: An Introduction to the Globalization Debate*, edited by David Held and Anthony McGrew, 1–50. Cambridge: Polity Press.

Held, David, et al. 1999. *Global Transformations: Politics, Economics and Culture*. Stanford, CA: Stanford University Press.

Hobson, John M. 2003. "Disappearing Taxes or the 'Race to the Middle'? Fiscal Policy in the OECD." In *States in the Global Economy: Bringing Domestic Institutions back in*, edited by Linda Weiss, 37–57. Cambridge: Cambridge University Press.

Jessop, Bob. 1998. "The Rise of Governance and the Risks of Failure: The Case of Economic Development." *International Social Science Journal* 50 (March): 29–45.

Johnson, Chalmers. 1987. "Political Institutions and Economic Performance: The Government-Business Relationship in Japan, South Korea, and Taiwan." In *The Political Economy of the New Asian Industrialization*, edited by Frederic C. Deyo, 136–64. Ithaca, NY: Cornell University Press.

Kohli, Atul. 2004. *State Directed-Development: Political Power and Industrialization in the Global Periphery*. Cambridge: Cambridge University Press.

Lau, Siu-kai. 2007. "In Search of a New Political Order." In *The First Decade: The Hong Kong SAR in Retrospective and Introspective Perspectives*, edited by Yue-man Yeung, 139–59. Hong Kong: The Chinese University Press.

Leftwich, Adrian. 1993. "Governance, Democracy and Development in the Third World." *Third World Quarterly* 14, no. 3: 605–24.

Little, I. M. D. 1981. "The Experience and Causes of Rapid Labour-intensive Development in Korea, Taiwan Province, Hong Kong, and Singapore and the Possibility of Emulation." In *Export-led Industrialisation and Development*, edited by Eddy Lee, 23–45. Geneva: International Labour Office.

Migdal, Joel S., Atul Kohli and Vivienne Shue, eds. 1994. *State Power and Social Forces: Domination and Transformation in the Third World*. Cambridge: Cambridge University Press.

Ohmae, Kenichi. 1995. *The End of the Nation State: The Rise of Regional Economies*. New York: Free Press.

Okimoto, Daniel I. 1989. *Between MITI and the Market: Japanese Industrial Policy for High Technology*. Stanford, CA: Stanford University Press.

Ranis, Gustav. 1985. "Employment, Income Distribution and Growth in the East Asian Context: A Comparative Analysis." In *Export-Oriented Development Strategies: The Success of Five Newly-Industrializing Countries*, edited by Vittorio Corbo, Anne O. Krueger and Fernando Ossa, 249–74. Boulder, CO: Westview Press.

Rueschemeyer, Dietrich, and Peter B. Evans. 1985. "The State and Economic Transformation: Toward an Analysis of the Conditions Underlying Effective Intervention." In *Bringing the State Back In*, edited by Peter B. Evans, Dietrich Rueschemeyer and Theda Skocpol, 44–77. Cambridge: Cambridge University Press.

Samuels, Richard J. 1987. *The Business of the Japanese State: Energy Markets in Comparative and Historical Perspective*. Ithaca, NY: Cornell University Press.

Strange, Susan. 1996. *The Retreat of the State: The Diffusion of Power in the World Economy*. Cambridge: Cambridge University Press.

United Nations Development Programme. 1997. *Governance for Sustainable Human Development*. Available at http://mirror.undp.org/magnet/policy/

Wade, Robert, and Gordon White, eds. 1984. *Developmental States in East Asia: Capitalist and Socialist*. Special Issue, *IDS Bulletin* 15, no. 2 (April).

Weiss, Linda. 1995. "Governed Interdependence: Rethinking the Government-Business Relationship in East Asia." *Pacific Review* 8, no. 4: 589–616.

———. 2003. "Introduction: Bringing Domestic Institutions back in." In *States in the Global Economy: Bringing Domestic Institutions back in*, edited by Linda Weiss, 1–33. Cambridge: Cambridge University Press.

White, Gordon, and Robert Wade. 1988. "Developmental States and Markets in East Asia: An Introduction." In *Developmental States in East Asia*, edited by Gordon White, 1–29. Basingstoke: Macmillan.

World Bank. 1992. *Governance and Development*. Washington, DC: World Bank.

———. 1994. *Governance: the World Bank's Experience*. Washington, DC: World Bank.

Chapter 1

Acemoglu, Daron, Simon Johnson and James A. Robinson. 2001. "The Colonial Origins of Comparative Development: An Empirical Investigation." *American Economic Review* 91 (December): 1369–401.

———. 2005. "Institutions as the Fundamental Cause of Long-Run Growth." In *Handbook of Economic Growth*, vol. 1A, edited by Philippe Aghion and Steven N. Durlauf, 385–472. Amsterdam: Elsevier.

Acemoglu, Daron, and James Robinson. 2006. *Economic Origins of Dictatorship and Democracy*. Cambridge: Cambridge University Press.

Aghion, Philippe, and Peter Howitt. 1999. *Endogenous Growth Theory*. Cambridge, MA: MIT Press.

Amsden, Alice H. 1989. *Asia's Next Giant: South Korea and Late Industrialization*. New York: Oxford University Press.

———. 1999. "The Specter of Anglo-Saxonization is Haunting South Korea." In *Korea's Political Economy: An Institutionalist Perspective*, edited by L. Cho and Y. Kim, 87–125. Boulder, CO: Westview Press.

———. 2001. *The Rise of "the Rest": Challenges to the West from Late-Industrializing Economies*. New York: Oxford University Press.

Angell, Marcia. 2004. *The Truth About the Drug Companies: How They Deceive Us and What to Do About It*. New York: Random House.

Bardhan, Pranab. 2005. *Scarcity, Conflicts, and Cooperation: Essays in the Political and Institutional Economics of Development*. Cambridge, MA: MIT Press.

Carson, Joseph G. 2003. "Manufacturing Payrolls Declining Globally: The Untold Story." Alliance Bernstein Institutional Capital Management, U.S. Weekly Economic Update, 10 and 24 (October).

Chang, Ha-Joon. 2002. *Kicking Away the Ladder: Development Strategy in Historical Perspective*. London: Anthem Press.

Chibber, Vivek. 2003. *Locked in Place: State-Building and Late Industrialization in India*. Princeton, NJ: Princeton University Press.

Di John, Jonathan. 2006. "The Political Economy of Taxation and Tax Reform in Developing Countries." UNU/WIDER Research Paper No. 2006/74.

Evan, Peter B. 1995. *Embedded Autonomy: States and Industrial Transformation*. Princeton, NJ: Princeton University Press.

———. 2004. "Development as Institutional Change: The Pitfalls of Monocropping and the Potentials of Deliberation." *Studies in Comparative International Development* 38, no. 4 (Winter): 30–52.

———. 2005. "Challenges of the 'Institutional Turn': New Interdisciplinary Opportunities in Development Theory." In *The Economic Sociology of Capitalist Institutions*, edited by Victor Nee and Richard Swedberg, 90–116. Princeton, NJ: Princeton University Press.

———. 2007. "Extending the 'Institutional' Turn: Property, Politics and Development Trajectories." In *Institutional Change and Economic Development*, edited by Ha-Joon Chang, 35–52. New York: United Nations University Press.

Evan, Peter B., and James E. Rauch. 1999. "Bureaucracy and Growth: A Cross-National Analysis of the Effects of 'Weberian' State Structures on Economic Growth." *American Sociological Review* 64 (October): 748–65.

Evans, Peter, and Sarah Staveteig. 2009. "The Changing Structure of Employment in Contemporary China." In *Creating Wealth and Poverty in Post-Socialist China*, edited by Deborah Davis and Feng Wang, 69–82. Stanford: Stanford University Press.

Fitzgerald, E. V. K. 2006. "Tax Reform in a Globalized World." Paper presented to the UN-DESA/FONDAD Conference on Policy Space for Developing Countries in a Globalized World." New York, 7–8 December 2006.

Ghosh, Jayati. 2003. "Exporting Jobs or Watching Them Disappear? Relocation, Employment and Accumulation in the World Economy." In *Work and Well-Being in the Age of Finance*, edited by Jayati Ghosh and C. P. Chandrasekhar, 99–119. New Delhi: Tulika.

Helpman, Elhanan. 2004. *The Mystery of Economic Growth*. Cambridge, MA: Harvard University Press.

Hoff, Karla, and Joseph E. Stiglitz. 2001. "Modern Economic Theory and Development." In *Frontiers of Development Economics: The Future in Perspective*, edited by Gerald M. Meier and Joseph E. Stiglitz, 389–459. New York: Oxford University Press.

Houtzager, Peter, and Mick Moore. 2003. *Changing Paths: The New Politics of Inclusion.* Ann Arbor: University of Michigan Press.

Hurst, William. 2004. "Understanding Contentious Collective Action by Chinese Laid-Off Workers: The Importance of Regional Political Economy." *Studies in Comparative International Development* 39 (June): 94–120.

Johnson, Chalmers. 1982. *MITI and the Japanese Miracle.* Stanford, CA: Stanford University Press.

Jones, Charles I. 2002. "Sources of U.S. Economic Growth in a World of Ideas." *American Economic Review* 91: 1–32.

Krippner, Greta R. 2005. "The Financialization of the American Economy." *Socio-Economic Review* 3 (2005): 173–208.

Kohli, Atul. 2004. *State-directed Development: Political Power and Industrialization in the Global Periphery.* Cambridge: Cambridge University Press.

Lee, Ching Kwan. 2007. *Against the Law: Labor Protests in China's Rustbelt and Sunbelt.* Berkeley and Los Angeles: University of California Press.

Lucas, Robert E., Jr. 1988. "On the Mechanics of Economic Development." *Journal of Monetary Economics* 22 (July): 3–42.

Negroponte, Nicholas. 1996. *Being Digital.* New York: Vintage Books.

Ostrom, Elinor. 1996. "Crossing the Great Divide: Coproduction, Synergy, and Development." *World Development* 24 (June): 1073–87.

Rodrik, Dani. 1999. "Institutions for High-Quality Growth: What They Are and How to Acquire Them." Paper presented at the International Monetary Fund Conference on Second Generation Reforms, Washington DC. 8–9 November.

Rodrik, Dani, Arvind Subramanian and Francesco Trebbi. 2004. "Institutions Rule: The Primacy of Institutions over Geography and Integration in Economic Development." *Journal of Economic Growth* 9 (June): 131–65.

Romer, Paul M. 1986. "Increasing Returns and Long-Run Growth." *Journal of Political Economy* 94 (October): 1002–37.

———. 1990. "Endogenous Technological Change." *Journal of Political Economy* 98 (October): S71–102.

———. 1993a. "Idea Gaps and Object Gaps in Economic Development." *Journal of Monetary Economics* 32 (December): 543–73.

———. 1993b. "Two Strategies of Economic Development: Using Ideas and Producing Ideas." In *Proceedings of the World Bank Annual Conference on Development Economics 1992,* 63–91. Washington, DC: World Bank.

———. 1994. "The Origins of Endogenous Growth." *Journal of Economic Perspectives* 8 (Winter): 3–22.

Sen, Amartya K. 1999. *Development as Freedom.* New York: Alfred A. Knopf.

Stiglitz, Joseph E. 2002. *Globalization and its Discontents.* New York: W.W. Norton.

Solow, Robert M. 1957. "Technical Change and the Aggregate Production Function." *Review of Economics and Statistics* 39 (August): 312–20.

Wade, Robert. 1990. *Governing the Market: Economic Theory and the Role of Government in East Asian's Industrialization*. Princeton, NJ: Princeton University Press.

Weber, Steven. 2004. *The Success of Open Source* Cambridge, MA: Harvard University Press.

Weber, Steven, and Jennifer Bussell. 2005. "Will Information Technology Reshape the North-South Asymmetry of Power in the Global Political Economy?" *Studies in Comparative International Development* 40, no. 2 (Summer): 62–84.

Wong, Joseph. 2004. *Healthy Democracies: Welfare Politics in Taiwan and South Korea*. Ithaca, NY: Cornell University Press.

Woo-Cumings, Meredith, ed. 1999. *The Developmental State*. Ithaca, NY: Cornell University Press.

World Bank. 1993. *The East Asian Miracle: Economic Growth and Public Policy*. New York: Oxford University Press.

———. 1997. *1997 World Development Report: The State in a Changing World*. New York: Oxford University Press.

Chapter 2

Amsden, Alice H. 1989. *Asia's Next Giant: South Korea and Late Industrialization*. New York: Oxford University Press.

Beeson, Mark. 2003. "The Rise and Fall (?) of the Developmental State: The Vicissitudes and Implications of East Asian Interventionism." Unpublished paper, University of Queensland.

Bello, Walden. 1998. "East Asia: On the Eve of the Great Transformation?" *Review of International Political Economy* 5 (Autumn): 424–44.

Berger Mark T. 2001. "The Post-Cold War Predicament: A Conclusion." *Third World Quarterly* 22 (December): 1079–85.

———. 2004. *The Battle for Asia: From Decolonization to Globalization*. London: RoutledgeCurzon.

Chung Moo-Kwon. 2001. "Rolling Back the Korean State: How Much Has Changed?" Paper presented to the 2001 Meeting of the IPSA Section of Structure of Governance, University of Oklahoma, Norman, 30–31 March.

Cumings, Bruce. 1998. "The Korean Crisis and the End of 'Late' Development." *New Left Review*, no. 231 (September–October): 43–72.

Erdogdu, M. Mustafa. 2002. "The South Korean Crises of 1997 and its Aftermath: The Legacy of the Developmental State and the Importance of State Capacity of Post-Crisis Adjustment." Paper presented at the VI.

ERC/METU International Conference in Economics. Ankara, Turkey. 11–14 September.

Evans, Peter B. 1993. Review of *States or Markets? Neo-Liberalism and the Developmental Policy Debate*, edited by Christopher and James Manor and *The Market and the State: Studies in Interdependence*, edited by Michael Moran and Maurice Wright. *American Political Science Review* 87 (June): 518–9.

———. 1995. *Embedded Autonomy: States and Industrial Transformation.* Princeton, NJ: Princeton University Press.

Fisher, Stanley. 1998. "The Asian Crisis: A View from the IMF." Address delivered at the Midwinter Conference of the Bankers' Association for Foreign Trade, 22 January. Available at http://www.imf.org/external/np/speeches/1998/0112298.htm.

Johnson, Chalmers. 1982. *MITI and the Japanese Miracle.* Stanford, CA: Stanford University Press.

Kim, Yun Tae. 2005. "DJnomics and the Transformation of the Developmental State." *Journal of Contemporary Asia* 35 (November): 471–84.

Lee, Yeonho. 2005. "Participatory Democracy and Chaebol Regulation in Korea: State-Market Relations under the MDP Governments, 1997–2003." *Asian Survey* 45 (March/April): 279–301.

Levinson, Mark. 2000. "The Cracking Washington Consensus." *Dissent* 47, no. 4 (Fall): 11–4.

Lie, John. 1991. "Review: Rethinking the `Miracle'—Economic Growth and Political Struggles in South Korea." Review of *Asia's Next Giant: South Korea and Late Industrialization,* by Alice H. Amsden. *Bulletin of Concerned Asian Scholars* 23 (October–December): 66–71.

Mauro, Paolo. 1997. "Why Worry about Corruption?" *IMF Economic Issues* 6. Washington, DC: International Monetary Fund.

Migdal, Joel S., Atul Kohli and Vivienne Shue, eds. 1994. *State Power and Social Forces: Domination and Transformation in the Third World.* Cambridge: Cambridge University Press.

Minns, John. 2001. "Of Miracles and Models: The Rise and Decline of the Developmental State in South Korea." *Third World Quarterly* 22 (December): 1025–43.

Moon, Chung-In, and Jongryn Mo.2000. *Economic Crisis and Structural Reforms in South Korea.* Washington, DC: Economic Strategy Institute.

OECD. 2000. *Pushing ahead with Reform in Korea: Labour Market and Social Safety-Net Politics.* Paris: OECD Publishing.

Öniş Ziya, and Ahmet Faruk Aysan. 2000. "Neoliberal Globalisation, the Nation-State and Financial Crises in the Semi-periphery: A Comparative Analysis." *Third World Quarterly* 21 (February):119–39.

Wade, Robert. 1990. *Governing the Market: Economic Theory and the Role of Government in East Asian Industrialization.* Princeton, NJ: Princeton University Press.

Wade, Robert, and Frank Veneroso. 1998. "The Asian Crisis: The High Debt Model versus the Wall Street-Treasury-IMF Complex." *New Left Review,* no. 228 (March–April): 3–24.

Woo-Cumings, Meredith. 1999. "Introduction: Chalmers Johnson and the Politics of Nationalism and Development." In *The Developmental State,* edited by Meredith Woo-Cumings, 1–31. Ithaca, NY: Cornell University Press.

Zhang, Xiaoke. 2002. "Domestic Institutions, Liberalization Patterns, and Uneven Crises in Korea and Taiwan." *Pacific Review* 15, no. 3 (August): 409–42.

Chapter 3

Aikman, David. 1986. *The Pacific Rim: Area of Change, Area of Opportunity.* Boston: Little, Brown.

Bickers, Robert, and Ray Yep, eds. 2009. *May Days in Hong Kong: Riot and Emergency in 1967.* Hong Kong: Hong Kong University Press.

Castells, Manuel, Lee Goh and R. Yin-Wang Kwok. 1990. *The Shek Kip Mei Syndrome: Economic Development and Public Housing in Hong Kong and Singapore.* London: Pion.

Chan, Cheuk-wah. 1998. *The Myth of Hong Kong's Laissez-faire Economic Governance: 1960s and 1970s.* Occasional Paper No. 79. Hong Kong: Hong Kong Institute of Asia-Pacific Studies, The Chinese University of Hong Kong.

Cheung, Anthony, B. L. 1992. "Public Sector Reform in Hong Kong: Perspectives and Problems." *Asian Journal of Public Administration* 14 (December): 115–48.

———. 2001. "The 'Trading Fund' Reform in Hong Kong: Claims and Performance." In *Public Sector Reform in Hong Kong: Into the 21st Century,* edited by Anthony B. L. Cheung and Jane C. Y. Lee, 203–28. Hong Kong: The Chinese University Press.

Cheung, Anthony, B. L., and Paul C. W. Wong. 2004. "Who Advised the Hong Kong Government? The Politics of Absorption before and after 1997." *Asian Survey* 44 (November/December): 874–94.

Chiu, Stephen W. K. 1994. *The Politics of Laissez-faire: Hong Kong's Strategy of Industrialization in Historical Perspective.* Occasional Paper No. 40. Hong Kong: Hong Kong Institute of Asia-Pacific Studies, The Chinese University of Hong Kong.

———. 1996. "Unravelling Hong Kong's Exceptionalism: The Politics of Laissez-faire in the Industrial Takeoff." *Political Power and Social Theory* 10: 229–56.

———. 1999. "State Building and Rural Stability." In *Hong Kong's History: State and Society under Colonial Rule,* edited by Tak-Wing Ngo, 74–100. London: Routledge.

Chiu, Stephen W. K., and Ho-fung Hung. 1997. *The Colonial State and Rural Protests in Hong Kong*. Occasional Paper No. 59. Hong Kong: Hong Kong Institute of Asia-Pacific Studies, The Chinese University of Hong Kong.

Deyo, Frederic C. 1987. "State and Labor: Modes of Political Exclusion in East Asian Development." In *The Political Economy of the New Asian Industrialism*, edited by Frederic C. Deyo, 182–202. Ithaca, NY: Cornell University Press.

Faure, David. 2003. "In Britain's Footsteps: The Colonial Heritage." In *Hong Kong: A Reader in Social History*, edited by David Faure, 658–78. Hong Kong: Oxford University Press.

Feng, Bangyan. 1997. *Xianggang Huazi Caituan 1841–1997* (Chinese conglomerates in Hong Kong). Hong Kong: Joint Publishing.

Friedman, Milton, and Rose Friedman. 1981. *Free to Choose: A Personal Statement*. Harmondsworth: Penguin Books.

Goodstadt, Leo F. 2000. "China and the Selection of Hong Kong's Post-Colonial Political Elite." *China Quarterly*, no. 163 (September): 721–41.

———. 2005. *Uneasy Partners: The Conflict between Public Interest and Private Profit in Hong Kong*. Hong Kong: Hong Kong University Press.

———. 2007. *Profits, Politics and Panics: Hong Kong's Banks and the Making of a Miracle Economy, 1935–1985*. Hong Kong: Hong Kong University Press.

Haddon-Cave, Philip. 1980. "Introduction: The Making of Some Aspects of Public Policy in Hong Kong." In *The Business Environment in Hong Kong*, edited by David G. Lethbridge, xi–xix. Hong Kong: Oxford University Press.

Haggard, Stephan. 1990. *Pathways from the Periphery: The Politics of Growth in the Newly Industrializing Countries*. Ithaca, NY: Cornell University Press.

Haggard, Stephan, and Tun-jen Cheng. 1987. "State and Foreign Capital in the East Asian NICs." In *The Political Economy of the New Asian Industrialism*, edited by Frederic C. Deyo, 84–135. Ithaca, NY: Cornell University Press.

Holliday, Ian, Ma Ngok and Ray Yep. 2002. "A High Degree of Autonomy? Hong Kong Special Administrative Region, 1997–2002." *Political Quarterly* 73 (October): 455–64.

Hong Kong Government. 1966. *Hong Kong Hansard*. Hong Kong: Hong Kong Government Printer.

Hospital Authority. 2007. *Hospital Authority Annual Report 2006/07*. Hong Kong: Hospital Authority.

Huang, Yasheng. 1997. "The Economic and Political Integration of Hong Kong: Implications for Government-Business Relations." In *Hong Kong under Chinese Rule: The Economic and Political Implications of Reversion*, edited by Warren I. Cohen and Li Zhao, 96–113. Cambridge: Cambridge University Press.

Huque, Ahmed Shafiqul. 1999. "Hong Kong's Policy of Positive Nonintervention: A Critical Appraisal of the 1998 Stock Market Intervention." *Issues and Studies* 35 (April): 152–73.

King, Ambrose Yeo-chi. 1975. "Administrative Absorption of Politics in Hong Kong: Emphasis on the Grassroot Level." *Asian Survey* 15 (May): 422–39.

Lau, Siu-kai. 1984. *Society and Politics in Hong Kong*. Hong Kong: The Chinese University Press.

———. 1999. "From Elite Unity to Disunity: Political Elite in Post-1997 Hong Kong." In *Hong Kong in China: The Challenges of Transition*, edited by Gungwu Wang and John Wong, 47–74. Singapore: Times Academic Press.

Lee, Eliza Wing-yee. 1998. "The Political Economy of Public Sector Reform in Hong Kong: The Case of a Colonial-Developmental State." *International Review of Administrative Sciences* 64 (December): 625–41.

———. 2000. "The New Hong Kong International Airport Fiasco: Accountability Failure and the Limits of the New Managerialism." *International Review of Administrative Sciences* 66 (March): 57–72.

Lee, Kin-ming and Jack Wai-chik Yue. 2001. "A Prolegomenon to the Study of the Role of Rhetoric in the Garbage-Can Policy Process: The Case of Hong Kong's Positive Non-Interventionism." *International Journal of Public Administration* 24, no. 9: 887–907.

Ma, Ngok. 2004. "SARS and the Limits of the Hong Kong SAR State." *Asian Perspective* 28, no. 1: 99–120.

———. 2007. *Political Development in Hong Kong: State, Political Society, and Civil Society*. Hong Kong: Hong Kong University Press.

Ngo, Tak-wing. 1997. "The Legend of a Colony: Political Rule and Historiography in Hong Kong." *China Information* 12, no. 1/2 (Summer/Autumn): 134–56.

———. 1998. "Jingji ganyu yu buganyu: Gangtai liangdi tongzhi celu bijiao" (Economic intervention and non-intervention: The ruling strategies of Hong Kong and Taiwan compared) (經濟干預與不干預：港台兩地統治策略比較). *Hong Kong Journal of Social Sciences* 12 (Autumn): 1–16.

———. 2000. "Changing Government-Business Relations and the Governance of Hong Kong." In *Hong Kong in Transition: The Handover Years*, edited by Robert Ash, et al., 26–41. Houndmills: Macmillan.

Schiffer, Jonathan R. 1991. "State Policy and Economic Growth: A Note on the Hong Kong Model." *International Journal of Urban and Regional Research* 15 (March): 190–96.

Scott, Ian. 1989. *Political Change and the Crisis of Legitimacy in Hong Kong*. Hong Kong: Oxford University Press.

———. 2005. *Public Administration in Hong Kong: Regime Change and Its Impact on the Public Sector*. Singapore: Marshall Cavendish Academic.

So, Alvin Y. 1986. "The Economic Success of Hong Kong: Insights from a World-System Perspective." *Sociological Perspectives* 29 (April): 241–58.

Tang, Shu-hung. 1991. "Fiscal Constitution, Income Distribution and the Basic Law of Hong Kong." *Economy and Society* 20 (August): 283–305.

Wilding, Richard. 1982. "A Triangular Affair: Quangos, Ministers and MPs." In *Quangos in Britain: Government and the Networks of Public Policy-Making*, edited by Anthony Barker, 34–43. London: Macmillan.

Woo, Tun-oy. 1977. "Imports from China: Its Impact on Hong Kong's Manufactured Export Performance, 1962–1974." MPhil thesis, The Chinese University of Hong Kong.

Youngson, A. J. 1982. *Hong Kong: Economic Growth and Policy*. Hong Kong: Oxford University Press.

Chapter 5

Bottomore, Tom. 1992. "Citizenship and Social Class, Forty Years on". In *Citizenship and Social Class*, T. H. Marshall and Tom Bottomore, 55–93. London: Pluto Press.

Cheung, Anthony B. L. 2000. "New Interventionism in the Making: Interpreting State Interventions in Hong Kong after the Change of Sovereignty." *Journal of Contemporary China* 9 (July): 291–308.

Cheung, Anthony B. L., and Ian Scott. 2003. "Governance and Public Sector Reforms in Asia: Paradigms, Paradoxes, and Dilemmas." In *Governance and Public Sector Reforms in Asia*, edited by Anthony B. L. Cheung and Ian Scott, 1–24. London: RoutledgeCurzon.

Chu, Yiu-Wai. 2010. "The Donaldization of Hong Kong Society." In *Contemporary Asian Modernities: Transnationality, Interculturality and Hybridity*, edited by Yiu-Wai Chu and Kit-Wah Man, 190–211. Bern: Peter Lang.

Delanty, Gerard. 2000. *Citizenship in a Global Age: Society, Culture, Politics*. Buckingham: Open University Press.

Eder, Klaus. 1993. *The New Politics of Class: Social Movements and Cultural Dynamics in Advanced Societies*. London: Sage.

———. 2001. "Social Movement Organizations and the Democratic Order: Reorganizing the Social Basis of Political Citizenship in Complex Societies." In *Citizenship, Markets, and the State*, edited by Colin Crouch, Klaus Eder, and Damian Tambini, 213–37. New York: Oxford University Press.

Evans, Peter B. 1992. "The State as Problem and Solution: Predation, Embedded Autonomy, and Structural Change." In *The Politics of Economic Adjustment: International Constraints, Distributive Conflicts, and the State*, edited by Stephan Haggard and Robert R. Kaufman, 139–81. Princeton, NJ: Princeton University Press.

Fung, Archon, and Erik Olin Wright. 2001. "Deepening Democracy: Innovations in Empowered Participatory Governance." *Politics and Society* 29 (March): 5–41.

Giddens, Anthony. 1982. *Profiles and Critiques in Social Theory*. Berkeley and Los Angeles: University of California Press.

Goodin, Robert E. 2003. "Democratic Accountability: The Distinctiveness of the Third Sector." *Archives Européennes de Sociologie* 44 (December): 359–96.

Habermas, Jürgen. 1989 [1962]. *The Structural Transformation of the Public Sphere: An Inquiry into a Category of Bourgeois Society.* Translated by Thomas Burger. Cambridge, MA: MIT Press.

Haddon-Cave, Philip. 1984 [1980]. "The Making of Some Aspects of Public Policy in Hong Kong" (Introduction to the First Edition). In *The Business Environment in Hong Kong,* edited by D. G. Lethbridge. Hong Kong: Oxford University Press.

Ho, Denny Kwok-leung. 2004. "Citizenship as a Form of Governance: A Historical Overview." In *Remaking Citizenship in Hong Kong: Community, Nation, and the Global City,* edited by Agnes S. Ku and Ngai Pun, 19–36. London: RoutledgeCurzon.

Hong Kong Special Administrative Region Government. 1998. *Chief Executive's Policy Address 1998.* Available at http://www.policyaddress.gov.hk/pa98/english/ speech2.htm.

Jessop, Bob. 1978. "Capitalism and Democracy: The Best Possible Political Shell?" In *Power and the State,* edited by Gary Littlejohn, et al., 10–51. London: Croom Helm.

———. 1990. *State Theory: Putting Capitalist States in Their Places.* Cambridge: Polity Press.

———. 1999. "The Changing Governance of Welfare: Recent Trends in Its Primary Functions, Scale, and Modes of Coordination." *Social Policy and Administration* 33 (December): 348–59.

———. 2002. *The Future of the Capitalist State.* Cambridge: Polity Press.

Jones, Catherine. 1990. *Promoting Prosperity: The Hong Kong Way of Social Policy.* Hong Kong: The Chinese University Press.

Ku, Agnes S. 1999. *Narratives, Politics, and the Public Sphere: Struggles over Political Reform in the Final Transitional Years in Hong Kong (1992–94).* Aldershot: Ashgate.

———. 2004. "Negotiating the Space of Civil Autonomy in Hong Kong: Power, Discourses, and Dramaturgical Representations." *China Quarterly* 179 (September): 647–64.

Ku, Agnes S., and Clarence Hon-chee Tsui. 2009. "The 'Global City' as a Cultural Project: The Case of the West Kowloon Cultural District." In *Hong Kong Mobile: Making a Global Population,* edited by Helen F. Siu and Agnes S. Ku, 343–65. Hong Kong: Hong Kong University Press.

Lee, Grace O. M. 2003. "A De-capacitated State? Systemic Constraints on Governance in Hong Kong." In *Governance and Public Sector Reform in Asia,* edited by Anthony B. L. Cheung and Ian Scott, 117–37. London: Routledge.

Mann, Michael. 1987. "Ruling Class Strategies and Citizenship." *Sociology* 21 (August): 339–54.

Marshall, T. H. (1950). *Citizenship and Social Class, and Other Essays.* Cambridge: Cambridge University Press.

McLaughlin, Eugene. 1993. "Hong Kong: A Residual Welfare Regime." In *Comparing Welfare States: Britain in International Context,* edited by Allan Cochrane and John Clarke, 105–40. London: Sage.

Miners, Norman. 1998. *The Government and Politics of Hong Kong,* 5th updated ed. Hong Kong: Oxford University Press.

Scott Ian. 2000. "The Disarticulation of Hong Kong's Post-Handover Political System." *China Journal,* no. 43, 29–53.

Sing, Ming. 2004. *Hong Kong's Tortuous Democratization: A Comparative Analysis.* London: RoutledgeCurzon.

Turner, Bryan S. 1990. "Outline of a Theory of Citizenship." *Sociology* 24 (May): 189–217.

Turner, Matthew, and Irene Ngan, eds. 1995. *Hong Kong Sixties: Designing Identity.* Hong Kong: Hong Kong Arts Centre.

Wagner, Antonin. 2004. "Redefining Citizenship for the 21st Century: From the National Welfare State to the UN Global Compact." *International Journal of Social Welfare* 13 (October): 278–86.

Chapter 6

Box, Richard C. 1998. *Citizen Governance: Leading American Communities into the 21st Century.* Thousand Oaks, CA: Sage Publications.

Chan, Elaine, and Joseph Chan. 2007. "The First Ten Years of the HKSAR: Civil Society Comes of Age." *Asian Pacific Journal of Public Administration* 29 (June): 77–98.

Chiu, Stephen W. K., and Tai Lok Lui, eds. 2000. *The Dynamics of Social Movement in Hong Kong.* Hong Kong: Hong Kong University Press.

Coleman, James S. 1986. *Individual Interests and Collective Action: Selected Essays.* Cambridge: Cambridge University Press.

———. 1988. "Social Capital in the Creation of Human Capital." *American Journal of Sociology* 94, supp.: S95–120.

Evans, Peter B., ed. 1997. *State-Society Synergy: Government and Social Capital in Development.* Research Series, no. 94. International and Area Studies, University of California, Berkeley.

Faure, David, ed. 1997. *Society: A Documentary History of Hong Kong.* Hong Kong: Hong Kong University Press.

Fung, Archon, and Erik Olin Wright. 2003. *Deepening Democracy: Institutional Innovations in Empowered Participatory Governance.* New York: Verso.

Hayes, James. 1996. *Teachers and Friends: Hong Kong and Its People 1953–87.* Hong Kong: Hong Kong University Press.

Jones, Catherine. 1990. *Promoting Prosperity: The Hong Kong Way of Social Policy.* Hong Kong: The Chinese University Press.

Lau, Siu-kai. 1982. *Society and Politics in Hong Kong*. Hong Kong: The Chinese University Press.

Leach, Robert, and Janie Percy-Smith. 2001. *Local Governance in Britain*. Houndmills: Palgrave.

Lee, Eliza W. Y. 2005. "Nonprofit Development in Hong Kong: The Case of a Statist-Corporatist Regime." *Voluntas: International Journal of Voluntary and Nonprofit Organizations* 16 (March): 51–68.

Leung, Beatrice, and Shun-hing Chan. 2003. *Changing Church and State Relations in Hong Kong, 1950–2000*. Hong Kong: Hong Kong University Press.

Leung, C. B. 1982. "Community Participation: from Kai Fong Association, Mutual Aid Committee to District Board." In *Hong Kong in the 1980s*, edited by Joseph Y. S. Cheng, 152–70. Hong Kong: Summerson Eastern Publishers.

———. 1986. "Community Participation: The Decline of Residents' Organizations." In *Hong Kong in Transition*, edited by Joseph Y. S. Cheng, 354–71. Hong Kong: Oxford University Press.

Morris, Elizabeth Willson. 1998. "Urban Redevelopment and the Emerging Community Sector." PhD diss., University of California at Berkeley.

Ngo, Tak-Wing, ed. 1999. *Hong Kong's History: State and Society under Colonial Rule*. London: Routledge.

Putnam, Robert D. 1995. "Tuning In, Tuning Out: The Strange Disappearance of Social Capital in America." *Political Science and Politics* 28 (December): 664–83.

———. 2000. *Bowling Alone: The Collapse and Revival of American Community*. New York: Simon & Schuster.

Sinn, Elizabeth. 2003 [1989]. *Power and Charity: A Chinese Merchant Elite in Colonial Hong Kong*. Hong Kong: Hong Kong University Press.

So, Alvin Y. 1999. *Hong Kong's Embattled Democracy: A Societal Analysis*. Baltimore: Johns Hopkins University Press.

South China Morning Post. 2003. United Challenge. 8 December.

———. 2004a. Chloe Lai, "Double Unhappiness: Critics Oppose URA's Plan to Raze 'Wedding Card Street'." 9 February.

———. 2004b. Chloe Lai, "Wedding Card Street Must Go: URA." 10 February.

———. 2004c. "Talk Back: Should Wedding Card Street Be Saved?" 11 February.

———. 2005a. "That's Typical." 12 September.

———. 2005b. "Building on Experience to Preserve the City's Heritage." 4 October.

———. 2006. "Jungle Fervour." 21 June.

Tsai, Jung-Fang. 1993. *Hong Kong in Chinese History: Community and Social Unrest in the British Colony, 1842–1913*. New York: Columbia University Press.

Tsang, Steve. 2004. *A Modern History of Hong Kong*. Hong Kong: Hong Kong University Press.

Weller, Robert P. 1999. *Alternate Civilities*. Boulder, CO: Westview Press.

Wong, Aline K. 1972. *The Kaifong Associations and the Society of Hong Kong*. Taipei: Orient Cultural Service.

World Bank. 2004. *State-Society Synergy for Accountability: Lessons from the World Bank*. Washington, DC: World Bank.

Chapter 7

Angel, Shlomo. 2000. *Housing Policy Matters: A Global Analysis*. New York: Oxford University Press.

Balchin, Paul, ed. 1996. *Housing Policy in Europe*. London: Routledge.

Barr, Nicholas. 2004. *Economics of the Welfare State*, 4th ed. New York: Oxford University Press.

Castells, Manuel, Lee Goh and R. Yin-Wang Kwok. 1990. *The Shek Kip Mei Syndrome: Economic Development and Public Housing in Hong Kong and Singapore*. London: Pion.

Cheung, Anthony B. L. 2000. "New Interventionism in the Making: Interpreting the State Interventions in Hong Kong after the Change of Sovereignty". *Journal of Contemporary China* 9 (July): 291–308.

Chua, Beng-Huat. 1997. *Political Legitimacy and Housing: Stakeholding in Singapore*. London: Routledge.

Consumer Council. 1996. "How Competitive Is the Private Residential Property Market?" http://www.consumer.org.hk/website/wrap_en2/hse9607/hse_e.htm

Doling, John. 1999. "Housing Policies and the Little Tigers: How Do They Compare with Other Industrialised Countries?" *Housing Studies* 14 (March): 229–50.

The Economist. 2005. "In Come the Waves", June 18, 73–5.

Fan, Kelvin, and Weng-sheng Peng. 2003. "Real Estate Indicators in Hong Kong SAR." In *Real Estate Indicators and Financial Stability*, 124–48. BIS Papers no.21. Bank for International Settlements. http://www.bis.org/publ/bppdf/bispap21.pdf.

Forrest, Ray, and James Lee. 2004. "Cohort Effects, Differential Accumulation and Hong Kong's Volatile Housing Market." *Urban Studies* 41 (October): 2181–96.

Forrest, Ray, and Alan Murie. 1988. *Selling the Welfare State: The Privatization of Public Housing*. London: Routledge.

Fu, Yuming. 2000. "Hong Kong: Overcoming Financial Risks of Growing Real Estate Credit." In *Asia's Financial Crisis and the Role of Real Estate*, edited by Koichi Mera and Bertrand Renaud, 139–58. Armonk, NY: M. E. Sharpe.

Harvey, David. 2005. *A Brief History of Neoliberalism*. New York: Oxford University Press.

Hong Kong Housing Authority. 1987. *Long Term Housing Strategy: A Policy Statement*. Hong Kong: Government Printer.

Hong, Yu-Hung. 2003. "Policy Dilemma of Capturing Land Value under the Hong Kong Public Leasehold System." In *Leasing Public Land: Policy Debates and International Experiences*, edited by Steven C. Bourassa and Yu-Hung Hong, 151–76. Cambridge, MA: Lincoln Institute of Land Policy.

Kemeny, Jim. 2001. "Comparative Housing and Welfare: Theorising the Relationship." *Journal of Housing and the Built Environment* 16 (March): 53–70.

Lee, James. 1999. *Housing, Home Ownership and Social Change in Hong Kong*. Aldershot: Ashgate.

———. 2000. "Housing Policy in the Post Asian Financial Crisis." *Public and Social Administration Working Paper Series* 2000, no. 2. Department of Public and Social Administration, City University of Hong Kong.

———. 2003. "The Home Ownership Scheme and its Continuing Needs." In *Fifty Years of Public Housing in Hong Kong*, edited by Yeung Yue-man and Timothy Wong, 259–282. Hong Kong: The Chinese University Press.

———. 2003/4. "Comparing East Asian Housing Systems: Some Implications on Theorizing Housing and Welfare." *Social Development Issues* 24 (Winter): 87–99.

———. 2010. "Social Security, Housing Policy and Asset-Building: Exploring the Relevance of Home Ownership for Elderly Income Protection." In *Social Policy and Poverty in East Asia*, edited by James Midgley and Kwong-leung Tang, 100–18. London: Routledge.

Lee, James, Ray Forrest and Wai Keung Tam. 2003. "Home-ownership in East and South East Asia: Market, State and Institutions." In *Housing and Social Change: East West Perspectives*, edited by Ray Forrest and James Lee, 20–45. London: Routledge.

Lee, James, and Ngai Ming Yip. "Home-ownership under Economic Uncertainty: The Role of Subsidized Sale Flats in Hong Kong." *Third World Planning Review* 23 (February): 61–78.

Lee, James, and Ya-peng Zhu. 2006. "Urban Governance, Neoliberalism and Housing Reform in China." *Pacific Review* 19, no. 1: 39–61.

Lee, Kim-Ming, and Jack Wai-chik Yue. 2001. "A Prolegomenon to the Study of the Role of Rhetoric in the Garbage-can Policy Process: The Case of Hong Kong's Positive Non-interventionism." *International Journal of Public Administration* 24, no. 9: 887–907.

Patten, Chris. 1998. *East and West: The Last Governor of Hong Kong on Power, Freedom, and the Future*. London: Macmillan.

Peng, Rutjue, and William C. Wheaton. 1994. "Effects of Restrictive Land Supply on Housing in Hong Kong: An Econometric Analysis." *Journal of Housing Research* 5, no. 2: 263–91.

Quigley, John M. 2001. "Real Estate and the Asian Crisis." *Journal of Housing Economics* 10 (June):129–61.

Renaud, Bertrand, Frederik Pretorius and Bernabe O. Pasadilla. 1997. *Markets at Work: Dynamics of the Residential Real Estate Market in Hong Kong.* Hong Kong: Hong Kong University Press.

Smart, Alan. 1986. "Invisible Real Estate: Investigations into the Squatter Property Market." *International Journal of Urban and Regional Research* 10 (March): 29–45.

Smart, Alan, and James Lee. 2003. "Financialization and the Role of Real Estate in Hong Kong's Regime of Accumulation." *Economic Geography* 79 (April): 153–71.

Tang, Connie P. Y. 2007. "Change and Inertia in Housing Policy: Japanese Housing System during Economic Crisis." In *The Crisis of Welfare in East Asia*, edited by James Lee and Kam-wah Chan, 71–99. Lanham, MD: Lyttleton Press.

Titmuss, R. M. 1958. *Essays on "the Welfare State".* London: Allen and Unwin.

Tsang, Donald. 1996. "Small Is Still Beautiful." *South China Morning Post*, 19 September, A13.

Tse, Raymond Y. C. 1998. "Housing Price, Land Supply and Revenue from Land Sale." *Urban Studies* 35 (July): 1377–92.

Wade, Robert. 2006. "Choking the South." *New Left Review*, ser. 2, no. 38 (March/April): 115–27.

Wong, Yue-Chin Richard. 1984. *On Privatizing Public Housing.* Hong Kong: City University of Hong Kong Press.

Yau, Cannix, and Carrie Chan. 2005. "Tsang Nips in the Bud of Ho's Drive for High Land Prices." *The Standard*, 21 June, A12. Available at http://www.thestandard.com.hk/stdn/std/Metro/GF21Ak07.html.

Index